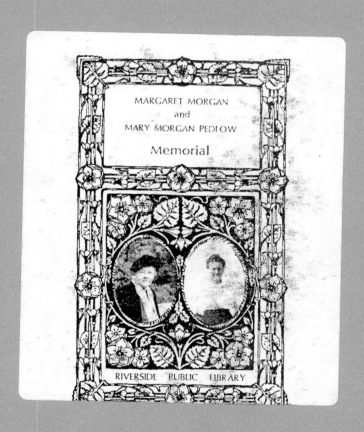

Happy cooking

CHEZ JACQUES

Traditions and Rituals of a Cook

❧ WITH 100 RECIPES ❧

JACQUES PÉPIN

PHOTOGRAPHS BY TOM HOPKINS

STEWART, TABORI & CHANG | NEW YORK

Published in 2007 by STEWART, TABORI & CHANG
An imprint of Harry N. Abrams, Inc.

Text copyright © 2007 Jacques Pépin
Photographs copyright © 2007 Tom Hopkins

Library of Congress Cataloging-in-Publication Data:
Pépin, Jacques.
    Chez Jacques : traditions and rituals of a cook / by Jacques Pepin ;
photographs by Tom Hopkins
        p. cm.
    Includes index.
    ISBN-13: 978-1-58479-571-1
    ISBN-10: 1-58479-571-9
    1. Cookery, French. I. Title.

TX719.P4575 2007
641.5944—dc22   2006028401

PRINTED AND BOUND IN CHINA
10 9 8 7 6 5 4 3 2

HNA
harry n. abrams, inc.
a subsidiary of La Martinière Groupe

115 West 18th Street | New York, NY 10011 | www.hnabooks.com

To "little one," whose smile in
the morning makes my day

Contents

ACKNOWLEDGMENTS

The writing of this book has truly been a labor of love for me, but it hasn't been a solitary undertaking. Many capable people have helped along the way, and their individual contributions are reflected on every page.

First, I want to thank Leslie Stoker, publisher at Stewart, Tabori & Chang. She understood and shared my vision of producing a book consisting of recipes for my all-time favorite dishes presented as friend-to-friend explanations, essays on topics of importance to me, and countless pictures of my food, my artwork, and of me enjoying life with family and friends. Thanks to her and Julie Stillman, our great editor and copyeditor who insisted on our reexamining and rewriting any recipe instructions that she found unclear, the book is far better than even I imagined it could be.

I have collaborated very closely with Norma Galehouse, my trusted assistant for nearly a quarter of a century. Again in this book she has diligently organized, reorganized, and edited the writing and the recipes to a strict and thorough standard of professionalism.

I've worked for twenty years on and off with my friend Tom Hopkins, who did all the photography for the book. He never disappoints, managing to capture the mouthwatering essence of the food, the beauty of the Connecticut outdoors, and the great fun I have at play with family and friends. He generously gave his time and expertise, working above and beyond on the project, and I am forever grateful. My special thanks, too, to Susi Oberhelman, our designer, who managed to turn my words and Tom's pictures into a beautiful and inviting package.

I am indebted to my many friends, most of them fellow *boules* enthusiasts, for their willingness to share food and wine and to appear on these pages. Especially, I thank Jean-Claude Szurdak and Jean-Michel Gammariello, good friends and willing helpers always.

I have dedicated this book to my wife, Gloria, who, more than anyone else, is present behind all the pictures and recipes, always suggesting and helping me with unfaltering love. She is the author of this book as well as I am, and it would not have been possible without her.

INTRODUCTION

Of all the cookbooks that I have written, this is certainly the most personal. It is more than a cookbook. It details my lifestyle and includes recipes, of course. But the recipes selected are ones that I have a connection with, recipes that bring images to my memories, recipes that mean something personal to me. Some of these recipes are variations of recipes that I have published in other books and that I keep making over and over again, but most are recipes for dishes that I remember from my youth or cooked with Gloria or with friends at my house.

The French epicure Brillat-Savarin said in one of his aphorisms, "You are what you eat." I believe that for many people I am what I cook, because I have been defined by food all my life, or at least for the last sixty years or so. Going back as far as my memory can take me, I see my mother, my aunts, and my cousins in their kitchens, and I can smell those kitchens. I see myself with my father in the cellar drawing wine, tending the garden with my brother, mushrooming with friends, or cooking with my wife Gloria or my friend Jean-Claude Szurdak. My cultural identity is in great part related to food, and that gastronomic culture includes a whole set of rules and habits that define my way of life. In this culture there are rituals, and special events, such as playing *boules,* picnicking, or going frogging or mushrooming. These rituals are expressed through traditional recipes and specific ways of doing things.

Although I was born in France and worked for more than ten years in restaurants there, I have been in the United States for so long that I feel more American than French. My life is made up of habits that I acquired as a child, but also those that I have adopted through all my years in New York and Connecticut and other parts of the United States. There won't be hundreds of recipes in this book, only the ones that count. The majority of people can live well with twenty or thirty recipes and, in fact, all of their family traditions and rituals are expressed through those recipes. For most people, the dishes that matter are the dishes that are cooked with love, dishes that are part of a family's structure, passed down from a grandmother, mother, spouse, aunt, uncle, or cousin. Those dishes remain much more embedded in our taste memory than the recipes and dishes of great restaurants, even for a professional cook like me. When I smell or see those traditional recipes, I also see my family—wife, daughter, brothers, mother—or friends; I see my father's garden or my gardens in upstate New York or Connecticut—there is no separating the food from the image.

What I see and remember more than anything else are markets. The Marché St. Antoine, along the Saône in Lyon, or the market in Antibes, where I remember a little woman from whom I bought perhaps the best apricot jam I've ever tasted. I recall the Wednesday market in Bourg-en-Bresse, and markets in Provence, like Arles, Avignon, and St. Remy. When I think of all the markets in the world—from the fish markets in Tokyo and Portugal, and the West African markets of Dakar, to the markets in Marrakech, Fez, or in Progresso on the Yucatán Peninsula—I realize my travels are always associated with local products and restaurants.

My recipes are always closely linked to my markets in Madison, the Connecticut town where I live, as well as Bishop's and Fonicello's, farm markets in neighboring Guilford, and the little farm nearby where I get my eggs from Rose, an elderly German lady who has the best eggs you could find anywhere. I go to a farm stand on the Hammonasett Connector, where I find wonderful fresh peas and corn in the summer, and the Lobster Landing in Clinton, where I buy lobsters. I look for freshness and quality in my markets—even the regular supermarkets have never been as beautiful as they are today, compared to the way they were in the early 1960s. At that time, there were no fresh mushrooms, leeks, shallots, or herbs, and there were only two salad greens: iceberg and romaine.

I visualize markets throughout the year, according to season and specific dishes that celebrate those seasons. In the spring, there is a

sweet smell to the earth when I plant my garden, and when those tiny seeds start emerging from the ground every year, it is still a miracle to me. In April nothing compares to the wild dandelion salad greens that I pick along the edge of the road, the tiny fresh peas from a nearby farm, and sweet baby carrots. During the summer, I like drowsing in the hot sun or walking in the cool grass, conjuring up mushrooms in the woods, and picking up little fish along the shore in Madison. I dream of steamed lobster, juicy and sugary corn, creamy new potatoes, and picnics with fried chicken, lukewarm plum tomatoes, and rosé wine along the Hammonasett River. There is a sweetness and gentleness to the fall. I love the fragrant smell of apple tarts, making cider, roasting a duck with sweet potatoes, the bursting yellow and red of the maple trees,

the tanginess of the Concord grapes, and, finally, the turkey of Thanksgiving, my favorite holiday. Winter in America will always call to mind the brilliant sun and blue sky with piercing cold and crisp air and the smell of chestnuts in the streets of New York City when I first arrived there in 1959. In Connecticut, winter is the smell of wood burning in the fireplace, comforting bean stew and split pea with ham soup, cheese fondue, and the feasts of the holidays, which we celebrate with oysters, capon or goose, foie gras, and chocolate truffles. This is the best time for small children, and I can see Claudine as a child making caramel candies in the snow. I recall lazy afternoons with a good book by the fireplace, and long walks with my dog along the deserted beach battered by cold wind under a gray and black sky.

It is always difficult and arbitrary to divide and organize a cookbook into different chapters, each with a different title. The more ambitious the cookbook, the greater the number of recipes, and the more divisions there are. An earlier book of mine, *The Art of Cooking,* is divided into stocks, soups, eggs, fish, shellfish, poultry, game, meat, bread, pastry, cakes, and more. But in this very personal and condensed cookbook, I wanted to make the groupings simpler, following the organization of a simple meal we enjoy at home, with the recipes divided among first courses, main courses, side dishes, and desserts. It is easy for the reader to look for ideas and find dishes with this organization, although it requires an open mind, because in the First Courses chapter there are many diverse dishes, from soup to fish to shellfish and pastry, that could be served as main courses as well by increasing the size of the portions. In the same way, many of the recipes in the Main Courses chapter can be reduced in size and served as a first course for an elaborate, elegant dinner.

In this book, I explain the recipes as I would if I were talking to a friend, rather than follow the conventional structure of a very organized and detailed set of quantities. My goal is to excite the imagination rather than set limits in a structured recipe. I want to give freedom to the cook, who can then imagine the recipe through my description and can take it further down the path and make it much more personal, intimate, and special. There is mystery and suspense in the making of a dish, and I do not want to take that away from the cook. The discoveries along the way will make that recipe unique and private. The same dish made with the same ingredients by ten different cooks will have ten outcomes. Some renditions will be dull and tasteless, and some brilliant, tasty, and original, depending on the talent and generosity of the cook. One has to cook with love and eagerness for the food to be exciting and flavorful, and this has to be controlled by good techniques.

Of course I have included the necessary ingredients and amounts in the recipes, with preparations and some cooking times as part of the story, but hopefully, not been specific enough to limit the cook's freedom. A recipe should always be read completely before starting to prepare the dish, although people seldom do it. In this book, more than in any of my other books, the recipes have to be read, understood, and visualized before the reader starts cooking. Though not always specified, it is a given that I use the best possible vegetables and fruits in season, unsalted butter, freshly ground black pepper, extra-virgin olive oil, great quality wine vinegar, and eggs from a farm.

This is an egocentric and personal book, and I have chosen recipes that I like to cook and eat. Some recipes are for four people, some for six, some for eight, depending on whether I am cooking for a picnic or for a couple of friends.

It is certainly in the French tradition to talk about food. In my family we talk about what we are eating, what we are going to eat, what we ate on a special occasion years ago, and on the pleasures of the table in general. In essays scattered throughout the book, I share my thoughts on various aspects of food, food history, and cooking, hoping to draw you in to some ongoing conversations with your family and friends on these topics.

For me, the greatest taste may be a perfect crunchy baguette slathered generously with the very best sweet butter, and the greatest dessert (besides dark, bitter chocolate) may be the succulent apricot or strawberry jams made with very ripe fruits and spread thickly on pieces of warm brioche. My favorite ritual is sitting every night at the dining-room table with my wife and sharing our meal and one, sometimes two, bottles of wine and discussing the events of the day. Throughout the last four decades, this daily ritual has been ingrained so profoundly within us that we could not live without it. I hope you will enjoy traveling with me down my memory lane and partaking of my food, my wine, and my friends.

The Anatomy of a Recipe

My purpose here is to discuss and try to define what a recipe is, what it is supposed to accomplish, and how it should be used. To most cooks, a recipe is a set of instructions, a formula explaining certain culinary processes or techniques used in the making of a dish. It has its uses, as well as its limitations. Certain recipes become friends to whom one comes back over and over again. Others have the equivocal quality of acquaintances with whom one is never totally comfortable. And some recipes feel totally foreign to one's style of cooking, taste, or culinary habits.

Somehow the mechanical and progressive process of adding one ingredient to another in well-defined and logical steps doesn't really equate with the final taste. There is a gap—a disconnect—between the step-by-step procedure and the completed dish, just as an artist cannot equate the technical process of painting with the finished work of art.

In addition to the method required in both cooking and painting, something intangible and elusive relating to the individual and his personal talent has to be part of the process. This intimate element determines the originality and concept of the dish. Yet for a beginner chef this structured, printed page that one calls a recipe is often necessary, even though it may take away the freedom of a dish. The formula is needed to control and replace the lack of experience of an often overenthusiastic amateur.

The interaction of ingredients—which differs from day to day—the mood of the cook, the functioning of the equipment, even the weather on the day the recipe is put down onto paper combine to dictate a particular formula. Thus a recipe is only the expression of one moment in time, and that moment can never be exactly duplicated again. Since the precise circumstances can't be duplicated, a dish can never be reproduced in exactly the same manner. That is the moment when the sense of taste of the cook should take over. As the recipe is made over and over, the nature of things changes. Temperature and humidity vary, available pots could be cast iron, stainless steel, or copper, and the heat source may be gas, electric, or radiant heat. The number of guests always differs, and the mood of the cook changes from day to day, as do the ingredients available at the market. All these variables result in subtle differences in the finished dish.

There cannot be great food without great ingredients. Although substitutions are often necessary, they can be tricky. Frozen butter, carrots, corn, or supermarket eggs are only pale copies of fresh butter, carrots, and corn just out of the garden, and eggs from free-range chickens. For the serious cook the search for good ingredients is perpetual. It is usually what distinguishes good cooking from great cooking. Even the best cook in the world cannot produce superlative cooking without superior ingredients.

The making of a dish entails many things. The goal is not to punctiliously follow instructions on a printed page; the goal is to duplicate a taste. That taste will not materialize if a formula is rigidly and blindly followed unless the exact set of conditions in place when the recipe was written are perfectly duplicated. Yet it is impossible to have a chicken with exactly the same amount of fat or to duplicate the same heat source or the same climatic conditions. To scrupulously follow a recipe is like making a painting with numbers; this process works only on a crude level and takes into account only the technical aspects of the process.

To create a dish, one starts with an idea and a number of ingredients. The "idea" in the Platonic context is a true model of what that dish could be. Of course, one never produces the "perfect" dish to match the Platonic model; yet the aim is to try to get as close as possible, and this is where the ingredients and techniques count. They are the assets, the tangible part of the recipe; the idea is the abstract part that concerns itself with the talent of the cook and the creation of a taste. With enough practice and knowledge, the making of a recipe happens first in the

Pot-au-Feu, recipe on page 168

head of the cook prior to the execution of the dish. This is the exciting time when one "creates" a taste in one's head. The dish can be "tasted" by the cook, just as a composer can "hear" his or her music at the moment of creation. One knows it will work, one knows that it will taste good, that it will taste right. In a written piece of music the beauty is there, inherent and invisible, just like the taste is in the written recipe. It is there within, waiting. In the large block of stone that Michelangelo is working on, the slaves are there, imprisoned, waiting. They are there, just as the taste in my recipe is there, "*en puissance*," waiting to be discovered and enjoyed through the proper techniques.

As the cook starts to proceed and combine ingredients, the food takes hold. Just as a painting reacts in a certain way when one color is added to another, a recipe progresses from one entity to another depending on the reaction of the ingredients at that particular moment, as well as the feel and knowledge of the cook. This is to say that small things like one more or one less tablespoon of flour and one different cut of the knife will create a new entity and situation. These "accumulated entities" or steps are determined by two things: how the food changes as the recipe moves forward and how the cook reacts to these changes.

Opportunity is an important factor. The method followed in creating a recipe often corresponds to an impulse, an insight. Ingredients get included because they happen to be there; a menu is created because of particular produce that happens to be beautiful at the market that day. So creating a recipe follows a logical order. To create a recipe is to work in a progressive way with ingredients and to transform and react to the ingredients by tasting, looking, and adjusting over and over again. One never controls a dish completely, but the more one knows about food, the better the control.

There is a contingency to the creation of a recipe, an elusive factor that is ever present and very important for the cook who doesn't follow a structured set of rules. One must progress from within the food, trying to make it move in a certain direction and acknowledge the changes. To write a recipe is simply to record objectively what is happening. All of these steps are determined by the look of the food and how the cook reacts along the way. When all is done, the finished product in the creation of a recipe is a printed page. For someone to start with that recipe, finished and structured, as a point of departure is to work in reverse of how the dish was created. Instead of starting with the ingredients and making them move in a certain direction, instead of working from within the food, one starts with everything already completely finalized. It is better to use the recipe only as a guide to secure the final taste.

Even when the combination of ingredients reaches the point where one thinks it is "right," it is not always easy to stop at the exact moment when the created taste is at its peak. It requires a certain detachment and objectivity as well as a clear palate to evaluate the same dish over and over again without dulling the taste buds. A good cook is able to follow the progression of taste, keeping the different elements separated until the moment when all the components blend together in a taste that coincides with or rejoins the original idea of the dish. This is the moment to stop; the taste is at its peak.

It is impossible for someone making a recipe from a book to be sure that the original taste created by the author is the same taste arrived at. Yet, if the result is appealing and satisfying, the recipe was made correctly. Isn't it true that "the proof of the pudding is in the eating"? I have had dinner many times at the homes of friends who cooked from one of my books and have often been amazed at how far away the dish has moved from the original recipe. It is not necessarily a negative experience; in fact, it is sometimes better than the original version, and I end up getting credit and thanks for a dish that has nothing to do with me anymore.

One of the most important steps in cooking is to taste again and again so that you acquire the memory of that taste and can store it somewhere in your memory bank. To make that recipe again is to duplicate that taste from memory, not to duplicate a printed page. This doesn't mean that the steps and procedures by which the recipe was created will be the same; more often than not, they will be different. Adjustments due to variations in ingredients, equipment, quantities, and cooking conditions will have to be made to reproduce, as closely as possible, the original taste. To learn how to cook is to learn the idea and taste behind a recipe. When the idea is understood and the taste controlled, one is able to duplicate a dish without a precise written formula to follow.

The cooking process is an art of adjustment, compensation, and, sometimes, recovery. The paradox is that the recipe tells the reader in a didactic way, "This must be done this way," when, in fact, to taste "the same" the recipe has to be changed each time to compensate for ingredients, working conditions, quantities, and the like. Hence, the act of writing down a recipe on a piece of paper, by definition, destroys the idea or essence of the recipe. Therefore, cooks have to rely on their palate and memory as they meander through all the variables in their search for the true taste.

A printed page of instructions knows nothing of the differences between a petrale, a lemon, or a gray sole, and it doesn't distinguish between an old and a freshly caught fish. If all the variables could be identified and explained, which is impossible, it could probably take many pages to write down a single recipe. The directions would be so confusing and impractical that even the most dedicated cook would find them useless. The true essence of the recipe is acquired and retained in the memory and this is where the professional chef goes to have consistency, recall, and harmony in the everyday routine of a restaurant kitchen. During my first job in the United States, at Le Pavillon in New York City, I wanted to duplicate dishes that I had prepared in Paris. I had no written formulas, but I had a quantity of taste memories to work from. By adding, tasting, adding, I achieved tastes that were as close as possible to the ones provided by my memory. For all intents and purposes, I *had* duplicated the dishes. Yet if someone had taken notes as I was making the same dishes in Paris and in New York, the quantities, explanations, and ingredients would have been quite different from city to city. But through memory and an understanding of the idea behind a recipe, the same taste—or a very close taste—was achieved.

The professional chefs who use their knowledge of food and memory of tastes should be able to duplicate the same dish anywhere in the world. They carry within themselves the knowledge and craftsmanship that enable them to make the proper adjustments to reach the right taste. When teaching cooking classes, I do not look at my recipes because I have the "idea" and the memory of the dish in my head. I know the process I want to follow and the taste I want to achieve. Therefore I take whatever steps are necessary to bring about the final taste.

What, then, is the purpose of a written recipe? A recipe is a teaching tool, a point of departure. You have to start somewhere to familiarize yourself with a new taste, new techniques, and the look of a new dish. So at first the recipe should be read completely before starting; a rule which is almost never observed and is the cause of many a downfall in the kitchen.

As you "formulate" a recipe for the first time, the author's instructions should be followed closely and faithfully. If the set of factors happens, coincidentally, to be close to the way things were when the author wrote the recipe down, it is likely that the dish will turn out well, partially by chance. In that case, you are likely to make the recipe again.

The second time the recipe is prepared, you have already acquired a familiarity or knowledge of the dish—what it tastes like, what it looks like, how the ingredients react with one another. You already feel a certain comfort with the dish. Because of that degree of confidence, you are likely to take a more casual look at the set of instructions the second time around. By the third time the dish is prepared, you start moving away from the original formula and making substitutions based on your personal impulses and taste. Eventually, as your knowledge of the dish increases, you forgo the original directions, and the recipe becomes more and more individualistic and personal. Finally, it is your own. By transforming the recipe progressively to suit your taste, you ultimately become the creator of a new recipe. This is a normal progression that is followed by the good home cook as well as the professional, and this is not plagiarism.

In his *Essays*, Montaigne, the great humanist of the sixteenth century, expresses the same idea. The bees, he says, gather the pollen from flower to flower, but they create their own honey. Likewise, there comes a time, after many personal transformations and adjustments, when a cook acquires an "in-depth" knowledge of a dish and transforms it into his own version of the dish.

All good cooks have this in-depth knowledge of some dishes. These are the familiar family favorites, dishes that are always welcome and that everybody loves—and they are never as good eaten anywhere else. Curiously, these dishes or ingredients often from our childhood, are so satisfying, so intrinsically part of ourselves, that they become inconspicuous and commonplace without the praise they rightly deserve. As a young man in France, I was never truly aware of the basket of bread and the carafe of wine that graced our daily table. It was only after I came to the United States and was invited to dinner at the home of a new American friend that I had met at Columbia University that I felt that

something was missing. We had been seated for a while and the first course had been served, and although I sensed that something was amiss, I could not pinpoint what it was. It was only when I extended my arm, in a conditioned reflex, for the basket of bread that I became aware that it was not there. Prior to this, it would have been unthinkable for me to sit at the table and go through a whole meal without bread and wine.

By making a dish again and again, the cook gains, often unconsciously, a thorough comprehension of it. Even if the telephone is ringing, the children are running through the house, or the ingredients are inconsistent, the cook adjusts easily and automatically, knowing what steps of the dish can be prepared ahead and what to do to increase the yield from four to forty.

Ingredients are what most often need adjusting. Preparation of pears in caramel sauce exemplifies the notion of adjustments in ingredients: the original "idea" is to peel pears, cut them in half, remove their seeds, and place the pear halves, sprinkled with sugar, in a roasting pan, which then goes into a hot oven. Exposed to the heat, the juice of the pears seeps out, combines with the sugar, and creates a syrup. As the syrup boils, the pears cook in the syrup and, by the time the syrup is reduced to a caramel, the pears should be just tender. Cream is added to the caramel to melt it, and the resulting silky, ivory sauce is poured around the pears in a serving dish. Eventually, as it cools, the sauce gets thicker and can be diluted with a dash of pear brandy or cognac to give it the proper taste and viscosity. The pears can be served in this manner with ice cream or crêpes, as well as flambéed.

When I first created this recipe, given the quality and ripeness of the pears, the temperature of the oven, and the type of roasting pan used, the pears cooked in 30 minutes. Therefore, the recipe reflects the 30 minutes of cooking as part of the instructions. This number reflects only what happened that particular day. Still, for someone

to make the dish and have the sugar transform into caramel and the pears become tender in exactly 30 minutes as explained in the recipe, would be purely coincidental and unlikely. What is essential, then, is to understand the goal or "idea" of the recipe: to create a syrup with the juice of the pears and sugar, to reduce it into a caramel, and to finish it with cream—all in the time it takes to cook the pears to perfect tenderness. With well-ripened Anjou or Bartlett pears, the juices will come out of the pears and create syrup after 8 or 10 minutes in the oven. The pears will be cooked enough by then. If the pears are cooked longer, they will fall apart before the amount of syrup around them has had time to reduce to a caramel. In this case, the adjustment is to transfer the cooked pears to a serving dish, place the syrup in a saucepan, and cook the syrup down on top of the stove until it turns into a caramel before finishing it with cream. In this way, the cook adjusts for very ripe pears. When using Bosc or Seckle pears, which tend to be quite firm and lower in moisture, the cook must make the opposite adjustment. After 5, 10, or 12 minutes of cooking, the pears will still be hard and will not have released any liquid, so the dry sugar may start to smoke and burn. To adjust for this lack of moisture, one must add water to the pan to create the syrup. By the time this syrup boils and reduces into caramel, the pears should be tender and properly cooked. If not, more water will have to be added and the pears cooked longer. Eventually, the pears will be cooked and the syrup caramelized so it can be finished with cream and brandy. Although the written recipe indicates a cooking time of 30 minutes, the ripe pears cooked in 5 minutes while the hard ones may have needed an hour to get tender. Yet for the good cook, who knows how to compensate, the three dishes taste and look similar when finished.

Equipment is the second factor most often in need of adjustment. The control and reaction of metal pots and pans to electric heat as com-pared to gas heat is different. The control is better with gas. Cooking in stainless steel rather than aluminum will change the cooking time as well as the taste and appearance of food. In dry roasting, aluminum will create beautiful crystallization of the juices, while they will have a ten-dency to burn in stainless steel. The oven temperature must be adjusted accordingly. Some metals tend to discolor food, others impart a metallic taste, while others will react to acid in the food and thus may be unsuit-able for certain dishes.

Finally, quantities require a great deal of adjustment. A veal stew for four people can be made in a medium-size Dutch oven, and the vegetables will brown along with the meat. The entire procedure can be done in one pot, and the dish will develop a specific taste and look done in this manner. To duplicate the same taste and look for twelve people, the procedure will be quite different. If the ingredients for twelve are cooked in the same pot, even if it is a large one, it is likely that the meat will not brown properly and the vegetables will fall apart. For lack of crystallization of the meat, the sauce will be light and weak. In order for the dish to taste and look right, it must be prepared in a completely different way. The meat and vegetables should be browned in different skillets, cooked different lengths of time, and, eventually, combined, all with one goal in mind: to recreate the same look and taste as the original smaller stew.

These variations are an habitual ritual, a common and daily prac-tice for most professional cooks. However, for neophytes, who depend entirely on that printed page we call a recipe, the making of this or another dish will depend not only on the explanations of the author but also on contingency factors that they are probably not aware of. You may be lucky enough to have a chicken with the same amount of fat or a pineapple with the same ripeness as those used by the creator of the recipe, but there are no guarantees. The situation at hand may be very close to or very far from the conditions that prevailed when the recipe was first created. This is why explaining a recipe so it is foolproof to a novice is basically impossible. With a pro, however, one can bypass most of the procedures and get directly to the "idea" or principle behind the directions. For example, it is sufficient to tell a chef that the pear dish is made by baking pears and simultaneously creating a caramel with the juice of the pears and sugar and, finally, melting that caramel with cream and brandy. All the contingencies, like the time of cooking and the quantity of sugar required (which depends on the sweetness of the fruit and the amount of moisture it contains), will automatically be understood.

A cookbook like the *Repertory of Cooking* is written in this manner and is intended specifically for the professional. In this very small book are packed 7,500 recipes written in a very elliptical style. Most of the recipes are one, two, or three lines, and give the cook the principles of the dish rather than specific directions. This type of writing presupposes a great deal of knowledge and craftsmanship on the part of the reader and would be worthless for beginners. At the other end of the spectrum, in *Mastering the Art of French Cooking*, Julia Child writes more than fifteen pages of instructions to explain to the readers all the intricacies of making a French baguette. Most writers of cookbooks will place themselves somewhere between the two extremes, as it is impossible to satisfy everyone's needs. Yet, when deciding what cookbook to buy, you face that dilemma. Depending on your own needs, desires, and knowledge, you may be more comfortable with the *Repertory of Cooking* while other people prefer *Mastering the Art of French Cooking*.

There are two approaches to the creation of a recipe: scientific and poetic. The scientific approach extols measurement to the sixteenth of a teaspoon of an ingredient and directs the cook in such a precise, determined way that it becomes excessive, specious, and, finally, does not work. Cooking cannot be treated as a mathematical formula (although baking is more likely to work with a structured formula than cooking). Pushed to the extreme, the scientific approach reduces the ingredients to numbers and the cooking process to a robotic sequence. The poetic approach, on the other hand, extols casualness. Throwing a little bit of this or that capriciously into a dish creates a hit-or-miss situation and usually leads to disaster. To an amateur, a professional chef—precise in movements and techniques—may seem to combine ingredients together very casually. Talking and cooking at the same time, not measuring ingredients, seems a very poetic approach. Granted, there is freedom in the cooking process of the professional, but this seemingly nonchalant attitude is controlled by many years of practice. It is a disciplined, directed, and "restricted informality," to create an oxymoron. This is the place where the technician joins the artist and creates the proper conditions for fathering great dishes.

The special accent given by each cook creates dishes with a signature. A dish is often a giveaway; it betrays the identity of the cook to a good taster who can recognize the certain style and seasonings of a particular chef. The "Grandma recipe" never tastes the same unless *she* makes it. Even if she explains to someone else exactly how to make it, that version will still be different because there is a certain "touch" that makes the recipe impossible to duplicate exactly.

There are contradictions in most cookbook recipes. Each recipe is a small story, a complete entity in itself with a beginning, a middle, and an end. Usually a recipe is written with instructions, as if the recipe will be served by itself as soon as it is finished. It is true that I have often sautéed a piece of fish till ready, divided it between two plates, and brought it to the table for my wife and me to enjoy for lunch or dinner. Yet, most of the time, recipes are served within the context of a menu. That is, while one dish is consumed, the next one may have to wait in the oven. Or, if I need the oven to broil the fish at the last minute, I may have to make the roast a bit earlier.

Some cookbooks cover some of these contingencies, especially if it is the type of book that leads the reader through making a whole menu. For example, "Start with your roast. While it is cooking, peel and boil your potatoes, then start the fish. Next, clean the salad and prepare the dressing. Then, finish your potatoes and remove the roast from the oven. By then the fish should be ready, so open the wine, slice the bread, and you are ready to serve." The problem with this type of cookbook is that it forces you to cook and consume a whole menu with combinations that you may or may not like. On the other hand, when writing a conventional cookbook, there is no way for the author to know whether or not the reader will serve each dish by itself or in combination with other dishes and if so, in what combinations. Therefore, recipes have to be thought through carefully and adjusted according to where they fit in a menu or whether they are going to be served by themselves immediately after cooking.

For a cookbook author, there is a disturbing finality in the writing of recipes. During the period when a cookbook is written and edited, things continue to evolve and change, and, by the time the book is published, most authors would like to be able to refine and adjust some of the recipes again. However, this is not possible. The recipes are now written "in stone." So, when the recipes are taken away to be published, they become somewhat alien to the author who is now stuck with them and has no possibility of changing or improving them.

In the best of circumstances, the role of the author is inherited by the cooks who will prepare the recipes from the book. By understanding the writer's ideas, the essence or concept of the recipes, and by cooking them again and again, the cooks will "improve" the recipes and eventually make them their own with their own personal touch and creativity. This is what good cooking and good eating are all about.

COOKING AND PAINTING

I have been cooking for more than half a century, and I have been painting sporadically for thirty or forty years. Cooking is fun, but also serious; after all, it is my métier. Painting is strictly fun, and I paint only when I am in the mood. I know I am a better cook than painter, because I know cooking much better than I know painting. I do not equate great painters and great cooks. Cooking is mostly a matter of craftsmanship with some talent added—and sometimes great talent emerges from the kitchen. However, cooking, like painting, sculpting, being a surgeon, mason, or jeweler requires a great deal of skill.

There are people who have great technical skill in the kitchen and not much talent. I have known chefs who have spent thirty years in their profession, can run a kitchen properly, and are quite good technically, but their food is never really great; they don't have the palate and the talent to take it further. This is not said pejoratively. People with some technique and some talent usually do well, while others with no technique and some talent, a situation I have found often in students and amateur cooks, who may have a great sense of taste, might turn out a very good dish occasionally, but they cannot control the quality and production of the food or run a restaurant. Likewise, art students who spend three years in school learning the rules of perspective, how to mix yellow and blue to make green, and how to use a brush and a spatula will be able to sit at an easel and create one painting after another. Does that make these people artists? No, they are craftsmen at this point. However, these trained hands now have the means to express talent, if they have it. It is the same with the chef apprentice.

In painting, individuals who have extraordinary technique and extraordinary talent, like Picasso or Matisse, are geniuses. In the kitchen, a few chefs have certainly gone further and achieved more than others, and they have become models, setting the criteria for other professionals. Chefs like Guérard in France and Thomas Keller in America are good examples.

In this book, I have been egocentric and partial to the food I love and the food that is very close to my sense of taste and aesthetics, without concerning myself too much with diversity, balance, or menu-making. With the recipe photos, I have tried to stay true to the food, without "torturing" it to make it look artistic. For me, by far the most important attribute of food, beside its physiological function, is taste. In painting, however, the visual is the most important and essential attribute. I always say in jest that food critics should be blind, so that they can go to the heart of the matter and know whether the food is good or not. Yet there is some truth in this statement. Some chefs tend to put too much food on the plate and place too much emphasis on the decoration and the visual elements of the food—often at the expense of taste. The food becomes muddy and loses its identity.

In Proust's affective memory as recounted in *Remembrance of Things Past*, look, touch, taste, smell, and hearing are of the utmost importance, and so it is for a chef. The smell, the taste, the look, and the touch merge into a dish. Good chefs are very aware of all their senses. However, talent is expressed only if technique is present. Endless repetition, a kind of mechanical process, is an investment of time, which is necessary for a chef. Eventually, the techniques become so much a part of the self that they will never be forgotten. Only after that fastidious process has been mastered can one think in terms of combinations of

Cooking and painting make me happy

ingredients, texture, color, harmony, and complementary *saveur*. As long as one is impaired by the tasks of slicing, cutting, and poaching, there is no space for talent to emerge.

When I have an idea about a dish, I can "cook it" in my head; I can follow the processes of putting the dish together, of cooking it, and thus avoid the pitfalls before actually starting the process. When I finally make the dish, the hammer may not fall exactly on the head of the nail each time, but it will fall close enough so that a couple of corrections usually produce the results I had imagined. On the other hand, as a painter I have very little technique. I have never invested the time and the endless repetition necessary to understand the primary, secondary, and tertiary colors and other tricks of the trade, like what can be done with a brush, a knife, a spatula, or a finger. I am a poor technician.

It is very hard for my hands to express the ideas I have in my head, because my technique is not good enough, and this is very frustrating. When one of my paintings turns out rather well, it's more fortuitous or accidental than controlled.

I read somewhere that cooking is a controlled creation, which is an oxymoron. However, I believe it to be true in cooking and painting as well. Although I get frustrated when I start a painting, occasionally something magical happens, and I end up with a picture that is partially satisfying. While I sometimes feel instinctively that I'm not quite "there," I don't know how to move forward. This is not the case with cooking, where I can analyze the process as I proceed and know if I need more viscosity, more seasoning, or more balance in a sauce to go further in the recipe. There is a process in starting a painting that is

kitchen utensils   *apricots of Provence*   *bowl of fruit*

difficult, even terrifying, sometimes, that I do not experience with cooking, because I know the processes so well.

Starting in the 1970s, nouvelle cuisine emphasized creativity in the making of a recipe and the presentation of the food on the plate. It also emphasized going to the market daily, not overcooking fish, vegetables, and meat, and being mindful of the health of your customers. Additionally, it advised chefs to streamline recipes and simplify sauces. This was all good advice. Unfortunately, many chefs remember only the creativity and presentation edicts.

Creativity is often a Pandora's box, giving license to chefs to combine the weirdest of ingredients, just for the sake of shock. Arranged on oversized plates, these ingredients are "overtouched," to quote Julia Child, and symmetrically arranged with tiny baby vegetables and meat

sliced ahead, which tends to bleed it, cool it, and dry it out. On these overdecorated plates the food becomes stagnant, losing its spontaneity and natural quality. It doesn't make you salivate when you look at it. However, I do not mean to denigrate all display; when the taste is secure, there is nothing wrong with a nice presentation, but never at the expense of taste.

Edmond Saillant, under his nom de plume, Curnonsky, wrote about regional and women's cooking in the early twentieth century. He famously said that food should have the taste of what it is, and there is certainly truth in his statement. There is nothing better than a tomato right out of the garden. Embellished with only the best possible olive oil and a dash of *fleur de sel*, it's all about the tomato. Yet, I remember eating my first piece of American apple pie shortly after I came to the

the dining room   the calm sea   kitchen tools

United States and feeling puzzled. The French apple tart, made with only apples, sugar, and butter, is all about the apple taste. My first impression was that American apple pie, with the addition of cinnamon, nutmeg, and/or mace, destroyed the taste of the apples, and it does to a certain extent. However, the combination of apples, butter, cinnamon, and mace creates a new, endearing taste. In that case, different flavors reach a crescendo in a harmony of their own. Other times, one simple ingredient is the key. To taste pork, enjoy a plain pork roast. Yet, when ground pork is mixed with cognac, shallots, wine, and other types of seasonings, the result is a pâté, which has a taste of its own—just as good as the simple roast, but different. There is value in both schools: simplicity and harmony. I am sometimes in the mood for simplicity, and other times crave a harmony of flavors and creativity.

I don't know whether my painting has helped my cuisine, or whether my cooking has helped my painting, and I don't know if one borrows from the other. All I know is that, certainly, for me, cooking and painting can live together in harmony. Both are different expressions of who I am and both enhance my life considerably.

It is great fun to fill the plates with paint instead of food

First Courses

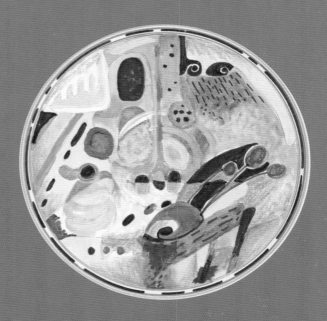

This chapter features a potpourri of dishes that includes stocks, soups, eggs, and various shellfish, like OYSTERS ROCKEFELLER and CLAM FRITTERS, which are perfect first courses. SMOKED TROUT AND SCRAMBLED EGGS is a great breakfast or lunch dish, and TRUFFLE AND PISTACHIO SAUSAGE WITH BUTTERED FINGERLING POTATOES makes a perfect lunch. Many of the recipes, from FRIED WHITEBAIT to the SAUCISSON OF PORK TENDERLOIN, are dishes often enjoyed with an aperitif before a meal, or are ideal for a large gathering, picnic, party, or when playing *boules.* Keep an open mind, and rearrange the recipes based on your own tastes and needs regarding whether they should be served as a first course or main course.

Small Oatmeal Breads, recipe on page 42

CHICKEN STOCK, BROWN STOCK, AND DEMI-GLACE

YIELD: ABOUT 4 CUPS OF STOCK, 2 CUPS OF DEMI-GLACE

Chicken stock is used more than any other stock in my house. We use it to deglaze a pan to do a sauce, as a base for a soup, to cook vegetables in, and to add to stews. It is a time-saver in the kitchen and the secret to many great soups and stews.

I don't really see much difference between the words stock, broth, and bouillon, and for me they are interchangeable. There are two types of stock: white stock and brown stock. They are both precious resources for the cook, although white stock is used more often than brown stock, and the difference is in the browning of the bones. White and brown stocks differ in the same way that boiled and roasted chickens do; a boiled chicken will produce a white stock that is lighter in taste and color than the darker, more deeply flavored brown stock from a roasted chicken. White stock is usually added to soups, sauces, or vegetables. Unsalted brown stock is often defatted and reduced by half, until syrupy and concentrated, to create a demi-glace.

Not too many years ago, you absolutely had to make your own chicken stock, but now there are good alternatives. There are several fairly good chicken stocks on the market with a minimal amount of salt—even some without salt—and they are pretty lean with a fairly good taste. I still like to make my own chicken stock, put it into containers, and freeze it. The whole house has a wonderful smell when Gloria or I make stock. When I buy a whole chicken and bone it out for a recipe, I freeze the carcass to make stock. I also make stock with the carcass from a roasted chicken along with other chicken parts that I can find at the market or in my freezer.

I used to get chicken bones at most markets, but they have become harder to find, so I buy gizzards, wings, and necks for my brown stock or use whatever chicken bones I have frozen myself. For small quantities of bones, it is easier to brown them on top of the stove in a large skillet or saucepan. When preparing a lot of brown stock (whether with chicken, veal, or beef bones), the easiest way to cook the bones is to put them in a large roasting pan and brown them in the oven. You want crystallization of the juice in the bottom of the pan. This solidified juice or glaze is released from the pan in the process of deglazing, which is adding water to the pan to melt the crystallized juice and create a stock.

Use a stainless-steel stockpot for stock, since it doesn't discolor the stock, as aluminum can. Some people bring the bones to a boil in cold water and then discard the water and start again. This is necessary only if the bones smell. In the first ten or fifteen minutes of cooking, most of the scum, which is coagulated protein, will come to the top. Skim it off, if you like. If you do not remove it, it goes to the side, and with the liquid at a very gentle boil, it stays there, getting smaller and smaller, and is removed when the stock is strained at the end. The important part is to start the stock with cold water and keep it at a very gentle boil, uncovered. If the stock comes to a rolling boil, the fat that rises to the top tumbles down into the liquid and emulsifies, getting incorporated into the stock. So keep the stock at a gentle boil. No salt should be added, and the pot should be uncovered or partially covered. Conversely, when reducing the stock to demi-glace, it doesn't matter if it boils strongly. The fat has already been removed from the stock, so there is no possibility of it being incorporated in the reduction.

Demi-glace is really unsalted brown stock that is reduced to the point where it becomes syrupy and concentrated. Thickened very lightly

when I smell chicken stock, I am home

with a pure starch, demi-glace is a vehicle used to create sauces. A piece of beef sautéed and deglazed with red wine and finished with demi-glace becomes beef with burgundy or bordelaise sauce. A chicken sautéed with tomato, tarragon, and white wine and finished with demi-glace becomes chicken with chasseur sauce. With a reduction of Madeira, the demi-glace becomes a Madeira sauce, and if you add truffles to the Madeira sauce, you have a truffle sauce, classically called Périgueux sauce, named for a town in the southwest of France where a lot of truffles come from.

In the last few years when I don't have demi-glace on hand I have experimented with a new technique. I use bottled or pre-made sauces in the finishing of dishes, like many Chinese cooks do. When sautéing venison or beef steaks, for example, I make a sauce with the drippings in the pan by adding balsamic vinegar, red wine, Worcestershire or steak sauce, a bit of ketchup, and some water and wine to create a sauce without a standard demi-glace, which people sometimes don't have at hand. However, sometimes it is impossible to make a sauce without demi-glace, as in the Parfait of Rosé Mushrooms with Sherry-Truffle Sauce, page 86, so I am including a recipe here.

———————————— ⁓⁓⁓ ————————————

CHICKEN STOCK | For 1 quart of potent stock, put 2 POUNDS OF CHICKEN CARCASS, NECK, GIZZARD, AND WINGS in a stockpot with 10 CUPS OF COLD WATER, and bring to a boil. As soon as the water comes to a boil, reduce the heat and maintain a very gentle boil at the surface of the liquid. Let boil, uncovered, for 10 to 15 minutes before adding any other ingredients. The scum will come to the top, and you can remove and discard it. Add 1 MEDIUM-SIZED ONION that has been cut in half and stuck with 4 WHOLE CLOVES, and then add 1 SPRIG OF THYME OR A LITTLE DRIED THYME, A COUPLE OF BAY LEAVES, 1 SMALL LEEK, and 1 RIB OF CELERY. Return the liquid to a boil, and boil gently for about 2 hours. Strain through a colander set over a bowl, and then strain again through a fine double-mesh strainer to remove any remaining bones. You should have about 1 quart of stock. Adjust with water if necessary.

Cool the stock overnight in the refrigerator, and then totally defat it by carefully spooning off and discarding all fat from the top. It should be a clear jelly. (If a recipe calls for a light chicken stock, dilute it with water to the desired concentration.) Divide among small containers, cover well, and freeze.

BROWN STOCK AND DEMI-GLACE | TWO POUNDS OF BONES—WINGS, NECKS, AND CARCASS—should fill up the bottom of a large, heavy, 12-inch saucepan. Start with A GOOD DASH OF CANOLA OR PEANUT OIL. The fat in the pan or on the skin of the chicken will be removed from the stock later on. At first the fat helps the browning. Brown the bones for 30 to 35 minutes on top of the stove over medium heat, until the pieces are nicely caramelized and the juice is crystallized in the bottom of the pan. Use a wooden spatula to loosen and scrape the bones in the pan as they cook.

Cut A LARGE ONION with the skin on into six pieces, and add to the pan along with 1 MEDIUM CARROT, washed, peeled, and cut into 2-inch pieces, and 6 TO 8 CLOVES OF UNPEELED GARLIC. Stir into

the bones, and continue cooking for 4 or 5 minutes, until you begin to smell the wonderful aroma of the onions, carrots, and garlic browning.

Pour the whole mixture into a colander to strain off the fat, or use a towel to hold the lid of the pan on top of the bones, so there is a small opening at the front. Pour the fat into a bowl, shaking the pan several times to remove as much fat as possible. To the bones in the pan, add 1 GALLON OF WATER, 1 SPRIG OF OREGANO, and 1 SPRIG OF FRESH THYME OR A TEASPOON OF DRIED THYME, A BAY LEAF, A RIB OF CELERY cut into 3 or 4 pieces, 1½ CUPS COARSELY CHOPPED FRESH TOMATOES, and 3 OR 4 TABLESPOONS OF KETCHUP (my secret ingredient), which adds a little sweetness and some of the color that I am looking for. Bring the mixture to a boil, and boil, uncovered, for about 1½ hours.

Strain the stock through a colander into a bowl, pressing on the solids to extract as much juice as possible, and then strain again through a double-mesh metal strainer to remove any remaining impurities. You should have a good quart of stock. Adjust with water, if needed. Cool for several hours or overnight in the refrigerator to allow the fat to come to the top. Remove the fat to reveal a beautiful jellied stock. You can freeze the stock, properly covered, at this point, or return it to a saucepan and boil it down to reduce it to a demi-glace.

To make demi-glace: Boil the stock until it is reduced to about 2 cups. It will be a beautiful reddish brown, light caramel color. Thicken with 1½ TEASPOONS OF POTATO STARCH OR ARROWROOT dissolved in 2 TABLESPOONS OF WATER OR RED OR WHITE WINE. This will thicken it just enough so that the viscosity of the demi-glace will be like heavy cream. Pour into containers, cover well, and refrigerate or freeze.

COOKING WITH WATER

There is a secret ingredient everlasting and present in most recipes; it is water. A good, generous, and free ingredient, water gives moisture, texture, and juiciness to food. It is responsible for enhancing the natural taste of food and is, therefore, a giver that does not alter or take away from the food.

Water is by far the most indispensable ingredient in a kitchen. Try to think of a restaurant kitchen without water for a minute. What would the sauce cook do for his stock? How would the soup and vegetable chef steam vegetables and make soup? How would the fish chef poach his fish? How would the beverage maker prepare his coffee? How could the pastry chef make puff pastry? Water goes into the dough, creates steam in the cooking process, and disappears, leaving thin, buttery, and tender flakes of pastry behind. What would the baker do if he couldn't spray water into the oven to make the bread expand and burst open, creating a thick crusty top and wonderful color and taste?

Water is the most modest of all ingredients. It helps highlight the flavor inherent in each product, without asking for recognition, as wine, juice, or stock does. The quality of water is often paramount to the quality of a dish. I'm lucky enough to have a well that is 350 feet deep, which supplies me with cold, clear, healthy, and delicious water. However, when I travel, I can taste chemicals in most towns' water when brushing my teeth or drinking a cup of coffee. If the water is really bad where you live, cook with bottled water.

Great water is needed to make great beer or whiskey. And for the true taste of vegetables, a vegetable soup should be made with vegetables and water, rather than stock. Great vegetable sauces are made by cooking one vegetable, like carrots, red peppers, or mushrooms, with water only and emulsifying the mixture, adding seasonings and butter. That's where the true taste is. In the great classic dish carrots Vichy, thinly sliced carrots are cooked in a little water, butter, salt, and a dash of sugar. The water creates the moisture to cook the carrots until tender and then evaporates along the way, so the cooked carrots are lightly glazed in the butter and sugar mixture at the end.

When making stocks or sauces, water is the medium that controls the end result. It is the medium because, to use the example of a plain beef stock, the bones have to cook a good six hours to release all the taste and nutrients necessary for a good stock, and water is the indispensable vehicle for the outcome. During the cooking, one adds water regularly to compensate for the evaporation. How much water is added is immaterial as long as the stock cooks long enough to get as much taste as possible from the bones. If, for argument's sake, the yield is supposed to be two quarts and is only one quart, additional water will bring the stock to a proper consistency and taste. Likewise, if the result is three quarts, reduction will bring it to the correct strength.

Water is paramount to deglazing solidified juices. For example, when a chicken has finished roasting, the accumulated liquid in the roasting pan consists of fat and encrustations, or glaze. Pour most of the fat off, add water, and bring the mixture to a boil to melt the glaze, and then strain the mixture. If too much water has been added, reduce it to the proper taste. One may be generous when adding water, because it is easy to correct. This is not so when deglazing with stock, wine, or liquor, because these liquids add flavor to the drippings. If too much wine is added, the juices will be acidic and harsh, and if the mixture is over-reduced, it will become strong, overpowering the natural taste of the roast. Wine and alcohol should be used in moderation and at the right moment.

Sometimes cooks turn their noses up disdainfully at water. They feel that deglazing with stock, Madeira, cognac, or deep red wine shows knowledge and sophistication. More often than not, mediocre dishes result from an excess of goodies rather than a lack of them. Too much reduction or an excess of butter, cream, wine, and cognac tend to muddy a dish and make it too rich, taking away from the clarity of taste.

There are recipes for cooking chopped onions, shallots, leeks, or scallions that advise sautéing them for a few minutes, until they are tender and translucent but not brown. The best approach is to put the onions in a skillet with butter or oil, add water to the mixture, and cook until the water evaporates. At that time, if the onions are not cooked enough, add additional water and continue cooking until the liquid evaporates again. When the mixture starts to sizzle or *chante* (sing), you know the evaporation is complete, and the onions will be transparent, tender, but still white. The water, a discreet and innocuous friend, will not have added any flavor of its own to the dish.

There is nothing like water to clean your palate between dishes or between sauces, so that you can distinguish between ingredients and nuances of taste. When one cooks behind the stove, with the heat of the kitchen, beer and wine are not the preferred beverages, and nothing will cool you off better than a couple of glasses of cool, fresh water. As an extra bonus, water is free, doesn't put any weight on you, and keeps you healthy. Enjoy it, and not in moderation.

ONION SOUP GRATINÉE

YIELD: 6 SERVINGS

I have many memories of late-night gratinée parties in our Lyon restaurant kitchen or at our house when I was a young man. When my brothers and I would go out at night, we usually came back with friends at 2 or 3 A.M. and traditionally prepared onion soup gratinée in the winter—and even in the summer—in the middle of the night. There are several versions of onion soup, and the ones served in restaurants rarely match the rich and crusty version we enjoyed as children.

My mother's recipe for this soup was made with water rather than stock. I liked it, although I have come to prefer the ones made with chicken stock. Using butter, she browned her onions more than anyone else I've ever seen, for 20 or 30 minutes, or until they were a mahogany color, with some of them almost black. She would then add a little sprinkling of flour, a little garlic, and some water, and cook this mixture for 30 minutes before putting it through a food mill. The result was a rich, dark, slightly thickened onion bouillon. She poured this into a large soup tureen containing a lot of sliced leftover country bread (*gros pain*) that she had browned in the oven. Half the tureen was bread, and the rest was filled with her broth. She then covered the broth with grated cheese and baked the soup for about 1 hour in a hot oven. Often, in the classic Lyon style, she would bring the large tureen of puffy golden soup to the table, make a hole in the center with her ladle, and pour in a mixture of egg yolks and port wine that she had combined in her soup plate. She then would stir the gratinée, crust and all, into a thick, hot mélange and serve it right away in hot soup plates. It was a meal in itself.

I make my gratinée the way we prepared it in Paris. It is baked in brown earthenware onion soup bowls that have a little ear or handle on either side. Do not use bowls with a straight edge; use slightly rounded bowls with a wide rim around the top. This is important, because it is on that wide rim that the grated cheese topping is pressed, hanging a little over the edge. As it cooks, the cheese sticks to the rim of the bowl, preventing the beautiful crust from sinking into the soup. Use a good chicken stock, flavorful, not too heavy, not too dark, and preferably homemade. I like yellow Bermuda onions; they have character but are not too acidic or strong in flavor.

In 1970, I opened a soup restaurant called La Potagerie on Fifth Avenue between 45th and 46th Streets in New York City. We prepared four different thick stewlike soups every day, but we made only thirty-six onion soup gratinées—we didn't have oven space to do more. They were made like this recipe and were ready at the beginning of the lunch service. When we brought them to the dining room, they disappeared in the first fifteen minutes of the service.

Gloria and I have to have onion soup a few times during the winter, and when we prepare it like this, it is essentially dinner. We usually enjoy it with a salad, a bottle of red wine, and fruit for dessert. Be careful not to burn yourself when eating through the brown, crusty cheese top that keeps this soup boiling hot.

Preheat the oven to 400°F. Cut A BAGUETTE into ½-inch slices, arrange the slices in a single layer on a cookie sheet, and bake in the oven for 8 to 10 minutes, until nicely browned.

Peel and slice about 1 POUND OF ONIONS by hand or in a food processor. Brown the onions in a sturdy saucepan with 1 TABLESPOON EACH OF BUTTER AND EITHER CORN OR PEANUT OIL over fairly high heat for about 15 minutes, stirring occasionally. The onions should be golden brown, soft, and have a wonderful aroma. Add about 8 CUPS OF CHICKEN STOCK and 1 CLOVE OF FINELY CHOPPED GARLIC (a little touch of garlic makes this soup taste more like my mother's). Bring to a strong boil, then reduce the heat and cook at a gentle boil for about 10 minutes. Add SALT AND PEPPER to taste. Using the big-hole side of a box grater to create thick threads, grate about ¾ POUND OF EMMENTHALER, GRUYÈRE, OR JARLSBERG CHEESE.

Preheat the oven to 425°F. Arrange six rounded onion soup crocks with about a 1½-cup capacity on a cookie sheet. Place 6 to 8 toasted baguette slices in each of the bowls, and sprinkle 1 or 2 tablespoons of the cheese on top. Fill the bowls to the rim with the soup mixture, adding water or chicken stock if you don't have quite enough liquid to fill the bowls completely. Just before putting the bowls in the oven, sprinkle about ½ cup of grated cheese on top of each. (You will notice that some of the bread will have risen to the top at this point, so you will have a bread base for the cheese.) Make certain that the cheese adheres to the rim of each bowl, pressing it around the edge with your thumb, so it will hold firm and melt there as it cooks. Let some of the cheese hang over the edge; it will form a crust. Place the tray in the oven, and bake for about 30 minutes, or until the cheese is golden, puffed, and crusty and the soup is very hot.

Onion soup gratinée and a glass of red wine for dinner

Clam Chowder and Small Oatmeal Breads

YIELD: 4 SERVINGS

I had never heard of or tasted clam chowder before I came to the United States. In fact, I had never had clams, although they do exist in France. At first I thought the flavor of clams was too strong compared to oysters, but after so many years in America, I now prefer clams to oysters and have become addicted to them.

Small littleneck clams are about 1½ inches in diameter at most, and cherrystones are 2 to 2½ inches in diameter. Large clams, quahogs, weigh up to 1 pound each and are sometimes cut into pieces for chowder or for spaghetti and clam sauce, one of my wife's specialties. I also puree large quahogs in a food processor, mix the puree with flour, baking powder, eggs, and seasonings, and fry them in oil for delicious clam fritters (see pages 60–61).

I learned how to make classic New England clam chowder at Howard Johnson's, where it was a specialty. Made and canned for the restaurants, it contained bacon, thyme, potatoes, clam juice, and a roux to thicken the mixture. The clams were added last, and the mixture was canned and cooked in the can for several hours, so the clams were tender. I featured Manhattan clam chowder, with a base of vegetables and tomato, at my soup restaurant La Potagerie in New York. I used about twelve different types of vegetables, from celery to eggplant, zucchini, onion, and tomatoes, and it was one of the most popular soups we offered.

In the area of Connecticut where I live, chowder is often made with potatoes, clam broth, thyme, and bacon, but without the roux and cream we used at Howard Johnson's; it is quite good. When I make New England clam chowder in the style of Howard Johnson's at home, even after 1½ hours of cooking the clams are still somewhat chewy. In my new way of making it, the clams and their juice are added to the hot soup just before serving, so they remain tender. The base is made quickly with butternut squash, leek, onion, garlic, milk, and a little cream.

With this chowder, I like to serve small oatmeal breads. I make these in small (2 tablespoon capacity) nonstick mini muffin pans or in the rubberized silicone mini muffin pans that are available in some markets.

CLAM CHOWDER | For four people, shuck 2 DOZEN CHERRYSTONE CLAMS. Set them aside in four small glass bowls, 6 clams per bowl, with about ¼ CUP OF CLAM JUICE in each bowl, leaving any sandy residue behind. In a stockpot cook about 1½ CUPS OF SLICED LEEKS in 1 TABLESPOON OF OLIVE OIL for a minute or so. Add 2½ CUPS OF DICED (¼-INCH) BUTTERNUT SQUASH, 1 CUP OF DICED (¼-INCH) MUSHROOMS, 3 CUPS OF MILK, A GOOD DASH OF SALT AND FRESHLY GROUND BLACK PEPPER, and 1 TABLESPOON OF CHOPPED GARLIC. Bring to a boil, then reduce the heat, and simmer for 3 or 4 minutes to cook the vegetables. Meanwhile, arrange 3 SLICES OF BACON on a ridged microwave tray, cover with a paper towel and microwave for 3 or 4 minutes, or until beautifully crisp. Transfer the clams and juice to four hot soup plates, and pour the boiling soup over them. Crumble about ½ slice of bacon on top of each serving.

SMALL OATMEAL BREADS | YIELD: ABOUT 12
Preheat the oven to 425°F. Put ½ STICK (4 TABLESPOONS) OF BUTTER in a large bowl with ½ CUP OF SLICED LEEKS, and microwave the mixture for about 1 minute to cook the leeks. Add ¼ CUP OF COLD MILK, which cools off the butter and leeks a little, and mix in 1 EGG, 1 TEASPOON OF SUGAR, ½ TEASPOON OF SALT, ⅓ CUP ALL-PURPOSE FLOUR, ½ CUP OATMEAL FLAKES, and 1 TEASPOON BAKING POWDER. Mix well, spoon into mini muffin cups, and bake for about 10 minutes.

POTAGE PARMENTIER (LEEK AND POTATO SOUP)

YIELD: 4 SERVINGS

If I had to choose one soup from among all my favorites, it would probably be leek and potato soup, potage Parmentier, named after the French agronomist Antoine-Augustin Parmentier, who developed the culture of the potato in France in the eighteenth century.

Leeks are essential to this soup; there is no replacement for them in this recipe. You can add a little onion, too, but leeks, potatoes, and stock are basically all you need. The hot soup is traditionally enriched with butter, and served with croutons and a sprinkling of chopped fresh chervil on top. If you don't have chervil, substitute chives or parsley, but the chervil lends a special anise taste. When I was a kid, my mother would prepare a rough leek and potato soup, cubing the potatoes and not pureeing them. We would pour cold milk into the soup at the table, and that was how we liked eating it. The milk would cool the soup off a little and give it that nutty, buttery taste of milk. Many restaurants finish the classic Parmentier with heavy cream, but I tend to prefer it finished with a little sweet butter.

For many years the cold version of this dish, the classic vichyssoise, was known in the United States but not in France. It was created by Louis Diat, who included a recipe for it in a book he wrote in the 1930s as the executive chef at The Ritz-Carlton in New York City. I worked at the Plaza Athénée hotel in Paris in the 1950s, and the chef there, Lucien Diat, was Louis' brother. The brothers came from the town of Vichy in France (famous during World War II for the temporary government of Henri-Philippe Pétain), and their mother used to make a creamy leek and potato soup and then serve it cold the following day with the addition of milk and chives. That recipe, which became known as vichyssoise in the United States, was also made at the Plaza Athénée in Paris because of the family history, but it was practically unknown in other restaurants at the time.

This is a simple, straightforward soup, and is a great first course when guests stop by unexpectedly. I like to use small Yukon Gold potatoes, which are soft and creamy, for this soup. A good, mild-flavored, homemade chicken stock that has been defatted is perfect for this soup. If the stock is strong, combine it with a little water. *Pluche* of chervil, meaning the whole leaf at the end of the chervil stem, is conventionally sprinkled on top of this soup. I like to place one *pluche* on top and croutons at serving time, but I also like to stir a little coarsely chopped fresh chervil into the finished soup to enhance the taste before adding the garnishes.

Potage Parmentier can be enjoyed not only hot, but with the addition of a little cold half-and-half and any leftovers can be transformed into a vichyssoise and served with chives on top.

As croutons for this dish, I prefer regular white bread (like Pepperidge Farm) cut into ¾-inch cubes. Sprinkle the cubes from 2 OR 3 SLICES OF BREAD with A LITTLE PEANUT OIL, spread them on a cookie sheet, and bake in a 400°F oven for about 10 minutes, or until the croutons are nicely browned.

Use 1 LARGE OR 2 SMALL LEEKS. Trim off some of the very green outer leaves (reserving them for stock), but be sure to use the tender green of the leek. Split the leek open and wash it well inside, so that there is no dirt or sand. Cut the leek into pieces of about ½ inch; you should have a good 2 to 3 cups of leek. Put the leek in a stockpot, and add ½ CUP SLICED MILD ONION and 2 CLOVES OF GARLIC, peeled and crushed. Add A LITTLE LIGHT OLIVE OIL OR PEANUT OIL, and cook over medium heat for 3 or 4 minutes, or until the leeks and onions begin to wilt. Pour in 3 CUPS OF GOOD CHICKEN STOCK and 1 CUP OF WATER to make the stock a little milder. At this point, add 1 POUND OF PEELED POTATOES that have been cut into chunks. Sprinkle with a good DASH OF SALT, bring to a boil, and then reduce the heat, cover, and let it boil very gently for 30 to 35 minutes. The vegetables should be very tender.

The best way to puree the cooked ingredients is with an immersion blender. Place the head of the blender directly into the pot, and process until the soup has a beautifully creamy consistency. Taste for seasonings, and add additional salt and some FRESHLY GROUND BLACK PEPPER, if needed. (Julia would want me to add white pepper to this because of the soup's light color, but I prefer the taste of black pepper.) At this point the soup can be poured into containers and frozen.

Finish the soup with about 3 TABLESPOONS OF THE BEST POSSIBLE QUALITY UNSALTED BUTTER, emulsifying it in the soup with the immersion blender. The soup can now be served in warm plates, garnished with croutons and CHOPPED CHERVIL and A FEW WHOLE CHERVIL LEAVES (*pluche*).

leek and potato soup, humble and best

GAUDES

YIELD: 4 SERVINGS

When I was a child in France, a specialty in the Bourg-en-Bresse and Jura Mountains regions, where I was born, was a kind of thick soup called *gaudes*, which was made of water and corn flour. This is one of the only areas of France where corn is eaten, and this is because chickens are raised there, and their diet is primarily corn. Because we ate corn and *gaudes*, we were called "yellow bellies," without the implications that phrase has here, implying only that we ate so much corn that our bellies turned yellow. *Gaudes* has the taste of my youth.

The first time Gloria went to France, she was pregnant with Claudine. I was anxious to have her try *gaudes*. The mixture was quite thick, made with only corn flour, salt, and boiling water, and was served with cold milk, which you add as you eat it. To my disappointment, she found it gross and coarse and wasn't at all taken by the taste. The corn flour for *gaudes* was bought already roasted, and my brother and I used to eat that nutty-tasting golden flour right out of the bag until we almost choked on it. My cousin, who has a restaurant in Bourg-en-Bresse, also used to make *gaudes*, and she used that roasted flour to bread fish as well as whitebait before frying it. Still available in France, this flour is good in corn muffins or corn bread. Because it is roasted, the flour has great intensity of taste.

I have refined the recipe somewhat. To reproduce that special flour, I brown fine masa harina (also called corn flour) in the oven to get the beautiful golden color of the flour I had as a child. I then cook the corn flour in stock and finish it at the end with some cream, fresh corn kernels, and a little chervil or parsley on top. It's more elegant, yet it still has the taste of the soup that I loved when I was young.

Preheat the oven to 300°F. Line a cookie sheet with aluminum foil, and spread 1 CUP (ABOUT 5 OUNCES) OF CORN FLOUR on the sheet. Bake the flour for about 40 minutes, stirring occasionally, until it is golden brown in color. Cool and taste the flour to confirm how good and nutty this roasted flour is.

Heat 2½ CUPS OF CHICKEN STOCK in a saucepan until it boils. Meanwhile, mix 1 CUP OF COLD WATER with ½ cup of the corn flour. (This helps keep the flour from lumping as you combine it with the stock.) When the stock is boiling, add the corn flour-water mixture to the pan, and combine with a whisk. Return to a boil, stirring occasionally, and boil gently for 6 to 8 minutes. Add SALT AND PEPPER to taste, and finish with ⅓ CUP OF CREAM.

For a garnish, remove the kernels from 1 EAR OF SWEET CORN (about ½ cup) and put them in a skillet with A TABLESPOON OF WATER. Cook over high heat for about 1 minute, until just cooked through. Add the corn to the soup. To serve, divide the *gaudes* among four bowls. Sprinkle with CHOPPED FRESH CHERVIL OR PARSLEY.

Gaudes is made with roasted corn flour

COLD COUNTRY OMELET

I like eggs in any form, and often when my wife and I don't know what to cook for dinner, I prepare an omelet. It can include anything available in my refrigerator or garden, from leeks to mushrooms, herbs, and/or cheese. We make classic French omelets with very fine curds, as well as coarse, country-style omelets with large brown curds. We also make poached eggs, hard-cooked eggs, and *mollet* eggs, which are soft-boiled eggs cooked just long enough to have a creamy delicious texture. All of these are made with local organic farm eggs produced by happy chickens and cooked in the best possible butter and olive oil.

Cold omelets are not too common in the lexicon of classic or home cooking, but for picnics, particularly, these were standard fare when I was a kid. When I prepare a picnic meal, cold omelets are often part of the menu. In Spain, the quintessential tapas is a tortilla—a flat potato omelet that is sliced into wedges—drizzled with olive oil, and served cold in bars from Madrid to Barcelona. My cold omelet is stuffed, rolled, and served at room temperature in thick slices, with a sprinkling of good olive oil, herbs, and black pepper on top. Using a nonstick pan to make omelets will make your life easier.

Combine 8 LARGE OR JUMBO EGGS of the best possible quality in a bowl with a good DASH OF SALT AND FRESHLY GROUND BLACK PEPPER. For the filling, mix together 1 CUP OF THINLY SLICED LEEKS (OR SCALLIONS IF YOU PREFER), including some of the tender green parts, and 2 CUPS OF LARGE MUSHROOM PIECES OR SMALL WHOLE MUSHROOMS (I use 2 cups, about 6 ounces, of freshly picked chanterelle mushrooms, but any mushrooms can be used).

Heat a good TABLESPOON OF OLIVE OIL in a 10-inch nonstick skillet, and add the mushrooms and leeks. The mushrooms will render a large amount of liquid. Let cook gently, covered, until all the liquid has evaporated, which will take 7 or 8 minutes. Remove the lid, and continue sautéing the mixture until it starts frying a little, gets glossy, and the leeks look pale beige. It should have a roasted nutty aroma. Add A DASH OF SALT AND PEPPER, and transfer the mixture to a bowl.

Heat 2 TABLESPOONS OF UNSALTED BUTTER in the same skillet used for the mushrooms until it begins to sizzle and just starts browning. Pour the egg mixture into the pan, and let the curds set for about 20 seconds before moving them. Then, using the tines of a fork (or the underneath rounded part of the fork to keep from damaging your skillet), stir the mixture, shaking the pan at the same time. Let the omelet cook without stirring for about 20 seconds more, and then stir again. Do this a couple more times, until the eggs form into curds, with the center still moist, glossy, and a little wet.

Spoon the cooked mushroom mixture across the center of the omelet in one long strip, and bring the side of the omelet closest to you back over the mushrooms, lifting the edge with a spatula or fork. Then bang the end of the handle closest to the pan with your hand to release the lip of the omelet on the far side of the pan, and fold it back over the mushrooms, too. If this maneuver is difficult, use a spatula to release the opposite side of the omelet. You want the mushrooms to be encased in the omelet. Add another dash of olive oil or butter (or both) to the pan, letting it slide under the omelet. Let the omelet brown in the pan for 30 to 40 seconds, then grasp the underside of the handle with one hand, place an overturned plate on top of the omelet, and invert it onto the plate. Let it sit for a minute or so to cool off a little, and then slide it onto a large piece of plastic wrap. Roll and tighten the omelet in the wrap until it measures about 9 inches long by 3 inches in diameter. Allow it to cool until ready to serve.

At serving time, remove the plastic wrap from the rolled omelet, place the omelet on a platter, and cut into 6 or 7 slices, each about 1½ inches thick. Arrange the cut slices flat on the platter, one slice next to another, and then coat generously with olive oil and A SPRINKLING OF CRACKED PEPPER AND CHOPPED CHIVES. Serve at warm room temperature, not ice cold, with a nice green salad and a glass of chilled rosé.

the only rule when entertaining is to make your guests happy

MELON AND PROSCIUTTO

✻ YIELD: 4 SERVINGS ✻

As I get older, I've come to realize how satisfying simple, straightforward food of the best quality can be. It is always in style and in fashion. With each passing year, I tend to limit the amount of ingredients on my plate, taking away from the plate rather than adding more and more, as some chefs do when they want to create new dishes that are unusual and different. I always choose good over different.

Prosciutto is one of my favorite foods, and I enjoy it anytime. I prefer it from the center of the round, where it is very moist, although some of my friends like prosciutto drier. I think the center of a Parma ham is excellent, as good as the Jamon from Spain, and the Pata Negra, or black feet ham, which comes from a half-wild pig that eats only natural, organic products like acorns, figs, and roots. I have seen hordes of these pigs crossing the roads in the mountains of Spain. They produce some of the best hams, fragrant, flavorful, with a deeper taste than the Parma ham, but maybe not quite as nutty or creamy. In Spain, the fashion is to slice the ham fairly thick, but I like mine paper-thin. But the ultimate ham in Spain is the Iberico, a ham aged several years from an organic pig of the highest possible quality raised under very strict conditions. Being aged a long time, the fat on the outside is almost transparent when the ham is cut, and it is more shrunken and drier than others. It has an extremely concentrated flavor that is definitely an acquired taste.

There are great hams in France also, especially the Bayonne ham from the southwest region of France, and in many other places, including the Savoy or the Alps. I remember as a youth the enormous cheeses called Comté that the farmers there made, and the hams hanging everywhere in the caves cut directly into the mountainside. I also enjoy long-cured hams from Kentucky and Virginia, and although they are conventionally cooked, I eat them raw like a good prosciutto.

I occasionally make my own prosciutto with whole hams, sometimes with venison, and also with shoulder hams, fattier and moist. I like my hams in the style of Italy, France, or Spain, rather than smoked in the German style. Ham has a special taste when cut thinly by hand. At the Boqueria, a market in Barcelona, we ate slices of Iberico ham with figs bursting with sugar. It was an extraordinary ham, sliced by an expert hand into very thin slices.

I like to combine prosciutto with the best possible melon. I have found some Charentais melons at my market in Connecticut. This heavily perfumed, flavorful melon weighs about one pound, has a small cavity in the center, and a good nose can detect one from several feet away.

———— ✻ ————

Pit and peel A RIPE MELON, so there is absolutely no green left on the flesh. Cut the flesh into 1-inch cubes, and sprinkle on A LITTLE LEMON JUICE, a lot of CRACKED BLACK PEPPER, and, at the last moment, just before serving, some COARSE SEA SALT to give the melon a crunch. Serve with SEVERAL VERY THIN SLICES OF PROSCIUTTO, arranging the slices on the melon and the plate like crinkling tissues falling on themselves. BREAD AND BUTTER are a must.

homemade prosciutto on buttered baguette for lunch

TORTILLA PIZZAS

YIELD: 3 PIZZAS, WITH 8 SMALL SERVINGS PER PIZZA

I enjoy making pizza from scratch and occasionally make a *pissaladière*, the famous pizza from the south of France. Garnished with rendered onion and a crisscross of anchovy fillets and black olives, it is a staple from Nice to Marseille. In the last few years, with the availability of many flatbreads at the supermarket, I have taken on the habit of making quick pizzas, sometimes using pita bread or lavash as a base, but more often than not using flour tortillas, because I always have a package of them in my refrigerator. They come in different sizes, from 6 to 10 inches, and even in 12-inch disks. These tortilla pizzas are ideal to serve when people come for drinks, or when we play *boules* and share a bottle of white wine.

The toppings for pizza are almost endless. I've made pizza with greens (from arugula to spinach), with red pepper, zucchini, and very thin slices of grilled eggplant. A few of my favorites are included here. One is a classic margherita pizza with tomato, mozzarella, and basil, and one is made with clams and shrimp and is fashioned after the delicious clam pizza available at Pepe's, a renowned pizza parlor in New Haven, Connecticut. Another famous pizza restaurant in town is Sally's, and there are endless debates about which is the best. I have had great pizza at both places! The oven at Pepe's is fueled with coal to 2000°F, so its clam pizza, made with regular pizza dough, is ready in 3 to 5 minutes. While you can't duplicate these results in your home oven, the version I have here is quite good. My third pizza is topped with thin slices of salmon that are "instant-cured" to produce a delicious gravlax. I use 10-inch tortilla disks as the base for my toppings and cook these pizzas at 500 degrees.

———

First, oil A TORTILLA ROUND FOR EACH PIZZA you plan to make: sprinkle OLIVE OIL on a sturdy cookie sheet or jelly roll pan, and press the tortillas in the oil on the tray to coat them well on one side, and then turn them over, so they are oiled on the other side.

MARGHERITA PIZZA | Preheat the oven to 500°F. Sprinkle 1 TABLESPOON OF GRATED PARMESAN CHEESE on top of an oiled tortilla. Add 1 THINLY SLICED 8-OUNCE TOMATO, a good sprinkling of SALT AND FRESHLY GROUND BLACK PEPPER, and A GOOD CUP OF GRATED MOZZARELLA (ABOUT 4 OUNCES); buffalo mozzarella is best, if you can get it.

Sprinkle on a little more salt and pepper, and top with about 1 TABLESPOON OF GOOD OLIVE OIL. You can cook the tortillas directly on the cookie sheet or directly on an oven stone, using a wooden peel to transfer them. Bake for 8 to 10 minutes, or until bubbly and crisp. Let the pizzas rest out of the oven for a couple of minutes, and then sprinkle with ¼ CUP SHREDDED BASIL (from about 12 leaves). Cut into 8 wedges, and serve with a glass of your favorite wine.

Everybody loves a hot and crusty slice of pizza

SEAFOOD PIZZA | I love to make seafood pizza in the summer, when there are plenty of clams. For one pizza, use 1 DOZEN SHUCKED CHERRYSTONE CLAMS and 8 MEDIUM-SIZE SHELLED SHRIMP left whole. Preheat the oven to 500°F. Sprinkle 1½ TABLESPOONS OF PARMESAN CHEESE on the oiled tortilla and arrange the shrimp and clams on top. (You can reserve the clam juice to use in a fish soup or to make a drink. My friend Craig Claiborne used to love "bullshots," which were drinks made with fresh clam juice and vodka.) Add 1 TABLESPOON OF COARSELY CHOPPED GARLIC (this is a lot of garlic, but it is needed!), A DASH OF HERBES DE PROVENCE, about 3 TABLESPOONS OF MINCED SCALLIONS, A LITTLE CHOPPED JALAPEÑO, if you like, OR A DASH OF TABASCO for heat. Sprinkle on another 1½ TABLESPOONS OF PARMESAN CHEESE, and then evenly drizzle 1 TO 1½ TABLESPOONS OF OLIVE OIL on top. Bake for 5 to 6 minutes, or until crusty. Let rest for a minute or so, and sprinkle with COARSELY CHOPPED FLAT-LEAF PARSLEY. Cut into 8 wedges, and serve.

CURED SALMON PIZZA | My third pizza, topped with gravlax, is served cold. For the gravlax, cut ½ POUND OF SKINLESS, BONELESS SALMON FILLET into 8 thin slices, and arrange them in a single layer on a flat plate or platter. Mix together 1½ TEASPOONS OF KOSHER SALT, 1½ TEASPOONS OF LIGHT BROWN SUGAR, and 1 TEASPOON OF FRESHLY GROUND BLACK PEPPER. Sprinkle half of this mixture evenly over the salmon slices, turn the slices over, and sprinkle with the remaining seasoning mixture. Spread A THIN COATING OF OIL on the slices, just enough to make the salmon shiny, and press a piece of plastic wrap directly on top of the salmon. Refrigerate to cure; it will be ready in an hour or less, although you can leave it overnight or even up to a day. (We are using only 4 slices of gravlax on our pizza. Make a second pizza, or enjoy the leftover gravlax with cucumber and/or sliced onion and buttered black bread.)

Preheat the oven to 500°F. Precook the tortilla for this pizza. Coat 1 TORTILLA with OLIVE OIL, using about ½ teaspoon on each side. Place the oiled tortilla on a cookie sheet and, to prevent it from curling up and bubbling in the oven without the weight of toppings to hold it down, place a rack or cake stand upside down directly on top of the tortilla. The rack will hold it flat as it cooks. Bake for about 5 minutes to brown the tortilla nicely and make it crisp. Let cool before continuing.

When the tortilla is cool, coat with about ¼ CUP OF SOUR CREAM, and then spread on about 1 TABLESPOON OF HOMEMADE HORSERADISH or store-bought bottled horseradish. (My friend Claude has enormous and pungent horseradish in his garden that he peels, grates, and puts in a jar with a little vinegar, salt, and water.) Arrange 4 slices of gravlax on top, so the salmon covers most of the surface, although it's attractive if a little sour cream shows through here and there. Sprinkle about ¼ CUP OF VERY THINLY SLICED RED ONION on top, and then cut about 6 BLACK OIL-CURED PITTED OLIVES into pieces and scatter them over the surface. Finally, coarsely tear 7 OR 8 FRESH BASIL LEAVES into pieces, and top the pizza with the basil. Cut the pizza into 8 pieces. Just before eating, I like to sprinkle on A LITTLE COARSE FLEUR DE SEL—that expensive but very flavorful salt—to give it a bit of a crunch.

Oysters Rockefeller

YIELD: 4 SERVINGS

I always enjoy going back to classic recipes and reinventing them in a more modern way closer to my own tastes, keeping most of the same ingredients but interpreting them differently. We have always loved oysters and often get them from Steve Milowski, who has a small family operation raising oysters on Fisher Island. Other times I get them in Branford, Connecticut, where John the fisherman sells me a whole case of oysters at a very good price.

Although Gloria and I like oysters best just plain on the half shell, occasionally we cook them. I like to make a great oyster stew with leeks, where the oysters are barely cooked by being added to the stew at the last moment. For this recipe however, I am redoing the old classic, oysters Rockefeller, although I don't serve the oysters in the shells, as they are served traditionally. Instead, I sauté spinach with garlic and a tiny bit of pepper flakes, salt, and pepper, arrange it in small mounds on individual plates, and top each mound with a raw oyster. I reserve the oyster liquid for soup or combine it with vodka to make a bullshot cocktail. The oysters in the spinach "nest" are then warmed in the oven while a sauce of butter and shallots is made to finish the dish along with some bacon bits.

Clean 10 OUNCES OF FRESH SPINACH, removing and discarding the larger stems. Heat 2 TABLESPOONS OF OLIVE OIL in a skillet over medium heat, and when it is hot, add the spinach to the pan. Cover with a lid; the spinach will start softening and reducing in volume. When it becomes soft, turn it in the pan, and add 1 TEASPOON OF CHOPPED GARLIC, SALT, and A PINCH OF RED PEPPER FLAKES. Cook, tossing and mixing it, for 1½ to 2 minutes, until it is wilted and just tender. Transfer to a bowl, and set aside.

Open 2 DOZEN MEDIUM TO LARGE OYSTERS. Drain off the juice, reserving it for other uses. Preheat the oven to 190°F.

On each of four ovenproof plates, spoon 6 small mounds of spinach inches apart, and press down on the tops gently to make an indentation or "nest" in the center of each mound. Place a raw oyster in each of these indentations, and put the plates in the oven to warm while you cook the bacon and the shallots and butter.

Arrange 4 SLICES OF BACON side by side on a ridged microwave tray. Microwave for about 5 minutes until nicely crisped, and then cut or break the slices into ¼-inch pieces.

To finish, melt 3 TABLESPOONS OF BUTTER in a small skillet over medium heat. Cook it until it starts changing color, becoming light brown. Add 3 TABLESPOONS OF CHOPPED SHALLOTS, stir, and cook for about 20 seconds longer, so the butter continues to cook along with the shallots.

Remove the hot plates of spinach and oysters from the oven, spoon a little shallot butter on top of each, and sprinkle on some bacon pieces. Serve immediately.

CLAM FRITTERS

When we used to vacation on the small island of Guadeloupe in the Caribbean, we became addicted to *accras,* little fritters of salted codfish. I often recreate these at home using large quahog clams, which we would collect in front of a beach house we owned in Branford, Connecticut. We would go out at low tide in water up to our knees and feel for the clams with our feet, picking up buckets of them that we would stuff, use for spaghetti and clam sauce, or make into these little fritters.

Large quahogs weigh between 12 ounces and 1 pound each, and are difficult to open unless you break off a piece of the shell to make room to insert the point of a knife to cut the abducting muscle that holds the shell closed. My friend Jean-Claude found a new way to open these large clams. He places a clam side to side between a vise. When a little pressure is applied, the shell opens slightly, just enough to slide a knife inside and cut the abducting muscle. If you try this, make sure to place a bowl under the vise to catch any juice.

Five large quahogs yield about 1 cup of clam meat and 1 cup of juice, which is what is needed to make 3 or 4 dozen fritters for a party of 8 to 10 people. I sometimes add about a quarter pound of salted codfish, which gives great intensity to the fritters. I like to season the batter with some hot pepper, usually jalapeño or serrano. In the islands

they serve the fritters with *petit* punch, which they call "ti punch," for short (see page 147). Consisting of white rum, lime juice, and sugar, and served ice cold, this punch can become as addictive as the fritters.

***

For 3 dozen small fritters, open 5 LARGE QUAHOGS to get about 1 cup of meat and 1 cup of juice (add water if there is not quite a cup of juice). Combine the meat and juice in a bowl, and vigorously stir the clam meat in its own juice several times before lifting it up out of the juice and pouring the juice slowly into another bowl, so you leave any shells or sediment behind. Put the clam meat in the bowl of a food processor, and process until you have a smooth puree. Combine with the juice in the bowl.

If you want to add SALTED CODFISH, soak A 4-OUNCE PIECE for 3 or 4 hours in tepid water, drain, cover with water in a saucepan, bring to a boil, and cook for about 3 minutes. Drain, and when cool enough to handle, break into small pieces or flakes. You should have about ½ cup.

Mix about 1¼ CUPS OF ALL-PURPOSE FLOUR with 1½ TEA-SPOONS OF BAKING POWDER, and add a good ¾ CUP OF CHOPPED ONION, 1 TEASPOON OF CHOPPED GARLIC, and as much FINELY CHOPPED JALAPEÑO PEPPER as you can tolerate. Mix in about ½ TEASPOON OF SALT and 3 TO 4 TABLESPOONS OF CHOPPED CHIVES. Stir in the pureed clams and their juice to give you a fairly thick batter. Mix in the flaked codfish, or *bacalao*.

Heat 3 CUPS OF CANOLA OR PEANUT OIL in a large skillet to 340 to 350°F. Add the batter as quickly as you can, letting it drop, a scant table-spoon at a time, into the hot oil. Cook for 5 to 6 minutes, until gloriously browned and puffy, turning the fritters over to brown them on both sides. Drain on a wire rack rather than paper towels, so they don't get soggy on the bottom. Arrange on a serving plate, and pass to guests. The fritters should be crisp on the outside and chewy inside—they are delicious and addictive.

SNAILS IN ARTICHOKE BOTTOMS

YIELD: 4 SERVINGS

When I was a kid, escargots, or snails, were often served for special occasions at home, or we ate them in restaurants, where they were considered a special dish. The classic way is to serve them in snail butter, which is butter combined with a lot of chopped garlic, and parsley, salt, and pepper. Often shallots are added, sometimes chopped almonds, sometimes a dash of Pernod, sometimes a little white wine, and sometimes a little chicken stock or the liquid from cooking the snails.

When cooked fresh, snails are served in those special metal plates with indentations to hold the snails steady. Spring-operated tongs are used to hold the snails, and a long two-pronged fork enables you to extricate them from their shells. Snails are usually bought in cans, drained, and placed with the snail butter into the empty snail shells, baked, and served piping hot with bread to soak up the butter. This is still one of the best ways to enjoy snails. It is also conventional to serve snails—whether canned or fresh—in a mushroom cap. Cook the caps for about 10 minutes in the oven, and then place the snails in the cooked caps, cover with snail butter, and bake in the oven until bubbling hot.

There are two types of snails served in France: the best are the *gros blanc,* the big whites, which are Burgundy snails often found in vineyards and picked up in the spring after hibernation, when they are really fat. Almost all protein, they are also the most expensive. Then there are the small gray snails, called *petit-gris,* which are slightly less expensive, quite flavorful, and the ones with black striations on the shells. These were usually the ones my brother and I would find along the edge of fields and forests when we were hunting for snails just after a rain, a conventional pastime in France for country kids.

Snails were apparently brought to California in the 1850s by French or Italian settlers, and though they are so plentiful there that they are usually considered a scourge by the farmers, snails never made it to the East Coast. The first time I went to California, in 1976, Gloria and I spent the weekend with friends in Eureka, a small coastal town that was similar to Brittany for me. In that misty area, where it often rains, I walked outside and found snails everywhere. I was so happy, I came back to the motel where we were staying, picked up the garbage pail, and went back out. I picked up four or five hundred snails, enough to fill up the pail, and returned excitedly to the room. Gloria was puzzled as to what I would do with all these snails, but I assured her everything would be fine. I set the pail in the bathtub, put a towel over it, and we went out for dinner.

When we returned after an evening of dining and listening to jazz with friends, I heard Gloria shriek as she walked into the bathroom. The snails were all over the walls and ceilings and I had to collect them all and return them to the pail. This time I secured the towel on top with a weight. The following day I went to a nearby liquor store and got some empty cardboard boxes. I bought some lettuce at the supermarket and fed it to the snails, as they should be fed for a couple of days to clean out their intestinal tract in case they have consumed something poisonous. I took them with me to Napa, California, where I was teaching for the first time at High Tree Farm in Rutherford in what would be the first in a series of the Great Chefs at Mondavi cooking classes that went on for decades. Charlotte Combe, who had a cooking school in Redwood City, was my assistant and friend. We blanched the snails, pulled them out of their shells, and removed and discarded the lower part of the intestinal tract (the *tortillon*). We cooked them in white wine and chicken stock with thyme, bay leaf, and onion very slowly for 2½ hours, until they were tender. The stock was concentrated and delicious.

Next to the cooking school was a field of artichokes. The farmer gave us permission to pick them so I could demonstrate how to prepare

artichoke bottoms. This is usually an expensive process, since it is costly to put artichokes into the hands of students who don't know how to trim them and tend to cut into the hearts. But the artichokes were free, and we prepared a lot of artichoke bottoms to serve with the snails and herb butter. In remembrance of that outing, I am preparing that ragoût of snails in artichoke bottoms. I hope this dish will become as memorable for you as it is for me.

Six snails per person are sufficient and fit nicely into an artichoke bottom, so you will need about 2 DOZEN SNAILS for four servings. (Be sure to buy real snails, not mud snails, which usually come from Taiwan or China. They are called *achatines* or *achate*. They have a muddy, bitter taste and a pasty texture.) When I prepare artichoke bottoms, I try to find artichokes in my market that are beginning to yellow and so are marked down, since I am going to trim off and discard the whole exterior anyway and use only the heart.

Trim the artichoke leaves from the heart as closely as possible without cutting into the heart itself. This is a relatively delicate technique. If you have never done this, it is best to pull the leaves off starting at the base, breaking them, and then pulling down on them carefully, making sure that you don't also pull out pieces of meat from the heart. When the heart or bottom is exposed, cut off whatever green remains with a small sharp knife or a good vegetable peeler. Cut off the central core of the leaves just above the heart, so all that remains is the heart with the choke inside. Rub with lemon to avoid discoloration.

Place 4 ARTICHOKE BOTTOMS in a saucepan. Add 1 CUP OF WATER, 1 TABLESPOON OF OLIVE OIL, 1 TABLESPOON OF LEMON JUICE, and A DASH OF SALT AND PEPPER. Boil gently, covered, for 20 to 30 minutes, or until they are tender. Allow to cool a little, then remove the choke (fuzzy part) with a small spoon. Place artichokes back in the cooking liquid, and refrigerate until ready to use. If the snails are canned, drain and rinse them briefly under cold water.

Heat about 2 TABLESPOONS OF OLIVE OIL in a large skillet. Add 1/2 CUP OF DICED MUSHROOMS, 2 TABLESPOONS OF CHOPPED SCALLION, and 2 TABLESPOONS OF CHOPPED SHALLOT, and sauté in the oil for 1 or 2 minutes. Add the snails, 1 TABLESPOON OF CHOPPED GARLIC, SALT, AND FRESHLY GROUND BLACK PEPPER, and cook for a minute or so. Using a slotted spoon, transfer the solids to a bowl while you deglaze the pan with 1/2 TO 3/4 CUP OF RED OR WHITE WINE. Cook for 4 or 5 minutes, until most of the wine is reduced.

Meanwhile, reheat the artichoke bottoms in their stock or in a microwave oven until heated through. Place one on each of four warm plates. Just before serving, add about 4 TABLESPOONS OF BUTTER (1 tablespoon per person, still less than is used in conventional snail butter) to the skillet, and cook for about 1 minute, until the butter is nicely incorporated into the sauce. Divide the snail mixture among the artichoke bottoms, spoon on some sauce, sprinkle with FRESHLY CHOPPED PARSLEY, and, if you like, some FRESH BREAD CRUMBS, and serve immediately.

after the Summer rain, my brothers and I would hunt for snails

Frog Legs with Garlic and Parsley (Grenouilles Persillade)

❊ YIELD: 1 SERVING ❊

A family tradition and summer ritual for me is catching *grenouilles,* or frogs, a pastime I enjoyed with my brothers every summer of our youth. We used to catch crawfish as well as frogs in the ponds and little streams near our home in Bourg-en-Bresse or in nearby Neyron. To catch crawfish, we tied together pieces of wood, creating a bundle two to three feet around and nearly the width of the little brook. We would stick pieces of meat and fish, eggshells—anything edible—into the wood and leave it there for a day or so, then lift the whole wood bundle out of the water and put it on the grass bank. When we opened it up and spread it out, we would find a dozen or so crawfish that had crawled through the wood pieces to retrieve edible bits and remained there. My mother would cook these in a very flavorful and highly peppered vegetable stock, and we would eat them with melted butter or mayonnaise and bread.

The frogs were the prize catch. The classic way of capturing them was with a string tied to a wooden pole. At the end of the string, we attached a little piece of red cloth. Frogs love the color red, and would clamp their mouths onto it. Then, with a flick of the wrist, we tried to make the frog jump out of the pond, or *botasse,* which had edges lined with water lilies and long reeds, perfect as a hiding place for frogs. We would get a few frogs this way, but eventually we devised a better method that we still use. We go out at night with a flashlight and a little net, and shine the light at the frog, getting as close to it as we can. Somewhat hypnotized by the light, the frog doesn't move. We clamp the net down over it, and then carefully remove it from the net.

When Claudine was very young and spent summers in France with her cousins, she learned to love the plump, juicy, and tender frog legs that she called *"les petites cuisses,"* or "tiny legs." She requested them each time we went to a small bistro or country inn in the Lyon area.

I have many frogs in my pond, but I have to fight the rest of nature to get them. Whether it is an egret, a heron, a hawk, or a raccoon, something seems to consume a great many of our frogs. Even though we have thousands of tadpoles in our little pond each spring, the frog population declines through the summer because of competition with nature. Yet we still get enough frogs once or twice a year to keep the tradition alive.

I do not enjoy killing animals, but I know how to kill a frog well and fast. Grab it by its back legs and bang its head a couple of times on a nearby rock. This kills the frog instantly. If you don't plan to catch your own frogs for this dish, you can find fresh or frozen frog legs at many fish markets and specialty stores, and they can also be purchased from online sources. Note that the yield for this recipe is for only one portion, which is often the case when I go hunting for frogs, as I usually end up with enough for one or two servings at most. Yet, if buying frogs for this dish, you can always extend the recipe to serve as many guests as you like.

Frogs are not served at a formal dinner; they are the ultimate finger food and a treat at home in summer or in the little bistros of the Lyon area, where *grenouilles persillade* is always featured on summer

Catching frogs and eating them in garlic butter is a Summer ritual

menus. There are many ways to prepare frog legs. Sometimes they are sautéed and garnished with stewed tomatoes, and in Bourg-en-Bresse they are poached in white wine and shallots and finished with tarragon and cream. Yet the classic way to serve frog legs is with a *persillade,* a combination of parsley and garlic.

To dress a frog, cut the skin down the back, and insert a finger of each hand under the skin. Pull in opposite directions until the skin slides off. Remove the guts, and using scissors, cut off the head and the feet. Discard the skin, head, and feet. Wash the legs well under cold water, and dry with paper towels.

For one person, you will need about 1 DOZEN FROG LEGS. Sprinkle them with SALT AND FRESHLY GROUND PEPPER, and dip them in FLOUR, preferably an instant variety, like Wondra, which gives a light coating and a nice crust. Heat about 2 TABLESPOONS OF PEANUT OIL in a skillet, preferably nonstick, and cook the frog legs for 2½ to 3 minutes on each side, until they are beautifully golden and lightly crusted. The flesh should remain moist and firm. Finish the dish with A GOOD TEASPOON OF CHOPPED GARLIC and 2 TABLESPOONS OF COARSELY CHOPPED PARSLEY, and stir in A TABLESPOON OF SWEET BUTTER. Add A DASH OF LEMON JUICE and serve.

I have prepared a similar dish, substituting chicken breast meat for the frog legs. I dredge cubes of chicken in flour, salt, and pepper, sauté them in oil for a total of about 3½ minutes (the chicken cooks faster than the frog), and finish them with butter, chopped garlic, and parsley, and a sprinkling of lemon juice.

CODFISH BRANDADE WITH
MOLLET EGGS AND MOUILLETTES

YIELD: 6 SERVINGS

Gloria loves *bacalao*, or salted codfish. Her mother was Puerto Rican and her father was Cuban, so *bacalao* (in several versions) is part of her culinary remembrance. When Gloria was small, *bacalao* was de rigueur for the Christmas holidays, so for many years now we have incorporated a salted codfish dish into our holiday entertaining. Usually we prepare *bacalao* in a Portuguese or Spanish style—flaked, sautéed with some red pepper, potato, garlic, onion, and black olives, and served on croutons.

A classic French dish made with codfish is *brandade*. This is a mixture consisting of salted codfish pureed with a bit of potato and a lot of garlic and finished with olive oil. *Brandade* is a classic dish at brasseries and bistros throughout France. It was also served in the center of France years ago, because salted codfish could be preserved when there was no refrigeration. The Brittany fishermen who went to St. Peter and Miquelon, in Newfoundland, would salt the cod there and bring it to French markets, as well as to Italian, Spanish, and Portuguese markets. *Brandade* is usually served on toast, and since it is loaded with garlic, is not a dish for the timid or for people who don't like really assertive tastes. This great spread is the perfect accompaniment for the robust and full-bodied Syrahs and Grenaches from the south of France.

When I prepare *brandade*, I usually make enough for Gloria to freeze two or three small gratin dishes of the mixture to serve with aperitifs when friends show up unexpectedly; it freezes quite well. Get the thickest salted codfish you can. These are usually found in Portuguese markets.

Gloria and I both adore eggs, and one of our favorite dishes is the *oeuf mollet*, which is similar in texture to a poached egg but is cooked in the shell for about six minutes (for jumbo eggs). The eggs are cooled in ice water, then peeled very gently, a delicate operation because the inside is soft. Use the best quality eggs for this dish. The eggs I buy at a local farm are far superior to those available at the supermarket. The yolks, a vivid yellow-orange, are high in lecithin and run thick and unctuous, and the whites are just custardy enough when cooked. As eggs cook, sulfur present in the whites gathers around the yolks to escape the heat, sometimes creating yolks tinged with green and smelling strongly of sulfur. This is especially prevalent in hard-cooked eggs with cracked shells. Ordinarily, because of the air stuck in the air chamber, when you lower an egg into boiling water, the air wants to escape and the pressure causes the shell to crack. To avoid cracked shells, before cooking make a tiny hole with a thumbtack or push pin into the rounder end of each egg to penetrate the air chamber inside.

I love *mollet* eggs with *brandade* accompanied by *mouillettes* of bread. *Mouillettes* are sticks of bread cut from six-inch chunks of fresh baguette. When my brothers and I were young, we were always served buttered *mouillettes* from fresh, crusty baguettes to dip into the soft-boiled eggs that my mother would prepare for us occasionally in the morning. The combination of *mouillettes*, *mollet* eggs, and *brandade* has the perfect taste contrasts and textures.

Getting eggs at Rose's — the best eggs come from free, happy chickens

CODFISH BRANDADE | Soak 1 POUND OF CODFISH in 5 TO 6 QUARTS OF COOL WATER for 4 or 5 hours, changing the water about halfway through this period. Don't leave it in the water much longer, because if you desalt the cod too much, you will have to add some salt in the cooking. Then place the fish in a medium saucepan, and cover it with water. Bring to a boil, and boil gently for about 3 minutes, just until the fish can be flaked. Drain in a colander and, when it is lukewarm, pull off the skin, and put it back in the saucepan. (The skin lends some richness, creaminess, and texture to the *brandade*.) Clean the fish, discarding the bones and sinew.

Add the fish to the saucepan with about 1½ CUPS OF MILK, about 1½ CUPS OF PEELED AND CUBED POTATOES, preferably Yukon Gold, 5 OR 6 CLOVES OF PEELED GARLIC, A GOOD AMOUNT OF FRESHLY GROUND BLACK PEPPER, and a little SPRIG OF FRESH THYME OR SERPOLET, a wild thyme that grows like a ground cover. (I brought some of this back from my friend Claude's field in upstate New York, where it grows wild, and now it covers a whole area of the walking path in my garden. The herb's beautiful purple flowers, great fragrance, and assertive taste work magic in many of my dishes.)

Bring the whole mixture to a boil, cover, reduce the heat, and boil very gently for about 30 minutes. Remove and discard the thyme sprig, and pour the rest of the mixture into the bowl of a food processor. Process until pureed, adding about ⅓ CUP OF THE BEST POSSIBLE EXTRA-VIRGIN OLIVE OIL (or concoct a mixture of half extra-virgin olive oil and half hazelnut or walnut oil, both of which lend a nutty taste to the dish). Add SALT AND FRESHLY GROUND PEPPER to taste. This should yield 3 to 3½ cups of *brandade*. Serve warm on toasts with aperitifs, or divide among a few small gratin dishes and freeze for later use.

To serve the *brandade* as a gratin, spoon it into a 4-cup gratin dish, and sprinkle on about 1 TABLESPOON OF GRATED PARMESAN CHEESE. Bake in a preheated 425°F oven for about 20 minutes, until nicely browned. Serve with the *mollet* eggs and *mouillettes*.

MOLLET EGGS | Carefully lower 6 EGGS into boiling water to cover in a saucepan. Return the water to a very gentle boil (otherwise the egg whites will toughen), and cook for about 6 minutes.

As soon as the eggs are cooked, pour out the water and shake the pan gently to crack the eggshells. Add water and ice to the pan, and set aside until the eggs are thoroughly chilled. During this cooling process, the sulfur will escape and disintegrate in the ice water if the eggs stay long enough. When cold, the eggs should be peeled carefully—remember they are soft inside. One of the best ways to do this is to remove some of the shell and break through the underlying membrane. Hold the eggs under a slow stream of cool, running water and peel. When the water runs between the membrane and the egg, it makes it easy to peel. Keep the peeled eggs in a bowl of cool water. When ready to serve, place the eggs carefully in a sieve, lower them into a saucepan of hot water, and warm them for about 2 minutes; at this point, the heat will have penetrated the eggs, and they will just be starting to get hot in the center. Remove the eggs from the water. Spoon out portions of *brandade* onto individual plates. Top each with an egg and surround with buttered *mouillettes*.

MOUILLETTES | Cut 6-inch chunks from A FRESH BAGUETTE. Cut each chunk in half lengthwise, and then cut each half into three or four pieces, each approximately 1 inch wide and about 6 inches long. If the baguette is not fresh and crunchy, brown the *mouillettes* in the oven to make them nice and crusty. Butter them just before they are served.

Fried Whitebait (La Petite Friture) with Fried Parsley

YIELD: 8 TO 10 SERVINGS WITH APERITIFS

La petite friture (tiny fried fish) has been truly a Pépin family ritual each summer for many years. *La friture* consists of very young fish, known collectively as whitebait, that we catch at the seashore with a net. I used to gather these as a young *commis* when I worked in the north of France, near Dauville, on the coast of Normandy. And when I was a child, my

brother and I caught freshwater fish of about the same size in a nearby river. Called *veiron* or *ablettes*, these were similar to gudgeon (small-bodied freshwater fish), about the size of a fountain pen in circumference and three or four inches long. We would press on the belly to extrude the insides, wash the fish in clean water, and fry them in peanut oil.

Eating these little fish along with a glass of cool white wine or sparkling cider is still a traditional summer activity on Sundays in the inns and bistros along the Rhône and Saône rivers in the Lyon area. My Aunt Hélène had a restaurant on a lake in Nantua, and one of her specialties was deep-fried *friture*, which she would serve daily to the *pétanque* and *belotte* (a card game) players in late afternoon. Instead of coating the fish with regular flour for frying, she would use *gaudes* (see page 46), the roasted corn flour that was used in this area of France. It gave a darker color and a nuttier taste to the tiny fried fish.

In Connecticut, at the end of the summer and into early fall, the whitebait, often small herring or smelt, come in. I fish them when the tide is coming in, pushing the whitebait toward the shore. My net is about eighteen to twenty feet long and about five feet wide, with lead in the bottom and floaters on top. I attach a strong six-foot stick at each end of the net and place the net in the water, with a person at one end standing in shallow water and one at the other end in slightly deeper water, about thirty feet from the shore. Walking parallel to the beach, we drag the net, staying close to the bottom, for about forty feet to catch the fish, and then the person in deeper water moves closer to make a circle with his partner, who stands still to enclose the fish, and then they drag the catch quickly toward the beach. The net is lifted up, and inside are little fish and, sometimes, a few crabs and small snapper, blues, or flukes, all of which we fry along with the whitebait. I like to clean our catch by the water so I don't make a mess at home. The fish are best eaten within the next six to twelve hours, or before the next high tide.

Whitebait are more readily available in Europe than in the United States, although they can sometimes be found in fish markets, particularly in the Chinatown area of large cities. If you can't collect whitebait yourself, your best bet is to try to convince a fisherman friend to net some for you.

Holding the fish just below the head between your thumb and index finger, push the guts out of the little hole in the lower part of the belly (if not gutted, the fish will taste bitter after frying). Wash well in seawater, and then wash the fish again at home and dry well with paper towels. For about 1 POUND OF FRITURE, mix about 1 TABLESPOON OF ALL-PURPOSE FLOUR into about 1 CUP OF MILK, and add a little SALT AND PEPPER. The flour gives just a little viscosity to the milk, thickening it just slightly.

Add the fish to the milk mixture, mix well, and then lift them out. While they are still wet from the milk, coat them in plenty of all-purpose flour. (Do this at the last minute, just before you are ready to fry the fish. Otherwise the coating will get gooey and wet.) I often put A GOOD CUP OF FLOUR in a plastic bag and, just before frying the fish, toss them with the flour in the bag, shaking the bag so that all the fish are well coated. Dump the contents of the bag into a colander, and shake the colander to remove excess flour.

Heat enough CANOLA OR PEANUT OIL to measure about 2 inches deep in a large skillet. Deep-fry the fish (a process that is best done outside, according to my wife) at 375 to 400°F for 3 to 4 minutes, moving the fish around with a skimmer until they are really crisp, like french fries, and beautifully brown. Drain immediately, sprinkle with FINE SALT, and serve with LEMON WEDGES and—if you want to be fancy occasionally—FRIED PARSLEY, celery leaves, or basil leaves.

To fry parsley, I clean CURLY OR FLAT-LEAF PARSLEY from my garden and dry it well before dropping it into the HOT OIL. I usually fry the parsley first, before frying the fish, in 275°F oil (no higher, because the parsley tends to burn at higher temperatures and get bitter tasting). Stir back and forth with a skimmer for about 1 minute, and then drain the leaves on paper towels.

My Aunt Hélène had a restaurant on a lake in Nantua

ABOVE LEFT: *Netted whitebait* ABOVE RIGHT: *Gutting the small fish* RIGHT: *Fried Whitebait with Fried Parsley*

SMOKED TROUT AND SCRAMBLED EGGS

YIELD: 4 SERVINGS

When we had a house in Hunter, New York, Gloria learned trout fishing from all the French chefs who spent weekends in the area. She loved the French way of fishing for trout, and began fishing regularly in the Schoharie and Esopus rivers, using a long French telescopic rod and regular worms I dug up for her in the garden. She walked slowly through the woods to get to the river, and snaked her line through tree branches so the trout could not see it and follow the line. She attached a little piece of red wool to the line, so that she could follow it in the current. She learned how to feel the bite and to hook the trout with a special twist of the wrist and drag it back gently and securely to the shore, where she slid her net underneath and got her prize.

The best fisherman of all was Pierre Larré. He was part of a restaurant dynasty in New York that existed long before I came to this country in the 1950s. He and his brother came from the southwest of France, and Pierre was the type of man who loved to go mushrooming, cured his own hams, and was an avid trout fisherman. He would catch trout in places where no one had ever caught trout before. Other fishermen would get closer and closer to him, and he would move away and go catch trout where they had tried unsuccessfully before.

Gloria adored Pierre and went off to fish with him in the early morning hours. I am not a morning person, so when she left at 5 A.M. to fish, I stayed snugly in bed. She would come back about 9 A.M., sometimes bringing all the other fishermen back with her, for a morning *casse-croûte* (snack). I would get up then and start making scrambled eggs and cleaning the trout. I would often smoke the trout, not for that morning, because it would take too long, but for another morning. During fishing season, we would always have smoked trout in our refrigerator. Some of the trout were smaller than others, of course, so the smoking and curing had to be adjusted a little to accommodate the size of the fish. While smoking trout is relatively easy to do, it is also available in specialty markets and gourmet shops around the country. If you want to smoke your own, buy a smoker or sacrifice an old roasting pan for this purpose.

I use dried herbs to smoke fish. In the fall, when the growing season is over but I still have basil in my garden, I pull out the plants, roots and all. First, I pull off and blanch the leaves, which I freeze for use during the winter. I hang the basil, thyme, and rosemary branches to dry out, and then break off pieces from these dried branches to burn during the smoking process. You can smoke fish using sawdust or wood chips of oak, cherry, or hickory (or any combination of these), along with the dried stems from the herbs that you've had in your garden during the summer. Sometimes I sprinkle a little dried thyme or a few dried bay leaves into the smoking mixture for extra flavor.

I smoke my fish, depending on size, for only 5 to 15 minutes, as I feel that the trout have absorbed enough smoky flavor at that point. However, I still continue cooking the trout in a covered pan until done. The trout take on a golden color on the surface of the skin and have a wonderful aroma and a light, delicate smoky taste. Trout smokes particularly well because it is a fatty fish, as are salmon and bluefish.

Serve about half a trout per person as a main course breakfast or brunch dish with two eggs per person, using the best possible organic eggs from a farm. I sometimes add mushrooms to my eggs, often using wild meadow or field varieties, including small chanterelles or honey mushrooms in early fall. I blanch the honey mushrooms in water for 10 minutes and rinse them under tap water before sautéing them in butter and oil.

There is nothing better than smoked trout and scrambled eggs with rich, black coffee for breakfast, a glass of Sauvignon Blanc for brunch, or, for a special treat, a glass of champagne.

SMOKED TROUT | Before being smoked, the trout has to be cured in salt. Dry curing is the process by which you sprinkle salt—either regular or kosher—directly on the fish. However, I like to make a liquid brine by adding salt to water until the water is saturated. This requires about 1½ CUPS OF KOSHER SALT to 3 CUPS OF WATER. I also add A HANDFUL OF BROWN SUGAR to the mixture to cut the harshness of the salt. Put 4 EVISCERATED TROUT in the brine mixture, and let them cure in it for about 1 hour for small trout (about 8 ounces or so). If you happen to catch or buy big trout (12 ounces to 1 pound each), leave them in the brine for 2 hours. Remove the trout from the brine, dry them with paper towels, and they are ready to be smoked.

I do my smoking outside, so I don't smoke up the house (something my wife appreciates!). Break the DRY HERB STEMS into pieces (or use wood chips, sawdust, or any combination of stems, chips, or sawdust) and put one or two handfuls (at most) into the bottom of an old roasting pan. Place a wire rack on top. If the rack doesn't have any feet, use some crumpled balls of aluminum foil to support it, so that the rack stands about 1½ inches above the herb stem pieces and/or wood chips. Arrange the trout in one layer on the rack, and cover it with the roasting pan lid or a piece of aluminum foil large enough to cover the whole pan and be tucked completely around it.

Place the pan on a gas grill set on medium. After 2 minutes or so, lift up a bit of the corner of the foil to see if the contents have started smoking. If they have, reduce the heat a little and continue smoking for 6 or 8 minutes depending on the size of the fish, at which point most of the wood and/or stems have burned away. Continue cooking for about 10 minutes for small trout and 12 to 15 minutes for larger trout. Shut off the heat, and let the trout steep for 30 to 60 minutes in the covered pan.

Cool, wrap in foil, and refrigerate the trout overnight. The skin will be slightly golden and beautifully leathery.

When ready to serve, starting at the belly where the fish is open from gutting, pull off the skin; it will pull off easily. Remove the head and tail. Running the long way down the middle of the trout is a line dividing the back and the belly fillets. Run your knife along this line, and push on one side of it to slide one of the fillets off the bone. (If it doesn't slide off easily, the trout is probably not cooked quite enough.) The small bones should stay attached to the central bone and the meat should slide off easily. Lift up and discard the central bone from the bottom fillet. I like my smoked fish slightly warm when serving it with eggs, so I put it in a 160°F oven to warm while I prepare the scrambled eggs.

SCRAMBLED EGGS | Beat 8 EGGS with SALT, FRESHLY GROUND BLACK PEPPER, and some CHIVES, and mix in 2 TO 3 TABLESPOONS OF SOUR CREAM. Melt 2 TABLESPOONS OF BUTTER in a nonstick skillet over medium heat, and sauté about 1 CUP OF DICED MUSH-ROOMS for 1 or 2 minutes. Add the eggs and, going along the edge of your pan with a whisk or rubber spatula, continue cooking and whisking to create medium-size curds and a creamy consistency.

Continue cooking your eggs for 3 or 4 minutes, or until the mixture comes together and is creamy and still slightly runny. At that point, remove the pan from the heat; there will be enough residual heat remaining in the pan to continue cooking the eggs. Add additional salt and pepper as needed and, to stop the cooking further, stir in a little more sour cream.

I like to serve these eggs with BAGUETTES that I cut into pieces 4 or 5 inches long and a couple of inches wide, toast in the oven or in a toaster, and spread with butter. Serve with the lukewarm trout.

MY MERGUEZ WITH PORK
AND GRILLED TORTILLA BREAD

YIELD: ABOUT 12 SAUSAGES

Nearly fifty years ago, when I left France, I was already familiar with *merguez*, the traditional lamb sausage of North Africa. That part of the world, called the Maghreb, encompasses Morocco, Algeria, and Tunisia, all of which were part of the French colonial empire for many years. After these countries gained their independence in the 1960s, many of the Arabs settled in France, where they have lived for several generations. Along with other North African dishes, like couscous and *mechoui* (a whole lamb barbecued on a spit), *merguez* is very popular in France. That little lamb sausage is a classic at any backyard barbecue or picnic there, as popular as the hot dog is in the United States.

Merguez are sometimes made only of lamb or a mixture of beef and lamb. I make my *merguez* with lamb and pork, which many Arabs would object to on religious grounds, but I feel that this combination works best.

One of the problems in making sausage is to find casings and a grinding machine with an attachment for stuffing them with the meat mixture. *Merguez* are about the size of breakfast sausages, and lamb casings of a little over an inch in diameter are traditionally used. As a different, delicious alternative, I make my *merguez* without casings, simply rolling the mixture into "sausages" about three inches long.

With the *merguez*, I like to serve bread, and often I prepare what I call grilled tortilla bread. It is great with any grilled food, as well as cheese.

MERGUEZ | Buy 1 POUND OF ITALIAN SAUSAGE, already ground, either hot or mild, and 1 OR 2 LAMB SHOULDER CHOPS, ABOUT 12 OUNCES TOTAL. These chops are a bit fatty, and give great flavor to the *merguez*. Bone the chops, and cut the meat into 1-inch pieces. You should have 9 to 10 ounces of lamb meat. Grind all the lamb, fat included, through a medium-size screen in a meat grinder, which I have as an attachment to my mixer. Alternatively, grind these pieces in a food processor for 10 to 15 seconds. Mix the ground lamb with the Italian sausage (if the Italian sausage is coarser than you like, you can grind it a little in the food processor).

To the combined meat, add 1½ TEASPOONS OF CUMIN POWDER, 1 TEASPOON OF PAPRIKA, ⅛ TEASPOON OF CAYENNE PEPPER, ¾ TEASPOON OF SALT, and 1 TEASPOON OF FINELY CHOPPED GARLIC. Mix together with your hands until well combined, and divide the meat into equal-size pieces, and form these into 3-inch sausages, each weighing about 2 ounces.

To cook the *merguez,* place the sausages on a very hot grill and cook for 5 or 6 minutes, turning them occasionally, so they brown evenly. They will get crusty and juicy, with a wonderful aroma. They should be cooked medium, with a juicy interior and seared exterior. Arrange on LETTUCE LEAVES, and pass around to guests. Alternatively, serve the *merguez* with grilled tortilla bread.

GRILLED TORTILLA BREAD | I use 6-INCH FLOUR TORTILLAS for this. I OIL the tortillas liberally on both sides, sprinkle on A DASH OF SALT and A LITTLE HERBES DE PROVENCE, and A DASH OF CUMIN OR CURRY if you like. Place on the hot grill with the *merguez*, and cook the tortillas about 30 seconds on each side. The surface of the tortillas will bubble as they brown. Just press on them with a spatula, and grill well. Cut into quarters, and serve with the *merguez*.

Truffle and Pistachio Sausage with Buttered Fingerling Potatoes

YIELD: 4 SERVINGS PER SAUSAGE

As Lyonnaise, we like to say that Lyon has the best charcuterie, not only in France, but also in the whole world. Of course, other areas of France pretend to have that same distinction, as do the Italians, Spaniards, Portuguese, Germans, and others. Yet, the charcuteries, the shops where pâtés, hams, sausages, and other pork products are sold, are particularly beautiful in Lyon, and the dried sausages—fat, red, salted, and a little spicy—that are made there are of great quality. The most common is a fat, short sausage known as *saucisson sec,* or dry sausage. Before it is dried, this mild but well-seasoned sausage is called *cervelas.* It is commonly poached or roasted and served at bistros in Lyon, usually with potato salad.

Cervelas was an important part of my youth. My mother, my aunt, and my younger brother all served these. Sometimes my mother pricked the whole fat sausage with a fork and roasted it, surrounded by small whole potatoes, in a large cast-iron vessel called a cocotte. More often than not, however, her sausage was poached over very low heat and then served with a potato salad or with boiled potatoes seasoned with butter and herbs. I liked all of these variations. For a very special occasion, the sausage was partially poached, encased in brioche dough, baked, and served in thick slices, often with a mushroom sauce, or, on a very special occasion, with a *sauce périgourdine,* or truffle sauce. For my taste, I still prefer the simple sausage, either roasted or poached, and served with new potatoes.

One of the problems with making sausage is finding casings to pack it in. A so-called "beef middle" casing of about 2½ inches in diameter is the right casing for this sausage, but I do not use a casing here, making the preparation much easier. The conventional sausage is made with plain ground pork flavored simply with pepper, a dash of garlic, a little wine, and special curing salt. However, at holiday time in Lyon, the charcuteries sell special sausages that also contain pistachios and black truffles, and the truffles give an incomparable flavor to the sausages. Black truffle season begins in France just after our Thanksgiving, and it goes on through February or March. Some of the best truffles are in the southwest of France and in upper Provence, in towns like Carpentras, where my friend Serge, who has a restaurant there, takes me truffle hunting. He taught me the best way to eat truffles: wash and thinly slice a raw truffle onto a plate, drizzle with the best olive oil you can find, and sprinkle on a little fleur de sel. Eat with slices of buttered baguette, or, better, slices of buttered brioche. This is a holiday treat for us, as perfect as it is simple, whenever I can get some fresh truffles from Provence. When I make these sausages, I usually enjoy a couple of them fresh in the weeks leading up to the holidays, and then dry the others in the cellar. After about eight weeks of drying, they are ready to eat sliced very thin with a glass of wine.

New potatoes just fresh from the garden are one of my greatest food memories. At my mother's home near Lyon, I remember her going into the garden at lunchtime with her *triandine,* a four-prong pitchfork, and unearthing those long, thin potatoes that we call fingerlings here but which are called *rattes* or *quenelles* in Lyon, named after the pike dumplings made there. In other parts of France, these are often called cornichon potatoes after the small, sour gherkins common in French cooking. My mother would rub the potatoes, fresh out of the earth, with her fingers, and most of the peel would slide off. Then she would sauté them in peanut oil and butter, adding a little salt at the end. Served with a curly chicory salad dressed with garlic, mustard, and oil, this was lunch for me, and what a lunch!

TRUFFLE AND PISTACHIO SAUSAGE | For two sausages, put 2 POUNDS GROUND PORK SHOULDER (sometimes called Boston butt) with 20 to 25 percent fat into a large mixing bowl. Grind, or have the butcher grind the meat for you through a medium-size screen. Add about ¼ CUP OF DRY AND FRUITY WHITE WINE, 1 TEASPOON OF FINELY CHOPPED GARLIC, 1 TEASPOON OF FRESHLY GROUND BLACK PEPPER, and about 4 TEASPOONS OF MORTON TENDER QUICK CURING SALT. I buy this over the Internet from Morton Salt, and it is essential if you want your pâté or sausage to be pink, like commercial hams, frankfurters, and pastrami. This salt, the curing agent, is composed of 99 percent salt, half of 1 percent sodium nitrate, and half of 1 percent sodium nitrite. If you use regular salt without a curing agent, the sausages will be fine to eat but will be gray in color rather than the appealing pink color achieved with the curing agent.

Add about ⅓ CUP OF SHELLED PISTACHIOS (not salted), and—if you can afford it—¼ CUP OF COARSELY CHOPPED BLACK TRUFFLE, preferably the *Tuber melanosporum*. Mix the ingredients together well with your hands. Divide the mixture in half. Form and press each half into a sausage about 8 inches long and 2 inches in diameter. Take care to press the mixture firmly enough to eliminate air bubbles, which would result in unsightly holes in the sausages. Wrap individually in plastic wrap, twisting the ends of the plastic wrap to enclose the sausages, and then roll each of them in aluminum foil, twisting the ends of the foil. Refrigerate for at least 3 days to cure. Freeze one of the sausages, if desired, and remember to thaw it slowly in the refrigerator before cooking.

The very important part of poaching these sausages is to do it at a low temperature for a long time. This makes a big difference in the taste and juiciness of the meat. Bring a pot of water to between 150 and 160°F. Lower the wrapped sausages into the pot, and place a heavy lid that is a little smaller than the top of the pot on top of the sausages to weigh them down in the pot and keep them immersed in the water. Cook in the same temperature range, checking the pot occasionally, for about 1 hour, or until the internal temperature of the sausages is close to the same temperature as the water, about 150°F. To keep warm, let the sausages sit in the 150-to-160°F water until serving time.

BUTTERED FINGERLING POTATOES | For the potatoes, use 4 OR 5 SMALL FINGERLINGS PER PERSON, ABOUT 1½ POUNDS TOTAL. Peel the potatoes, wash them, put them in a pot, and cover with cold water. Bring to a boil, reduce the heat, and boil gently for 20 to 25 minutes. Check them by piercing with the point of a sharp knife to assure that they are tender; they should be firm enough to hold together but cooked enough so they are creamy inside. When the potatoes are cooked, drain, holding the potatoes back with a lid while you pour out the water. Return the potatoes to the stove to cook for about 1 minute, shaking the pan occasionally, to evaporate whatever moisture remains, so the potatoes are not watery. Add 2 OR 3 TABLESPOONS OF THE BEST POSSIBLE UNSALTED BUTTER and A COUPLE OF TABLESPOONS OF MINCED FRESH CHIVES. Stir, add A DASH OF SALT AND PEPPER, and mix well.

To serve, transfer the potatoes to a small platter, unwrap the sausage, cut into slices, and arrange on top of the potatoes. Serve immediately, dishing up a couple of sausage slices with a few potatoes for a simple, unpretentious dish with great substance.

Knockwurst with Warm Potato Salad

YIELD: 4 SERVINGS

I am crazy about any type of cold cut: sausage, salami, mortadella, pâté, and, particularly, the fat, pink boiled ham of my youth. It was boiled very gently, bone in, and sliced by hand for each order. I also love different types of prosciutto shoulder or hind leg, as well as *cervelas* (see page 81), a moist sausage served hot, plain, in a crust, or in brioche with lentil or potato salad. I love hot dogs, knockwurst, and bratwurst, as well.

When I am in New York City, I often make a point of stopping at Katz Delicatessen on Houston Street, my favorite place in the city for pastrami and corned beef sandwiches. Go to the counter, give a buck to the man who is cutting the pastrami, and ask him to give you slices from the part of the pastrami or corned beef that has a little fat. The sandwich he will make from this will be practically a foot tall, with the meat contained between two slices of soft and fragrant rye bread and the sandwich accompanied by a fat, sour gherkin; it just doesn't get much better.

Very often when my friend Jean-Claude comes to visit, I make a warm potato salad for lunch with a couple of knockwursts. He loves sausage as much as I do. I shop at Ferraro's in New Haven, where I can get really thick, big knockwursts of very good quality. I like them just warmed up in hot water, or cut in half, briefly sautéed in a skillet, and served with potato salad.

I am a great lover of potato salad and prepare three or four different types. I particularly like the one I make with small Red Bliss potatoes or fingerlings with the skin on or off. I like sautéed leeks in my potato salad and a lot of parsley, onion (red torpedo or a milder onion, like a Walla-Walla or Vidalia), chopped garlic, lots of Dijon mustard, a little white wine, a good red wine vinegar, lots of chives, ground pepper, and plenty of good extra-virgin olive oil, the best you can get. This potato salad is best lukewarm.

WARM POTATO SALAD | Cover 1 TO 1½ POUNDS OF RED BLISS POTATOES with water, add A DASH OF SALT, and bring to a boil. Reduce the heat, and cook gently, uncovered, until the potatoes are tender to the point of a knife, about 30 minutes. I like my potatoes tender, and would rather have the slices breaking down a little than have them undercooked. Drain the potatoes while boiling hot, so whatever moisture is left in them will evaporate. While the potatoes are still lukewarm, cut them, peeled or unpeeled, into fairly thick slices, ¼-to-½ inch thick. I like the Bliss potatoes because they absorb the dressing well.

I prepare the dressing separately. Sauté 1 CUP OF SLICED LEEK in 2 TABLESPOONS OF OLIVE OIL for 2 to 3 minutes, or until it softens. Transfer to a bowl, and mix with 3 OR 4 TABLESPOONS EACH OF CHOPPED ONION, PARSLEY, AND BASIL OR CHIVES, 1½ TEASPOONS OF FINELY CHOPPED GARLIC, 2 TABLESPOONS OF DIJON-STYLE FRENCH MUSTARD, 2 TABLESPOONS OF WHITE WINE, 1 TABLESPOON OF RED WINE VINEGAR, A GOOD DASH OF SALT, and A FAIR AMOUNT OF FRESHLY GROUND BLACK PEPPER. To this, gently mix in ¼ CUP OF THE BEST OLIVE OIL you have. Combine the potatoes and dressing, mixing gently so as not to crush the potatoes too much.

KNOCKWURST | Heat 4 KNOCKWURST in hot water for 6 to 8 minutes, or split into halves lengthwise, and heat in a DASH OF OIL in a skillet. Serve with the lukewarm potato salad and extra mustard. A glass of cool white wine or beer is always welcome.

a Juicy knockwurst with potato salad and a beer for lunch

PARFAIT OF ROSÉ MUSHROOMS WITH SHERRY-TRUFFLE SAUCE

YIELD: 6 SERVINGS

This is a dish that I serve for special occasions; it is very elegant and deep in flavor. I have made it with regular white button or cremini mushrooms, which are fine to use, especially if the mushrooms are partially open underneath. These riper mushrooms have more flavor than oyster or shiitake mushrooms. However, in late summer I pick meadow or field mushrooms, called "*rosé*" because they are pink underneath, and I use those in this recipe. These are the wild variety of the regular supermarket white mushrooms. These gilled mushrooms can be confused with poisonous mushrooms, so unless you are knowledgeable about mycology, don't go mushrooming for *rosés* for this recipe. The small variety, *Agaricus campestris,* and the larger one, *Agaricus arvensis,* the so-called horse mushroom (a wild variety of portobello) come at about the same time, and either of these has a dense, deep taste that is perfect for this recipe.

I make a puree of the mushrooms, add cream, eggs, and seasonings, and cook them, much like a custard, in a water bath. This can be done ahead and the custard can be reheated gently over water on top of the stove. I coat the custard, or parfait, with a demi-glace flavored with truffles and a reduction of sherry wine. I serve this dish with a glass of sherry, which pairs well with it. For the sauce, I use black winter truffles, *Tuber melanosporum,* from France. I keep in my freezer the truffles that I foraged for and smuggled through customs when I returned from France. They are fragrant and have a wonderful flavor. Do not buy the summer truffle, *Tuber aestivum,* for this dish; it is less expensive but has very little taste. It is worth paying good money to have the real taste of a truffle.

The combination of demi-glace, sherry reduction, truffle, and a little butter makes an elegant, rich, deep sauce, and a little of this goes a long way. A couple of tablespoons of the sauce over each parfait of mushrooms are enough.

I served this dish recently as the first course of a fine dinner and followed it with the Steamed Lobster with Herb Sauce, Lobster Bisque, Corn, and Fingerling Potatoes (pages 123–127) as a main course. Afterward, I served cheeses and a bit of arugula from my garden tossed with a little walnut oil, and a fruit dessert. It made a splendid menu.

You will need A GOOD POUND OF MUSHROOMS for six guests. If you can't find the *rosés*, which will render a great deal of water, use regular white or cremini mushrooms. Wash and cut the mushrooms into large pieces, leaving them whole if they are small. Put them in a saucepan, and cook over medium heat, partially covered, until almost all the moisture has come out of them and evaporated, which will take 20 to 30 minutes. Wild mushrooms should always be cooked longer, as people sometimes can have a reaction to certain types if they are undercooked. At the end of the cooking, there should still be about ¾ cup of juice with the *rosé* mushrooms.

While the mushrooms are cooking, sauté about ⅓ CUP OF CHOPPED SHALLOTS in 1 TABLESPOON OF OLIVE OIL for 30 to 40 seconds. Add 2 TEASPOONS OF CHOPPED GARLIC, mix well, and then transfer to the bowl of a blender (better for this process than a food processor) with the cooked *rosés* and their juice. Blend into a smooth puree. (Note: This can be done ahead, even the day before, so you have it ready.) You should have 1¾ to 2 cups of this mixture.

When ready to prepare the parfait, butter six to eight ½-cup porcelain or stainless-steel ramekins. To the pureed mushrooms, add 1 CUP OF HEAVY CREAM and 4 EGGS. Mix well in the blender or by hand. You should have about 4 cups. Fill the ramekins to the rim and place them in a large skillet or roasting pan with lukewarm water surrounding them and extending halfway up the sides. Cook in a low oven, 300 to 325°F degrees, for 50 to 60 minutes, or until they are really set on top, and a toothpick or the point of a knife inserted into the center comes out clean. It can still appear slightly wet in the center, because it will continue cooking for a while as it cools. Set the parfaits aside in the water. They can be reheated at the last moment.

For the accompanying sauce, mix 1 CUP OF DEMI-GLACE (page 37) with ⅓ CUP OF SHERRY in a small saucepan. (There are different types of sherry: while the Manzanilla is a very dry white sherry, I like to use the Amontillado, which is slightly sweet, not quite as dry, and has a darker color.) Boil the demi-glace and sherry together for 4 or 5 minutes.

Meanwhile, if adding truffle, peel A MEDIUM TO LARGE TRUFFLE, and chop the peel very fine. Chop the remainder of the truffle a little more coarsely, because the peel is rougher in texture. You should have a good 2 tablespoons of chopped truffle. Add the truffle and whatever juice there is to the sauce. Add 1 TO 2 TABLESPOONS OF UNSALTED BUTTER, and whisk it in to finish the sauce.

Unmold the mushroom parfaits on warm plates, spoon 2 or 3 tablespoons of sauce on top, and enjoy.

PÂTÉ OF PHEASANT

YIELD: 2 PÂTÉS (SERVING 20 PEOPLE)

When I was an apprentice, the making of pâté, terrines, and *pâté en croûte* was a very sophisticated endeavor for the seasoned chef who had a great deal of knowledge and astute cooking wisdom. In fact, a pâté is a sophisticated and elegant "meat loaf."

Pâté de campagne, the ordinary country pâté, is available in most supermarkets in France. It is usually comprised of pork liver, pork fat, and pork meat. A terrine is always a bit more complex and is actually the name for the earthenware dish in which the forcemeat is cooked and served. By extension, it takes on the name of its cooking vessel. Terrines are generally more elegant and are often served with aspic, while the country pâté makes you think more of cornichons (sour French gherkins), and hot Dijon mustard. *Pâté en croûte* is more elaborate and is served, often warm, at special banquets and weddings. A mousse is a mixture of sautéed liver and fat emulsified into a type of liverwurst. Pâtés and terrines can be very mundane and simple or sophisticated with the addition of goose liver foie gras, as well as truffles, special mushrooms, and cognac.

Pâtés and terrines are served at the beginning of classic French meals and are often served for special occasions. Most people buy their pâtés in specialty stores, where they are readily available and often quite good. A pâté is always made with relatively fatty pork meat. Beyond the pork, a pâté can contain any meat, from veal to venison to woodcock to partridge to pheasant, as well as liver and sweetbreads.

When making pâté, the most important factors are the proportion of fat to meat and proper seasoning. Cook a little bit of the mixture in a skillet to check the seasonings before molding the pâté. It should be slightly overseasoned and oversalted. By the time it is cold, it is just right. Another important factor is to cook the pâté at a low temperature for a long time. If it is cooked too fast, the fat melts out of it, and the pâté is dry and crumbly.

Once or twice every winter, especially around holiday time, I make game pâté because I have several friends—including Claude—who go hunting and supply me with pheasants. Pheasant meat is lean, so it is important that the pork contain enough fat. I almost always have duck fat or back fat in my freezer to add to my pâtés if needed. When buying a pork roast at the market, trim the fat from the top and keep it in the freezer for adding to your pâté. I usually make two small pâtés, one of which I cook, and one I freeze uncooked. With the exception of mousse, cooked pâtés do not freeze well.

A small pheasant, which usually comes to me with the feathers still on and eviscerated, weighs about two pounds. Pheasants are delicate to pluck, and the skin tears easily. Since I do not need the skin for the pâté, I let my pheasants age for a few days in the refrigerator to improve the taste before cutting through the feathers and the skin and removing both of them together.

After the meat is removed from the bones, the carcass is cooked to make a stock, which is reduced to a glaze and added to the forcemeat. The used bones are re-cooked in water and made into an aspic to serve with the pâté. I love aspic, not only with pâté, but also with poached eggs and fish as well. To my pâté I add chopped truffles that I bought in the market

if the pâté is moist and well seasoned, the cook has talent

in Carpentras, France, and stored in my freezer, along with lightly roasted and skinned hazelnuts, and some chicken livers or duck livers.

Use curing salt, like Morton Tender Quick, available on the Internet or in restaurant supply houses. Quite good, it is 99 percent salt, half of 1 percent sodium nitrate, and half of 1 percent sodium nitrite. These are curing agents that keep the pâté looking beautifully pink inside.

TWO PHEASANTS (ABOUT 2 POUNDS EACH with the feathers on) will yield two small pâtés, each serving about ten people. Cut through the feathers and skin, and pull them off. Clean the birds up completely, removing any remaining feather pieces, then wash the pheasants, taking care to remove buckshot where the flesh is bruised and black. Separate the legs and the breast, and cut the breast meat off the carcass. Bone the legs, reserving the thigh meat and scrape as much meat as possible from the drumsticks. (There are nerves in the way, so only a little meat can be retrieved.) Remove and discard any sinew. The pheasants should yield approximately 1 pound of breast meat, about ¾ pound of leg meat, and about 1¼ pounds of bones.

Cut the bones into large pieces, and put into a large saucepan with an additional POUND OF CHICKEN BONES—NECKS, CARCASSES— and 1 TABLESPOON OF CANOLA OIL. Brown the bones gently over medium to high heat for about 30 minutes, stirring them occasionally with a wooden spatula. The bottom of the pan should be nicely crystal-lized and the bones brown and crusty. At this point, pour off any fat into a bowl, holding back the bones with the pan lid.

Add about 5 CUPS OF WATER to the saucepan, bring to a boil, and boil gently for 25 to 30 minutes. Strain, and return the bones to the saucepan in which they were cooked. You should have 2 to 2½ cups of stock. Boil to reduce this to about ⅓ cup of concentrated glaze, and set aside to add to the forcemeat. Add 2 QUARTS OF WATER to the pan containing the bones, boil gently for about 1½ hours, and then strain to use later in the aspic. You will have about 3 cups. Adjust with water if necessary. Set aside.

Cut the breast meat into 1½ inch cubes, and combine in a bowl with 1½ POUNDS OF GROUND PORK BUTT that should be nearly 40 percent fat. Add additional fat if necessary. Grind the leg meat, and add it to the bowl. Add ⅓ CUP OF DRY WHITE WINE, 2 TABLE-SPOONS OF GOOD COGNAC, 2 TABLESPOONS OF POTATO STARCH, 1 TABLESPOON OF CHOPPED GARLIC, ¼ CUP OF FINELY CHOPPED SHALLOT, 2 TABLESPOONS OF CHOPPED TRUFFLE, and about ¾ CUP OF ROASTED AND SHELLED HAZELNUTS. (Remove the skin by rubbing the nuts in a dish towel while they are still hot from the roasting, and don't worry if a little of the skin remains on them).

I grind my own seasonings in a small spice or coffee grinder. Drop 2 BAY LEAVES, broken into pieces, into the bowl of a grinder with 1 TEASPOON OF BLACK PEPPERCORNS, ½ TEASPOON OF DRIED

a slice of game pâté is the perfect start for a Fall dinner

OREGANO (I like the oregano that I buy in Mexico), ½ TEASPOON OF DRIED THYME LEAVES, and 1 TABLESPOON PLUS 2 TEASPOONS (5 TEASPOONS) OF CURING SALT. (Note: This amount of salt is needed.) Grind to a powder, and add to the forcemeat along with the concentrated glaze reduction from the bones. Mix well. Separate 3 OR 4 CHICKEN OR DUCK LIVERS into halves, and place on top of the meat. Cover with plastic wrap, and refrigerate for at least 3 days to develop the proper taste and aroma.

This is enough to make two pâtés, each about 4 cups. Fill the molds about halfway with the forcemeat, and arrange a row of livers down the center. Cover with more forcemeat to fill the terrines. Place a bay leaf and a sprig of thyme on top of each mold, cover tightly with plastic wrap, and then wrap in aluminum foil. Freeze one of the uncooked pâtés, if desired. (Freezing a cooked pâté results in a dry, crumbly pâté.) Allow the frozen pâté to thaw for 1 or 2 days in the refrigerator before cooking it.

Preheat the oven to 200°F. Place the wrapped pâté mold in a saucepan and surround it with warm water, so it comes about halfway up the mold. Put the pan in the oven, and bake for about 1¾ hours. The water around the pâté should remain at about 180°F, and the internal temperature of the pâté when completely cooked should be about 140°F. This will rise to at least 145°F 15 to 20 minutes after the pâté is removed from the oven. Cool at room temperature for a couple of hours, and then remove the foil and plastic wrap, cover the pâté with clean plastic wrap, and refrigerate until ready to serve. It should rest for at least a day or so before it is served. It will keep, refrigerated in the terrine, for a good week, with slices being removed as needed. To keep it for up to two weeks, remove it from the terrine, clean up all the juice and liquid around it, and wrap tightly in plastic wrap.

For the aspic, bring the 3 CUPS OF PHEASANT STOCK to a boil. Meanwhile, pour 2 ENVELOPES OF PLAIN, UNFLAVORED GELATIN (about 1½ tablespoons) into a stainless-steel saucepan with 2 EGG WHITES, ¾ CUP OF VERY COARSELY CHOPPED GREEN OF LEEK, ½ CUP OF CELERY GREENS, and about 1 CUP OF COMBINED FRESH PARSLEY, TARRAGON, CHIVES, AND BASIL, coarsely chopped. Stir in about ¾ TEASPOON OF BLACK PEPPERCORNS, coarsely crushed with a skillet, and A GOOD DASH OF SALT. Mix in ¼ CUP OF COLD WATER.

The aspic is prepared quickly, like an herb infusion. Pour the boiling stock on top of this mixture, and stir well. Place on the stove, and cook over high heat, stirring almost constantly until it comes to a strong boil. At this point stop stirring, and don't disturb it anymore. The impurities in the mixture and the egg whites will form a raft or crust on top. The liquid below the crust will be quite clear.

Line a small sieve with a wet paper towel, and pour the aspic through it into a bowl. You should have about 2½ cups of crystal-clear aspic. Allow it to cool, and then cut into a small dice for serving with your pâté. Good bread and an old Burgundy or a Napa Cabernet Sauvignon would be ideal accompaniments.

PÂTÉ OF FOIE GRAS WITH ROSE HIP JAM

There is a great deal of controversy about foie gras in different parts of the United States. Foie gras is the oversized liver of web-footed birds, specifically ducks and geese. The enlarged liver occurs as a natural process that was discovered by the Egyptians centuries ago. They realized that when birds were killed just before migration, their livers were large, fatty, and absolutely delicious. The animals had been force-feeding themselves for two or three weeks before migrating so they wouldn't have to stop too often and be exposed to predators. The fat, oversized liver returned to its original size once the bird reached its destination. This natural process has been duplicated by farmers from time immemorial in different parts of Europe, like Hungary and Israel and, certainly, in the southwest of France and Alsace. The animal is force-fed a mush of corn and duck fat for about three weeks before it is slaughtered. It eats willingly and doesn't suffer, which would affect the quality of the liver. In my opinion, livers from the Hudson Valley in upstate New York are the best in the United States.

A large liver usually comes vacuum-packed and weighs about $1\frac{1}{2}$ pounds at most. Foie gras is often sliced, sautéed, and served hot or used in stuffing. It is also served raw, cured with salt. It is best served in slices very cold with a sweet marmalade of apple or some fig jam, and some bread or brioche. Along Hammonasset Beach, near where I live, I pick a lot of rose hips in the fall, when they are dark red and very ripe. People often make jelly with these, but I make them into a sweet jam that is a great accompaniment for my foie gras.

In this recipe, the foie gras is cooked *sous-vide* or "under vacuum," although I also give instructions for poaching it without vacuum packing it. *Sous-vide* is a technique used by many chefs now for cooking meat as well as vegetables and fish. Whatever is to be cooked is first vacuum-packed and then poached in a low-temperature water bath with excellent results. This requires a vacuum-packing machine, and I use a small one at home that Gloria uses to vacuum-pack food for the freezer because it keeps better. In professional kitchens, there are machines with probe-type thermometers equipped with very thin needles that are inserted into the food being cooked, so an exact reading of the temperature is possible. The water in which the food is cooked is in an electric container where the temperature is controlled precisely.

PÂTÉ OF FOIE GRAS | Leave a 1½-POUND FOIE GRAS out at room temperature for 2 to 3 hours to soften. Remove it from the plastic bag it comes in, and open it to separate the two sides of foie gras in the package. Feel with your fingers to find the sinews, nerves, and veins inside, and pull them out. Don't worry if you are crushing the foie gras to do this; it will be packed together eventually. When the foie gras is totally open and you have denerved and deveined it to the best of your ability, mix together in a small bowl 1 TEASPOON OF REGULAR SALT, ½ TEASPOON OF SUGAR, and ½ TEASPOON OF FRESHLY GROUND BLACK PEPPER. Sprinkle this mixture on the foie gras, inside and out, and add 1 GOOD TABLESPOON OF BOURBON OR COGNAC. Wrap the foie gras in plastic wrap, and press it with your hands into a tube shape 8 or 9 inches long and 2 to 2½ inches in diameter. At this point, the uncooked foie gras can be refrigerated for 24 hours, sliced, and served as is.

If you have a vacuum-packing machine, place the foie gras in one of the special plastic bags provided by the machine manufacturer and seal it tightly in the bag according to the manufacturer's instructions. If you do not have a vacuum-packing machine, wrap another layer of plastic wrap around the foie gras to ensure that the package is waterproof.

Heat the oven to 175°F. Put the foie gras package in a pan of water that is between 150 and 160°F, and put an inverted plate on top of it to hold the foie gras down (otherwise it may float). Place in the oven for about 20 minutes. At this point, check the internal temperature, which should be about 130°F at most. Put the bag containing the foie gras in ice-cold water for 1 hour or so to cool off, then refrigerate it.

When ready to serve the foie gras, open the bag. There will be some yellow, fragrant fat all around it that has separated from the meat. Remove and reserve this; it is extremely savory and delicious for sautéing potatoes or as an addition to a stew or soup.

Cut the foie gras into ¾-inch slices, and serve on very cold plates with ROSE HIP JAM or a little fig jam, TOAST OR BRIOCHE SLICES, and some ROASTED, CRUSHED HAZELNUTS pressed into the top and around the sides of the foie gras. Sprinkle with a few grains of FLEUR DE SEL. This is best with a sweet wine, like a Sauternes or with a glass of champagne.

ROSE HIP JAM | First boil the rose hips whole in water for 1 to 1½ hours, until they are soft and tender, drain, and then push them through a food mill to strain out the flesh and separate it from the skin and seeds. For 1 POUND OF ROSE HIP FLESH, add about ½ POUND OF SUGAR, bring the mixture to a boil, and boil it for 5 minutes. Spoon it into jars, cover it with a little melted wax, and store it in the cellar.

landscapes are part of my happy memories

Headcheese Jean-Victor with Ravigote Sauce

I don't remember my father doing much cooking. My mother cooked all the time, of course, and my father would get involved when there were wild mushrooms he had picked up, little fish he had caught in a local stream for frying, or to make *fromage fort* with leftover cheese. He marinated the cheese in leek broth and white wine in an earthenware jar in the cellar and eventually mashed it up with a lot of garlic and more white wine to make a creamy, strong-flavored mixture that we ate on toast or browned in a hot oven.

Another dish he loved and made occasionally was headcheese with pork jowls, ears, snout, and tongue. I am naming this simple recipe after him because he would like this chunky, wholesome version. At my market I'm fortunate to find pork snouts, cheeks, and other parts of the pig's head, including ears and tongue, although the snouts and cheeks are about the best choice for this recipe. The recipe also includes cornichons, which are the tiny salted gherkins that Gloria preserves in the summer. When they are no bigger than her little finger, she picks the cucumbers from the garden, puts them in salt for six to eight hours, then rubs them with a coarse kitchen towel. She then packs them in a jar with vinegar, a sprig of tarragon, and a few black peppercorns. We serve these cornichons, or sour gherkins, with cold cuts and pâté, or use them in the headcheese.

Headcheese improves greatly if the meat is cured with salt and a curing agent, like Tender Quick, made by Morton Salt. This makes the headcheese beautifully pink, and the curing gives it a great aroma.

When I make it, I usually cook enough for two headcheese and freeze one of them. However, when it defrosts it doesn't have the proper consistency unless it is remelted, brought to a boil, and remolded. When this is done, it will have the texture of the fresh headcheese.

In the following recipe, we will make two headcheese, or *civier*, the name it is given in Bourg-en-Bresse. This recipe is divided and molded in two bowls; although it can be molded into any shape, I prefer my headcheese round, because that is the way my father made it. It makes an ideal lunch with crusty bread, Dijon mustard, and a glass of cold white wine. As a first course for a meal, I serve it with a *ravigote* sauce, which is a vinaigrette with mustard, onion, capers, and garlic. This invigorating sauce can be used on top of poached fish, with other cold cuts, or mixed with salad greens.

HEADCHEESE JEAN-VICTOR | Put 2½ POUNDS OF PIG SNOUT, cut into 2-to-3-inch pieces, into a plastic bag with 3 TABLESPOONS OF TENDER QUICK (this is a lot of salt, but you need this amount), 1 TABLESPOON BROWN SUGAR, ½ TEASPOON OF CAYENNE PEPPER, and 1 TEASPOON OF OREGANO (I like Greek or Mexican oregano). Cure for at least 24 hours in the refrigerator, turning occasionally, so that the flavor infuses the meat. Then take the pork out of the bag and rinse it very briefly under cold running water.

Put the pieces of pork in a pot with 3 CUPS OF WATER. Bring to a boil, reduce the heat, and boil gently, covered, for 1 hour. It should be tender to the point of a knife, but still a bit firm.

While the pork is cooking, prepare the vegetables. You will need 1 CUP OF COARSELY CUT ONION, 1 CUP OF DICED (½ INCH) CARROT, ½ CUP OF SLICED SCALLION, and 2 TABLESPOONS OF COARSELY CHOPPED GARLIC. Add these vegetables to the pot, along with A CUP OF DRY, FRUITY WHITE WINE. Bring to a boil again, and boil very gently for about 30 minutes, partially covered, so the liquid evaporates a little. Add about ¼ CUP OF SLICED CORNICHONS.

Divide the mixture between two bowls, each with about a 4-cup capacity. Cover tightly with plastic wrap, and allow to set overnight in the refrigerator. The headcheese should be very firm, and a great deal of fat will have come to the surface. Scrape it off with a spoon, and run a knife around the edge to unmold the *civier*. When a little air goes between the knife and the headcheese, it will fall out of the overturned mold. Cut into wedges, and serve as a first course, plain, with mustard, or with *ravigote* sauce.

RAVIGOTE SAUCE | For 1 cup of sauce, in a bowl combine ¼ CUP OF FINELY CHOPPED RED ONION, 2 TABLESPOONS OF DRAINED CAPERS, ¼ CUP OF FINELY MINCED SCALLION, 1 TABLE-SPOON OF DIJON MUSTARD, 2 TEASPOONS OF FINELY CHOPPED GARLIC, ¼ CUP OF CHOPPED PARSLEY, 2 TABLESPOONS OF RED WINE VINEGAR, ⅓ CUP OF OLIVE OIL, 2 TABLESPOONS OF WATER, and SALT AND PEPPER to taste. Mix well, and serve with the head-cheese or use as a dressing for salad greens.

Saucisson of Pork Tenderloin

YIELD: 2 SAUSAGES

Saucisson, a dried sausage of the salami type, is usually made with pork in France. There are dozens of different kinds of *saucisson* in the markets throughout the country, some smoked, some made only with pork, some made with a mixture of pork and beef, and some containing lamb. Years ago in Lyon, a special dried sausage used to be made from a combination of donkey meat and pork.

I have made *saucisson* through the years, putting the meat in casings, drying the sausages out on the porch or in the refrigerator. I have made them small, long, and fat as well as skinny. When stuffing the mixture by hand into pork casings, there are often pockets of air, and the *saucisson* gets dark spots as it dries out.

A few years ago at a market in Provence, I saw sliced *saucisson* that looked like thinly sliced, very lean prosciutto, and I realized that it was done with a whole pork tenderloin. This is what I have been making ever since. It is easy to make, the meat dries beautifully, and it is the leanest dried sausage one can have.

Buy the largest pork tenderloins you can find at the market, ones that weigh a pound or more. I cut about three inches off the tails and sauté these end pieces for dinner. The rest of the fillet should be about two inches in diameter and close to a foot long.

Remove any silver skin from 2 PORK TENDERLOINS, EACH ABOUT 1 POUND, and cut 2 to 3 inches off the tails, reserving them for another use. Put 1 CUP OF KOSHER SALT in a plastic storage bag (or use ½ CUP OF MORTON TENDER QUICK CURING SALT, which has a curing agent that keeps the meat beautifully pink). Add 2 TABLESPOONS OF LIGHT BROWN SUGAR to the salt in the bag, and mix well. Slide the tenderloins into the bag, close tightly, and shake to coat the meat with the salt mixture. Refrigerate overnight.

After 12 hours or so, remove the tenderloins from the bag, and wipe them dry with paper towels. Rub the meat with about 1 TABLESPOON OF COGNAC, and sprinkle on about 1 TABLESPOON OF CRACKED BLACK PEPPER and 1 TABLESPOON OF HERBES DE PROVENCE, dividing these ingredients between the two tenderloins.

Wrap each piece of meat in a cotton cloth to protect it from insects, tie it with kitchen twine, and hang in an area where there is good air circulation, like a cellar with a window that can be opened, or a porch. This is best done in cooler weather, but if that is not the case, place the tenderloins in your refrigerator on a rack where the air can circulate around them.

The tenderloins will dry out in five to six weeks. I like them when they are still a little soft, not too dry. Slice them very thin, and enjoy with bread and butter and a glass of cool wine.

THE LEGACY OF NOUVELLE CUISINE

To study the cuisines of the world is to study the cultures, traditions, and habits of different civilizations. All social studies can be filtered through the study of food. It is studied by practitioners in so many different disciplines, including: the anthropologist examining ancient civilizations; the historian exploring the history of trade in the New World; the sociologist considering food in different strata of society; the politician looking into embargoes on food and import/export trade; the student of religion studying food taboos in the Bible; the philosopher looking into the applications of a specific lifestyle; and the physician comparing foods that cure and foods that kill.

I entered apprenticeship in August 1949. Food rationing and the need for special stamps or coupons to buy scarce items, like butter, sugar, bacon, or ham were realities until 1947, and in 1949 ingredients and professional know-how were still in short supply because of World War II. Lifestyles were changing rapidly in this permissive postwar period, and people were looking for excitement and new horizons. I believe that nouvelle cuisine can be traced back that far because the war changed everything, and people never went back to the lengthier menus and more complicated, heavy food of the pre-war period.

It is interesting to realize that there was a nouvelle cuisine that flourished at the end of the seventeenth and the beginning of the eighteenth centuries, with many similarities to the nouvelle cuisine that erupted onto the scene in the early 1970s: "shorter" sauces (less complicated, thinner, and a smaller amount served); the reduction of cooking times (particularly for fish and vegetables); the combining of fruit and meat; a certain preoccupation with health; and a great emphasis on novelty and creativity. Great books were written by the chefs of that time, among them Menon, who wrote *La Cuisine Nouvelle* in 1742, and Marin, author in 1739 of *The Gift of Comus*. Just as it is now in 3-star Michelin restaurants, it was practiced by professional chefs for an elitist group of patrons. It was a nouvelle cuisine in the context of a haute cuisine, with all its complicated structure and subcuisines requiring dozens of helpers and apprentices.

There has really not been a haute cuisine as it was thought to be in the eighteenth and nineteenth centuries—during the time of Carême—since the end of the Belle Epoque. Viewed in the context of the past, the cuisine practiced by the great chefs prior to 1970 was, at most, haute cuisine bourgeoise.

Even though the elements were there, one had to wait until the early 1970s for someone to coin a name and cement the components into a new creed. The intellectuals of the moment, journalists Jean Gault and Christian Millau, not only extolled this new way of cooking worldwide in numerous articles and in their restaurant guide, but they set down nouvelle cuisine's bylaws with the help of some of the great chefs of France, particularly Paul Bocuse and Michel Guérard.

Most of what was advocated under a new name was essentially a return to a way of cooking that has always been practiced by great cooks of any ethnic group. Chefs in restaurants were instructed to have the freshest possible ingredients (that is, to shop every day); to offer shorter menus for the benefit of specific dishes (this was to compensate for a lack of helpers due to the expense, and a disappearance of the sub-cooking that was too expensive and time consuming); to have shortened cooking times, especially for fish and vegetables; to avoid, whenever possible, complicated cooking procedures; to investigate regional recipes, but be open to preparing them with new techniques and new equipment, such as the blender or food processor; to make leaner sauces; to be mindful of the health of your customer; to create new dishes with new ingredients, new combinations, with an open mind toward ethnic influences; and to present the food as artistically as possible. All of these were good rules, but they were rules that would lend themselves to many misunderstandings.

Nouvelle cuisine also simplified the food, serving it by presenting it on plates instead of platters, thus enabling the chef to give the right proportion of sauce and garnishes and make sure the food would be served hot. This simplification continued the trend that had started in the eighteenth century by the chefs of the nobility, who, having nobody to patronize after the French Revolution, started opening restaurants that could not concentrate on elaborate presentations as they had before, since they were now serving larger groups. It also continued the trend of *service à la Russe,* a sequential service that replaced the French service, or *service en confusion,* in the middle of the nineteenth century. It basically did away with the dining room and the great maître d's, who were so important in restaurants until the First and Second World Wars. Escoffier had already simplified cooking at the beginning of the twentieth century, and it was a continuation of the trend. It was the beginning of the *patron* chef, the owner chef, like Bocuse.

For people like me, who started cooking before nouvelle cuisine, this "new" cooking had great assets, especially for people who had had a taste of the way kitchens were forty or fifty years ago: too structured, too confining, and too autocratic. Nouvelle cuisine allowed chefs to individualize their cooking and show off personal talents and training, all with a new respect for the ingredients.

Health as part of cooking is better understood now, and has a great deal to do with the choice of the freshest possible ingredients, preferably organic, and serving smaller portions consisting of leaner meats, more vegetables and fish, and less butter and cream. Techniques are important, too, especially in vegetable and fish cooking, where faster ways of cooking using steam, microwave, or convection ovens tend to preserve the natural attributes of the food for a better diet.

The arrival of nouvelle cuisine in the United States coincided with social changes that were taking place in the early 1970s. During the 1960s era of radicalism, people began to object to canned food and rubberized TV dinners. Organic gardens and health-food stores became fashionable, and people started reading the labels on cans. And with this new emphasis on health and "self" came a concern about what one was putting in one's own body. Women's liberation opened the door to the mostly men's world of professional cooking, but it also opened the door to the home kitchen, which prior to this time was primarily the domain of women. This crisscrossing made it acceptable for men to start cooking at home, and, conversely, for women to move into the world of professional cooking.

The job of the cook, once considered dirty, uninspired, and lowly, took on the quality or character of artistry, personal expression, individualism, creativity, and even genius. All of a sudden, cookware shops, cooking schools, and new restaurants proliferated, along with new food magazines, weekly food pages in most daily papers, and an astounding crop of new cookbooks, and this trend continues.

Yet for all of nouvelle cuisine's positive contributions, it is commonly criticized by chefs and food writers nowadays because it is badly understood. At its onset, nouvelle cuisine was overpraised by journalists and liberated young chefs, but it was also misunderstood then, as it is now. It is not the low-calorie cooking of Guérard's *cuisine minceur,* which is an offshoot of nouvelle cuisine with its own codes or rules. Guérard applied that new style of cooking but with a low-calorie angle. For many people, nouvelle cuisine ended up representing undercooked, overdecorated food served on oversized plates, looking like a well-planned French garden.

For the sake of personal expression and originality, many chefs prepared a type of cuisine that they had fought fiercely against, namely standardized food. What used to be called, ironically, *cuisine de palace* ("hotel food") years ago in France to describe the boring, repetitious food, involving thick sauces, pale and overcooked vegetables, and piped potatoes around the periphery of the plate has been replaced by a boned slice of meat or poultry surrounded by undercooked, underseasoned baby vegetables and topped with a sprinkling of berries, all over an over-reduced brown stock with little dots of a different sauce here and there. This standardization of food under the name of individualism is repeating the same mistakes that it was supposed to oppose.

It is probably constant invention and creativity, dogmas of nouvelle cuisine, that are least understood and most responsible for its exaggeration. Creativity hides the lack of technique and basic knowledge of many chefs behind strange, unusual combinations under the guise of originality. If, according to Pascal, "imagination is the mother of invention," it can only be positive when the imagination is thoroughly grounded in basic knowledge. The creation of that new dish should be a controlled creation governed by the craftsmanship of the cook, not his whims or feelings that day.

Another problem that arises with nouvelle cuisine is semantics. We used to have names on menus that clearly indicated specific dishes with specific garnishes. Now these listings are confusing. To excite the intellect of patrons, words that were once associated strictly with desserts, such as cake, custard, or parfait, are now used to define first courses or main courses, like a "cake of sweetbreads," a "custard of leeks," or a "parfait of chicken." Conversely, the names usually associated with main courses, like soup or roast, are now used for desserts: a "soup of strawberries," "roasted pears," etc. This certainly makes it more difficult for the patron to make selections from a menu, and often the choices are made based on names that titillate your intellect but don't deliver when the food arrives. Unfortunately, for many young chefs, nouvelle cuisine was a way of mixing the wildest and most esoteric ingredients to create combinations intended to shock and surprise the diner with something unusual regardless of the taste.

However, when properly understood, nouvelle cuisine has been a great asset in the world of the kitchen, and it has left its imprint upon today's cuisine, from the use of the freshest possible food to using organic ingredients, to being inventive, to seeking variety in the kitchen, and insisting on lightness in sauces. Cooks are becoming aware of what constitutes quality ingredients and are demanding them, and supermarkets are responding to the requests of an increasingly sophisticated clientele, regularly providing ingredients that were practically unknown fifteen or twenty years ago. Often a chef in a good restaurant will provide a degustation menu; instead of serving three standard dishes, eight different small dishes are served to better reveal the talent, versatility, and knowledge of the chef.

Young people, spurred on by the elevated status of chefs today, are entering the trade. Their choice of career is further motivated by the appearance of countless articles on food in daily newspapers, magazines, books, and on the Internet, where food is discussed daily on various websites and in chat rooms.

New and increasingly sophisticated equipment, like mini-chops, fast blenders, steam-injected ovens, and great knives oblige the growing demands of both amateur and professional cooks. To satisfy a more knowledgeable clientele, restaurants offer unusual ingredients in different combinations and try to produce authentic ethnic dishes and special creations.

The mini cooking revolution that we call nouvelle cuisine was inevitable. It followed social changes occurring in the 1970s, and the ethnic restructuring of America caused by the Asian and Hispanic influx. Modern chefs will be better for understanding the positive aspects of nouvelle cuisine and will move ahead with the changes while respecting their heritage and art.

Main Courses

In this chapter, I begin with pasta and continue on with recipes for fish, shellfish, and lobster. Poultry comes next, with dishes like FRIED CHICKEN SOUTHERN-STYLE, CHICKEN WITH MOREL SAUCE, and CHICKEN LIVER TIMBALE, which we always serve as a main course at my house. There are recipes for squab, duck, rabbit, and sweetbreads, as well as pork, lamb, and beef. You will find many "recipes within the recipes." For example, there are two additional tripe recipes that are made from the same preparation as used for TRIPE WITH POLENTA AND SPICY TOMATO SAUCE. Another bonus recipe is for a REUBEN SANDWICH, which can be made with leftovers from the CORNED BEEF WITH POTATOES, ONIONS, AND CABBAGE recipe. Some of the recipes in this chapter are complete meals: the STEAMED LOBSTER recipe includes LOBSTER BISQUE, CORN, AND FINGERLING POTATOES; and the ROAST CHICKEN is served with BOILED POTATOES and a BOSTON LETTUCE SALAD. Often portion size is the determining factor in whether a recipe is listed under First Courses or Main Courses, so if you love a particular main course recipe but don't want to serve it as an entrée at a dinner party, make the portions smaller and serve the dish as a first course.

Roast Rabbit with Mustard Crust, recipe on page 156

Linguine with Basil and Walnut Pesto

I rarely used basil in France. In the cooking of the 1950s, it was considered unusual and esoteric. Tarragon, chervil, parsley, and chives were the favorite herbs. I learned to appreciate basil after I came to the United States, visiting the homes of friends who were of Italian descent and used basil regularly. I started growing it and have since become addicted to basil. I plant tiny bush basil, red basil, and regular basil in my garden during the summer, and we make pesto often for dinner, usually on the spur of the moment. I keep herbs for the winter, drying some in the microwave, but basil is best frozen, providing it is blanched first, otherwise it turns an unappealing khaki color. Blanching also takes some of the bitterness out of the pesto (see sidebar).

I don't like to freeze finished pesto; the nuts, cheese, and garlic tend to get rancid in the freezer after a few weeks. The puree of fresh basil keeps beautifully green in the freezer, and I add the nuts, cheese, additional olive oil, and garlic to my basil just before using it. Sometimes I add flat-leaf parsley as well, and occasionally a few leaves of verbena, which grows next to my basil. I have experimented with all nuts, but go back to pignoli nuts mixed with walnuts or pecans. I like to use a lot of garlic, plenty of olive oil, and always include some jalapeño or serrano pepper in my pesto. Use the best possible Parmesan cheese, and make sure that your serving plates are very hot.

For a main course, use one pound of linguine for four people. You can make this dish with penne or spaghetti, but I like linguine best. At our house, pasta is usually the main course, and we follow it with a tomato or zucchini salad in summer and cheeses and fruit for dessert.

Bring 3 QUARTS OF SALTED WATER to a boil—this will be used both to blanch the basil and cook the pasta. Drop 4 CUPS OF BASIL LEAVES, lightly packed, into the boiling water. Push the basil down into the water, cook for about 20 seconds, and then lift it out with a skimmer, and rinse under cold water. Put into the bowl of a food processor. Add at least 4 CLOVES OF PEELED GARLIC, A SMALL JALAPEÑO, SEEDED, and about a ¾-CUP MIXTURE OF PIGNOLI NUTS AND WALNUTS OR PECANS. (Make sure to taste your nuts, since they can turn rancid pretty quickly.) Process on high, using a rubber spatula to push down any of the mixture that collects on the sides of the bowl. Add 3 TO 4 TABLESPOONS OF THE BEST POSSIBLE OLIVE OIL and A FEW TABLE-SPOONS OF WATER to make it combine better, and process until you have a beautiful green puree.

When ready to cook the pasta, drop 1 POUND OF LINGUINE into the boiling water, and while it is cooking, grate ABOUT 1 CUP OF PARMESAN CHEESE. When the pasta is almost cooked to your liking (I like mine firm, but not raw in the center), set a stainless-steel bowl near your pasta cooking pot, and spoon 2 TO 3 TABLESPOONS OF THE BEST POSSIBLE OLIVE OIL into the bowl. Add A GOOD DASH OF SALT AND BLACK PEPPER, and then scoop out ¾ CUP OF THE PASTA COOKING LIQUID and add it to the oil in the bowl. Drain the pasta in a colander, shaking it to remove excess water. Transfer the pasta to the bowl containing the oil and pasta cooking liquid and toss. The cooking liquid will be absorbed by the pasta. Add the pesto and a good handful of the Parmesan cheese, mix well, and taste again for seasonings. It should be well seasoned and the pasta should be quite moist. Serve immediately in hot deep plates, sprinkled with extra Parmesan cheese. Although it is an overload of carbohydrates, I like to eat bread with my pasta. Followed by a nice salad, this is one of our signature summer menus.

BLANCHING BASIL

To blanch basil for freezing, drop about 10 cups of clean basil leaves into boiling water, and push them down into the water, so they are submerged. Cook for 1 minute or so—the water may not even come back to a boil—until the basil is soft. Drain, and cool under cold water. Drain again, press lightly to remove some of the water, and then put into the bowl of a food processor with a good dash of salt and a couple of tablespoons of oil. Process, pushing the basil back into the bowl with a rubber spatula, until it is pureed. Freeze in small packages about the size of a deck of cards for use in making pesto, or in 2-tablespoon-size packages for use in soups, salads, or sauces during the winter.

Pasta with Mussels and Shrimp

YIELD: 6 SERVINGS

It is well known in our family that Gloria makes the best linguine with clam sauce, and I have published her recipe in a book and included it in a public television series that Claudine and I worked on together. When Claudine was small, she would request this dish several times during the summer, as did my brother, Roland, when he visited us in the United States. As for me, I enjoy it enormously anytime she wants to make it. Gloria and I like pasta, particularly with fresh vegetables and, sometimes, fresh fish and shellfish. I often use the large quahog clams, which I cut into pieces and cook briefly in the sauce at the last moment. The trick with clams is that to remain tender, they have to be cooked either a minimal amount of time or for a couple of hours. Cooked between these two extremes, clams tend to be rubbery, unless you are using razor clams, which usually stay tender.

One of our favorite shellfish, and also one of the least expensive, is mussels, and I use them with shrimp in this pasta recipe. I try to get mussels that are small and heavy; often the very large ones, called *bouchots,* have a tiny, shrunken mussel inside, which tends to be chewy. The small ones, especially if they are heavy, are usually full and juicy. One of the best mussels in France is shiny black with a little amber and golden color on the sides. Occasionally I see similar small mussels like that in markets here and buy them each time.

Sometimes when you cook mussels, a lot of juice will come out, and other times you have to add some water to the liquid to get the needed amount. Some mussels are briny and salted, but sometimes, depending on where they grow, they tend to need extra salt, which should be added at the end of the cooking. Most of the mussels available now are grown on wires and don't touch the bottom of the sea. Consequently, there is no problem with muddy and sandy mussels, as there used to be. Yet I still wash them carefully in cold water.

At my mother's restaurant in Lyon, she served mussels at least once a week, often with chopped onions, white wine, and butter, and at other times *poulette,* which was in a creamy white-wine sauce. Occasionally, she would combine shelled mussels with the *poulette* sauce and serve this on rice.

Generally, pasta with shellfish is not served with Parmesan cheese, but we like cheese at our house and always mix some freshly grated Parmesan into this dish just before serving and then sprinkle on additional cheese at the table.

Shrimp tails are what we usually find at the market, and uncooked fresh or frozen shrimp can be used in this recipe, although fresh is always better. If using frozen shrimp, thaw them slowly under refrigeration. I suggest medium to large shrimp here, which means they average about thirty per pound.

For six people, use 4 POUNDS OF MUSSELS. Wash the mussels by rubbing them together under cold water, and then put them in a large stainless-steel pan. Cover, and cook over high heat (no liquid is needed) for about 5 minutes, tossing them in the pan a couple of

times. Most of them should have opened at this point. Transfer the mussels to a colander set over a bowl to catch the juices. When they are cool enough to handle, remove them from the shells. You will notice that there may be a handful of mussels that have not opened or have just opened slightly. If you tried to pull them open, you would tear the meat apart, as it's not cooked enough. So put these unopened or partially opened mussels back in the saucepan, and cook them, covered, for a few additional minutes to make them open. Drain again in a colander, and allow to cool off before removing the meat from the shells. Discard any unopened mussels at this point.

When the juice settles a little, pour it gently (there is no need to strain it through paper towels) over the mussels, leaving the sediment behind. You should have about 2 cups of juice; if not, adjust with water. The recipe can be prepared earlier in the day to this point, and the mussels refrigerated.

For the sauce, pour about 1/3 CUP OF GOOD OLIVE OIL into a saucepan. Add 1 1/2 CUPS OF CHOPPED ONION, 1 TABLESPOON OF FRESH THYME LEAVES, and about 1/4 CUP OF LOOSE FRESH OREGANO LEAVES (I love to use fresh herbs, which are plentiful in my garden in summer, but if unavailable, substitute a bit of dried thyme and oregano), and 1 1/2 TABLESPOONS OF COARSELY CHOPPED GARLIC. Cook gently over medium to high heat for a couple of minutes, and then add 1/2 CUP OF DRY WHITE WINE (a fruity Pinot Grigio is great), the 2 CUPS OF MUSSEL JUICE, and a good grinding of BLACK PEPPER. Taste for salt, adding some if needed. Bring to a boil, and then reduce the heat and simmer for 3 to 4 minutes. Set aside.

Cut 1/2 POUND OF MEDIUM TO LARGE UNCOOKED SHELLED SHRIMP (about 15) in half.

To finish, cut 2 CUPS OF ARUGULA coarsely into 2-inch pieces, and set aside. Cook 1 POUND OF PASTA (like medium-size shells) in 3 1/2 QUARTS OF SALTED WATER until firm but tender, about 8 minutes.

While the pasta is cooking, bring the sauce to a boil, add the shrimp and mussels, and return the sauce just to a boil. Remove from the heat, and stir in the arugula.

When the pasta is cooked, drain in a colander, and shake it well to remove as much water as possible. Return the pasta to the pot in which it was cooked, and pour the sauce over it. Add 1/3 CUP OF GRATED PARMESAN CHEESE, mix well, and add additional salt and ground black pepper to taste. Ladle the pasta into warmed pasta plates and garnish with PARSLEY LEAVES. Add EXTRA CHEESE and RED PEPPER FLAKES—a favorite with Gloria—to the plated pasta if desired.

Small, heavy & shiny mussels are full and flavorful

FUSILLI WITH POUTARGUE

YIELD: 4 SERVINGS AS A LIGHT ENTRÉE

Poutargue or *boutarge* in French, *botargo* in Italian, and *tarama* in Greek is a pressed caviar made from the salted and dried roe of gray mullet or tuna and resembles a somewhat flattened sausage. In my opinion, the mullet roe is much better than the tuna and is the only one I use. The roe, packed in its own sac, has a concentrated taste and is fairly expensive. The last *poutargue* I bought was at the airport in Nice, and it came vacuum-packed. Some, from Yugoslavia, come packed in red wax, like cheese from Holland, and as a result it is sometimes called "red caviar." When removed from the wax shell, it is ready to use. *Poutargue* can be found in some specialty stores in the United States and through Internet sources.

I had some *poutargue* in Greece recently. Sliced very thin, like prosciutto, it formed big curls that were truly delicious served on a salad. In this recipe, I use a vegetable peeler to make shavings of *poutargue* to decorate the top of my pasta, and grate the rest of it on the big holes of a box grater to mix with the pasta. It is very important that the pasta be served as hot as possible on very hot plates.

I make a pasta sauce from anchovy fillets and a fair amount of garlic, then sprinkle fresh, coarse, roasted bread crumbs on top of the pasta at serving time for a great texture. Tiny cubes of bread are sautéed in a skillet with a dash of olive oil, salt, and pepper, until nice and crisp. This recipe is quite good when made with the anchovy sauce and bread crumbs minus the *poutargue*, if it's unavailable. Yet, it is a special treat and a great taste, if you can get it.

Bring a pot of water to a boil for cooking the pasta. Meanwhile, for the sauce, pour the OIL FROM A 2-OUNCE CAN OF ANCHOVY FILLETS into a large glass bowl. Chop the anchovies coarsely; you should have about 2 tablespoons. Add them to the oil in the bowl with an additional ¼ CUP OF OLIVE OIL, 1 TABLESPOON OF CHOPPED GARLIC, and 3 TABLESPOONS OF MINCED FRESH CHIVES.

Take 1 ROE OF POUTARGUE (you will need half a 6-ounce package, or 3 OUNCES). Using a vegetable peeler, peel off a dozen or so shavings from the roe to decorate the top of your pasta. Grate the remaining roe through the big holes of a box grater. Set this aside for mixing with the pasta.

Salt the water in the pot, drop ¾ POUND OF FUSILLI into the boiling water, mix, and cook according to the directions on the package or your own tastes. (I like mine cooked for about 10 minutes, until it is just slightly al dente.) Meanwhile, in a skillet sauté 1 CUP OF ¼-INCH BREAD PIECES in 2 TABLESPOONS OF OLIVE OIL with A DASH EACH OF SALT AND PEPPER until brown and crispy. Set aside.

When the pasta is nearly cooked, place the bowl containing the anchovies in a microwave for about 1 minute to warm it and cook the garlic a little. Reserve about ⅓ cup of the pasta water, and add it to the hot anchovy-garlic mixture. Drain the pasta well, and add it to the bowl along with some salt and pepper and the grated *poutargue*. Toss carefully, and divide among four very hot plates. Sprinkle with the shavings of *poutargue*, and serve immediately. Garnish at the table with GRATED PARMESAN OR GRUYÈRE CHEESE.

Fettuccine with Chicken Livers

Pasta is one of our favorite summer dishes. At the end of a hot day when we don't know what to cook, the garden always appeals to us, whether we make pesto, a fresh tomato sauce, or use zucchini, hot peppers, or simply herbs. What we find in our garden is, more often than not, served over pasta. It is a rich, comforting summer dish.

I love pasta with raw tomato sauce, a dish that I learned from my friend Ed Giobbi, who makes a tomato salad and tosses it with pasta. Through the years I have made all kinds of variations of this recipe, using different vegetables as well as different pastas, from bow-tie to linguine to spaghetti. Here I use fettuccine, combining it with summer tomatoes and herbs just out of the garden.

To give the recipe more depth, I add crisp bacon and chicken livers, a special favorite of ours that we often enjoy sautéed and sliced on toast with aperitifs. I like to put my raw tomato sauce in a large glass measuring cup or bowl and heat it in a microwave oven for a couple of minutes to make it tepid, so the sauce doesn't cool the warm pasta too much when it is tossed with it. Make sure that the plates for the pasta are hot.

For the sauce, peel about 2 POUNDS OF TOMATOES by dipping them in boiling water for a few seconds to loosen the peels. Set them aside for a few minutes to cool, then slide off and discard the skin. Cut the tomatoes in half, press out the seeds, and chop the flesh coarsely into ½-inch pieces. (If you prefer, don't peel or seed the tomatoes, but just coarsely chop them.) Put the tomato pieces in a glass bowl large enough for serving the pasta. Add 1½ TEASPOONS OF FINELY CHOPPED GARLIC, 1 TABLESPOON OF BUTTER, SALT AND PEPPER, and 3 TABLESPOONS OF SHREDDED BASIL. Set aside.

Bring a pot of water to a boil for cooking the pasta. For serving four people as a first course, I cook about ¾ POUND OF FETTUCCINE. Arrange 8 SLICES OF LEAN BACON on a ridged microwave tray and cover with a paper towel. Microwave until crisp, about 5 to 6 minutes, depending on the thickness of the bacon. Break into ½-inch pieces and set aside.

Add SALT to the boiling water, and cook the pasta for 12 to 15 minutes, or until it is firm but not too raw. Meanwhile, separate 6 CHICKEN LIVERS into halves, and then cut each in half again. Chop enough ONION to have ¼ CUP.

Heat 2 TABLESPOONS OF OLIVE OIL in a large nonstick skillet over high heat, and sprinkle the chicken livers with salt and pepper. When the oil is very hot, add the chicken livers to the pan. Cook for about 1 minute on one side, then turn, and sprinkle the onions around and on top of the livers in the pan. Cook for an additional minute, and set aside off the heat.

Add 3 TABLESPOONS OF OLIVE OIL to the tomato mixture in the glass bowl, and microwave the mixture for 2 to 2½ minutes to warm it. Drain the pasta carefully in a colander, and add it to the tomato sauce with about 2 TABLESPOONS OF GRATED PARMESAN CHEESE and 2 TABLESPOONS OF CHOPPED CHIVES. Toss well, and divide among four hot plates. Sprinkle with the chicken livers (including the juice) and bacon, and serve with EXTRA PARMESAN CHEESE.

CODFISH WITH BLACK BUTTER

Codfish is called *morue* in French, and what we call *bacalao* or salted codfish in the United States is *morue salée* in French. When I was a child, my mother would occasionally make salted codfish, but more often than not she served fresh cod that she dredged in flour and sautéed in butter. It is the classic fish you will find in bistros throughout France.

Cod is still one of my favorite fish. I like to use cod steaks cut from fillets from the back of the fish, which are thicker (up to 1½ inches and weighing 5 or 6 ounces) than fillets from the belly of the fish. These can be poached, braised, steamed, or baked, and always turn into a wonderfully flaky fish that stays moist even if overdone. Cod is not the type of fish that you want to serve undercooked. It should be cooked just enough so that it barely separates into flakes when served. Similar in texture to scrod and haddock, this versatile fish has larger moist flakes and is very tender.

One of my favorite ways to prepare cod, and a recipe I used to prepare at Gloria's French Café, the restaurant we operated in Madison, Connecticut, in the early 1980s, was to sauté it and serve it with *beurre noisette* (nut brown butter), or *beurre noir*, sometimes called black butter, which gives the fish a wonderful nutty taste. The recipe has capers, red wine vinegar, ground pepper, coarse salt, and a chiffonade of basil on top.

Use 1 COD STEAK PER PERSON, selecting thick steaks from the back, if possible, EACH 5 OR 6 OUNCES. For four servings, measure out 2 TABLESPOONS OF SMALL DRAINED CAPERS (the larger capers are softer and absorb too much of the vinegar in the jar). Bring a small pot of unsalted water to a boil. When it boils, drop the steaks in and let the water come back to a boil. This will take 3 or 4 minutes. When the water starts boiling, turn off the heat, and let the fish steep in the hot water for 2 to 3 minutes, until it is barely cooked, just enough so that you can see the flakes.

Meanwhile, prepare the butter. Melt about ¾ STICK (6 TABLE-SPOONS) OF UNSALTED BUTTER in a skillet, and cook until the butter foams and begins to brown. The foam will disappear, and the butter will begin to darken slightly to a darker brown. It is ready.

Drain your fish steaks on paper towels to absorb excess water, and arrange one on each of four warmed dinner plates. Sprinkle the capers on and around the fish, and pour the very hot brown butter on the fish. Pour about 1½ TABLESPOONS OF RED WINE VINEGAR into the hot skillet, and shake it around. Most of it will evaporate, but pour the remainder on the fish. Sprinkle on some FRESHLY GROUND PEPPER, a little coarse SEA SALT, and some SHREDDED BASIL, and serve right away. This favorite way of serving cod also works well with other fish, from salmon to trout.

LOBSTER SOUFFLÉ

YIELD: 6 SERVINGS

One of the old classic recipes that I still prepare once a year or so is lobster soufflé, a specialty of the Plaza Athénée in Paris. I don't prepare it exactly as we used to there because the lobster was overcooked in the original recipe, although I didn't know it at the time. It was cooked first in a stew, shells and all. Then the meat was extracted, combined with the sauce, and cooked again under the soufflé for 30 minutes or so. It was finally presented with medallions of lobster tail and truffle slices on top. It was quite good, but the lobster meat was always chewy.

There were fifty chefs in the kitchen, and the goal for each of us was to be able to make the lobster soufflé. The beauty of the system was that when the soufflé was done properly, any one of the chefs could have prepared it. It would have the same smell, the same look, and the same taste. At that time, the learning represented teamwork; it was the work of "many" instead of the expression of "one." This lobster dish is still made at the Plaza Athénée today in the same way, and it still costs diners a small—or not so small—fortune.

The original lobster soufflé was sometimes called *Armoricaine,* the old name of Brittany, and other times called *Américaine,* or in the style of America. The lobster *Américaine* was supposedly created by a French chef named Pierre Freisse, who lived in America in the nineteenth century. Back in France, he devised the lobster soufflé in remembrance of his time working as a chef in Chicago. Whatever name is given to this dish—*Américaine* or *Armoricaine*—it begins with a stew of lobster flambéed with cognac and containing white wine, tomatoes, garlic, onions, and tarragon. As a child, I remember my cousin Merret preparing a similar stew for a very special occasion using spiny lobster, *langouste,* rather than the standard lobster, which was not readily available and was even more costly than the *langouste.* Never transformed into the more elegant soufflé, her stew was served on the shell, as it is still served in bistros, where patrons eat it with their fingers and suck the sauce off the shells.

The Plaza Athénée soufflé was more elegant. Although the stew was prepared in much the same way, the meat was removed from the shells after 15 to 20 minutes of cooking, and the sauce was strained and enhanced with butter. Some of that sauce was served with bite-size pieces of lobster that were arranged in a rectangular silver gratin dish, called an *escoffier* in honor of the great nineteenth-century chef of that name. A soufflé mixture—basically, a cheese soufflé made with Gruyère or Emmenthaler—was poured directly over the warm lobster pieces and sauce. This two-layer soufflé was then baked immediately in a hot oven until puffed and brown.

When removed from the oven, the top was garnished alternately with thin medallions of lobster tail and slices of black truffle. A little additional sauce, consisting of some of the original sauce, re-strained and finished with cream and brandy, was served with the soufflé. An elaborate dish and a great creation and specialty of the Plaza Athénée, lobster soufflé was usually served as the special main course of a menu, or as a first course in smaller portions.

The specific smell of the lobster *Américaine* with its cheese soufflé topping baking in the oven will remain ingrained in my memory and always make me visualize the kitchen of the Plaza Athénée.

In my variation, I steam the lobsters very briefly in water, and then remove the barely cooked meat from the claws and tails, and set it aside. At this point, the flesh of the lobster bodies is still undercooked. I make the *Américaine* sauce with the shells and steaming water, and cook the cheese soufflé on the side by itself. At serving time, I combine the lobster meat, sauce, and soufflé in warm soup plates, and serve immediately.

This is a complex, sophisticated dish that is not prepared on the spur of the moment but for a really special occasion. It is a dish to enjoy with good friends, and to remember for a long time.

For six people, buy THREE 1½-POUND LOBSTERS. Put them in a large stainless-steel pot, and add about 4 CUPS OF WATER. Cover, and bring to a strong boil, which may take nearly 10 minutes. Reduce the heat to medium, and continue boiling gently, still covered, for about 5 minutes. Set aside, covered, for 30 to 45 minutes, until the lobsters in the pot are cool enough to handle. Retain the broth for use in the sauce. Break off the tails and claws from each of the lobsters, and crack the shells, taking care to retain any liquid released and add it to the broth. Remove all the meat, split the tail in half lengthwise, and remove and discard the intestinal tract. Cut each half tail into three or four pieces, and halve the claw meat. Arrange all the meat in a gratin dish lined with plastic wrap. Set aside. The recipe can be prepared ahead to this point and refrigerated.

For the *Américaine* sauce, heat A COUPLE OF TABLESPOONS OF OLIVE OIL in a very large saucepan. Cut the lobster bodies open, and remove and reserve any liquid tomalley or roe in a bowl. Cut each body into four or five pieces and add to the pan along with the shells from the tails and claws. Sauté over high heat for 10 to 12 minutes, until the shells begin to brown and become crusty, and most of the moisture has evaporated. There is a wonderfully rich, nutty smell that is specific to the browning of the shells, and you want to have that piquant smell to give intensity to the sauce. Add A COUPLE OF TABLESPOONS OF COGNAC, and light it to flambé the shells; the aroma will intensify. Add 1 CUP OF COARSELY CHOPPED ONION, ½ CUP OF COARSELY CHOPPED CARROT, and A CHOPPED CELERY RIB. Cook with the shells for 4 to 5 minutes, and then add 1½ CUPS OF COARSELY CHOPPED FRESH TOMATO, A BIG SPRIG EACH OF THYME AND TARRAGON, A FEW BAY LEAVES, 2 OR 3 TABLESPOONS OF TOMATO PASTE, and about 1½ CUPS OF WHITE WINE. Pour in the juice that the lobsters were steamed in, as well as all the reserved liquid that came out of the lobsters. Bring the mixture to a boil, and boil gently for 40 to 45 minutes. Add SALT AND PEPPER to taste.

Strain the mixture through a colander set over a bowl, and shake the colander to get as much juice from the solids as possible. Then, strain the juice again, this time through a very fine strainer. Pour all of that liquid into a saucepan, and reduce it to about 3 cups. (If you are miserly in the kitchen, as I am, you may want to make a stock from the leftover shells. Instead of discarding them, as is conventionally done, put them in a large stockpot with 4 quarts of water, bring to a boil, and boil gently for a good hour. Strain this second stock and freeze for use as a base for a lobster chowder, bisque, or consommé.)

Bring the 3 cups of reduced liquid to a boil, and thicken it lightly with about 1 TABLESPOON OF POTATO STARCH, ARROWROOT, OR CORNSTARCH dissolved in 3 TABLESPOONS OF WATER. This will give the sauce a viscosity slightly thicker than heavy cream. Bring to a boil, and stir in ½ CUP OF HEAVY CREAM, SALT AND PEPPER to taste, and 2 TEASPOONS OF COGNAC. The sauce is now ready. Break A FEW TABLESPOONS OF FIRM UNSALTED BUTTER into pieces and distribute them on top of the sauce. When the butter has melted, spread it lightly on the surface of the sauce with the tines of a fork. This will prevent the sauce from forming a skin or discoloring. This butter will be stirred into the sauce at serving time.

When you are ready to complete the recipe, melt HALF A STICK (4 TABLESPOONS) OF BUTTER in a skillet, and pour it gently over the reserved lobster meat (leave it in the plastic wrap, which allows you to use less butter than if using an open gratin dish). Add A DASH OF SALT and FRESHLY GROUND BLACK PEPPER, and sprinkle on about 1½ TEASPOONS OF CHOPPED FRESH TARRAGON. Bring the plastic wrap back over the lobster meat, so the meat is held tightly together and can soak in the butter.

For the soufflé, begin by making a béchamel sauce: Melt 3 TABLESPOONS OF UNSALTED BUTTER in a saucepan, and cook until light brown in color to give some intensity to the sauce. Add 4 TABLESPOONS OF ALL-PURPOSE FLOUR, mix well, and stir in 1½ TO 1¾ CUPS OF MILK and A DASH OF SALT AND FRESHLY GROUND PEPPER. Mix well with a whisk, bring to a boil, and boil for about 30 seconds. Meanwhile, separate 6 LARGE EGGS, preferably jumbo organic eggs. Add 4 of the egg yolks to the hot béchamel, and stir well to incorporate them. (Reserve the remaining 2 yolks for another recipe.) You need about 1 CUP GRATED GRUYÈRE OR EMMENTHALER CHEESE and about ¼ CUP OF GRATED PARMESAN CHEESE.

Preheat the oven to 375°F. Lightly butter a 6-or-7-cup gratin dish, and sprinkle in 2 to 3 tablespoons of the grated Parmesan cheese, tilting the dish so the cheese sticks to the butter and coats the bottom and sides. Tap out and reserve any excess cheese for use on the top of the soufflé. Beat the 6 egg whites until firm but not dry. Add about ⅓ of the whites to the béchamel, and mix with a whisk to incorporate. This will lighten the sauce and make it easier to fold in the remaining whites. Add the remaining whites and the grated Gruyère cheese, and fold in with a large rubber spatula. It's important to work quickly at this point, so the beaten egg white gets incorporated into the mixture without getting grainy. Pour into the prepared gratin dish, and sprinkle on the remaining Parmesan cheese. Place in the center of the oven, and bake for about 35 minutes, or until golden, crusty, and brown.

While the soufflé bakes, place the lobster meat in a 170°F oven for 20 to 25 minutes, or just until it is warmed through, leaving it in the plastic wrap. The lobster should be warm, but not hot. If heated too fast or at too high a temperature, it toughens. Just before serving, warm six soup plates in the oven.

Divide the lobster meat among the warmed soup plates, bring your sauce to a boil, and spoon it over the lobster meat in each plate. Spread out the meat to create a little space in the center of each plate, spoon about 1 cup of the soufflé, along with some of the crust, into the middle of the lobster on each plate. If you feel generous, garnish each serving with A SLICE OF TRUFFLE on top, and serve immediately.

This classic French dish is great with a Chardonnay that is a bit aged and "oakey." It needs it to withstand the strength and intensity of the *Américaine* sauce.

STEAMED LOBSTER WITH HERB SAUCE, LOBSTER BISQUE, CORN, AND FINGERLING POTATOES

YIELD: 6 SERVINGS

The great classic summer dish of New England, steamed lobster, is found in the best restaurants, as well as in little summer shacks near the ocean or on the Boston Post Road. It is usually served with baked potatoes and corn on the cob. We enjoy it often during the summer at restaurants and at home, and I have created an interpretation of it that is easier for guests to eat. I remove the lobster from the shell and serve it with a buttery herb sauce and those wonderful fingerling potatoes that are relatively new in the United States but that I remember well from my boyhood as *quenelles*. They are so named because they have the same shape as a Lyon specialty, pike dumplings, which are called *quenelles*. They are also called *rattes*, after the name for a mouse, with a similar shape. I grow these potatoes in my garden. They are dense and firm, and they never seem to fall apart when cooked. I serve them boiled with this dish, but they are also great sautéed in butter and oil in a skillet, as my mother used to prepare them right out of the garden, served with an escarole salad loaded with garlic and mustard.

Try to get female lobsters, as they have delicious roe and are usually more tender. Use lobsters weighing 1½ to 1¾ pounds, and serve one for two guests. To tell a male from a female lobster, turn them over. Female lobsters are slightly wider where the tail meets the body, and the last two little appendages are smaller than on the bodies of the males. A fishmonger can show you the difference. If possible, use hard-shell lobsters, which have more meat than soft-shell lobsters. I have even cooked the lobsters the night before and kept the meat tightly packed in plastic wrap. The shells are transformed into a rich bisque that also can be made the day before, except for a few last-minute additions. This is an ambitious menu but well worth the effort, especially since much of it can be prepared ahead.

STEAMED LOBSTER | For six people: Place 3 LOBSTERS, ABOUT 1½ TO 1¾ POUNDS EACH, preferably hard shell, in a nonreactive pan, like stainless steel, and add 4 CUPS OF WATER. Cover, and bring to a boil over high heat. It is important to realize that it may take a while, maybe as long as 10 to 15 minutes, for the liquid to come to a boil. If the lobsters are turning red at this point, move them around a little in the pan to get the ones on top into the hot liquid underneath. Boil gently for 1 or 2 minutes, and then remove them from the heat and let cool in the liquid, covered, for about 30 minutes, or until they are cool enough to handle. Reserve 2 cups of the cooking liquid for the herb sauce and the remaining liquid for the bisque.

To shell the lobsters, first remove the two claws and the tail from each. A great deal of liquid (about 1½ cups) will come out; reserve this for the bisque. Press on the shell of the tail to crack it, and remove the meat from the shell. The meat should be barely cooked. Split the tail in half lengthwise and remove the vein or intestinal tract.

Cover the claws with a kitchen towel, and break them with a heavy object—a can, meat pounder, or skillet. (Placing a towel on top keeps the juices from splattering all over.) When the claws are cracked, try to remove the meat in one piece. Remove and discard the piece of cartilage that is inside each claw. The knobby articulation or joint that connects the claw to the body contains the finest meat in the lobster. Crack or cut this area with scissors, and remove the meat.

In a gratin dish lined with plastic wrap, arrange the meat in per portion groupings, with half a tail, 1 claw, and some of the pieces from the articulation placed tightly together in one layer in the dish. Cover tightly with the wrap, and refrigerate, if preparing the day before.

When ready to reheat the lobster, melt 1½ STICKS OF GOOD UNSALTED BUTTER, and pour it over the lobster meat in the gratin dish. Cover again tightly with plastic wrap, so the lobster pieces are soaked in butter. Warm in a very low (150 to 160°F) oven. The lobster should reheat slowly so it can be served warm and remain very tender. If reheated in hot liquid or in too hot an oven, the meat tends to seize and toughen, so it is important to reheat it slowly and in butter, which will be used to make the herb butter sauce at serving time.

LOBSTER BISQUE | For the bisque, discard all the shells except the lobster bodies, where all the appendages are attached. Cut the bodies into four or five pieces each, and place them in one layer in a large saucepan with 1 TABLESPOON OF GOOD OLIVE OIL. Cook for 7 or 8 minutes, until the moisture has evaporated and the bodies start to brown. There will be a wonderful aroma from the browning. Cook for 12 to 15 minutes for the pieces to brown properly, and then add 1 CUP EACH OF COARSELY CHOPPED ONION, LEEK, AND CELERY, and 4 OR 5 CLOVES OF GARLIC, crushed with the skin left on. Cook for 2 to 3 minutes. To that, add ½ CUP OF WHITE WINE, 1 CUP OF TOMATO JUICE (I sometimes use Bloody Mary mix, which gives some zip to the sauce), the reserved juice (about 1½ cups) from shelling the cooked lobsters, and what is left of the cooking broth from the lobsters (beyond the 2 cups already reserved for the herb sauce). Add 1 TEA-SPOON HERBES DE PROVENCE, 1½ TEASPOONS DRIED TARRAGON (or a big sprig of fresh tarragon), and A GOOD DASH EACH OF SALT AND CAYENNE PEPPER. Bring to a boil, and cook gently, partially covered, for 30 to 40 minutes.

Strain in a colander, pressing on the solids with a spoon to extract all the liquid. Discard the lobster shells, and strain the mixture again through a double-mesh strainer, so it is very smooth. Cover and refrigerate if not serving immediately. When ready to serve, add about ½ CUP OF HEAVY CREAM and 1 TABLESPOON OF COGNAC, bring to a boil, and taste for salt and pepper.

hard-shell lobsters have more meat and more flavor

HERB SAUCE | To make the sauce, reduce the 2 CUPS OF RESERVED LOBSTER BROTH to 1 cup to intensify the taste. Thicken it with 1 TEASPOON OF POTATO STARCH dissolved in 1 TABLESPOON OF WATER. This can be done ahead. When ready to serve, add 1 TABLESPOON EACH OF CHOPPED PARSLEY, CHIVES, AND TARRAGON to the sauce. Pour the butter used for reheating the lobster into the sauce, and return the lobster to the warm oven. Bring the sauce to a boil; the butter will be emulsified into the liquid and create a smooth, creamy, and delicate sauce. Add some SALT AND FRESHLY GROUND BLACK PEPPER to taste. If available, add 1 TEASPOON OF ASIAN GARLIC-CHILI PASTE. It gives a special accent to the sauce.

FINGERLING POTATOES | Peel about 1 POUND OF FINGERLING POTATOES, and cook them in salted water for 20 to 25 minutes, depending on size. Drain at serving time, and place them back on the stove for 20 or 30 seconds, so the heat will absorb whatever moisture remains.

CORN | Use 1 EAR OF CORN PER PERSON. Cut the kernels off the cob; a good ear of corn will yield about 1 cup of kernels. Heat 1 TABLESPOON OF OLIVE OIL in a large skillet, add the corn kernels and A DASH OF SALT AND PEPPER, and cook over high heat, partially covered, for 3 to 4 minutes, until a crust begins to form in the bottom of the pan from the release of sugar from the corn mixing with the oil. This gives it a wonderful aroma and that delightful taste of roasted corn.

To serve the meal: Spoon the corn into the bottom of six hot dinner plates, place the lobster meat on top, and spoon on some of the sauce. Arrange the potatoes around the corn. Serve the bisque in small cups next to the lobster as an accompaniment.

ROAST CHICKEN WITH BOILED POTATOES AND BOSTON LETTUCE SALAD

YIELD: 4 TO 6 SERVINGS

I was born near Lyon in the town of Bourg-en-Bresse, famous for its "chickens of Bresse," which have white plumage, red combs, and blue feet, the colors of the French flag. In my apprenticeship, I can't recall any customers coming into the restaurant who didn't order chicken in one form or another. We always had roast chicken, some roasted especially to serve cold with a light aspic and a salad. Chicken with white wine cream sauce and mushrooms, chicken with tarragon, and chicken with red wine sauce were all part of the daily offerings. We didn't serve fried chicken, one of my favorites; I would learn later how to make it as part of my American experience (see pages 134–136 for a recipe).

When I go to Boston University to teach a group of culinary arts students, I often demonstrate what I call "a perfect meal," and the students are eager to duplicate it afterward. The meal is roast chicken served with a salad and boiled potato. It is straightforward, simple, and good when done properly, especially if you use an organic farm-raised chicken, or at least the best quality chicken available.

A few years ago, Jean-Claude and I raised chickens near his house in upstate New York. The smell of those chickens cooking in the oven took me back to my apprenticeship and earlier, when I was a small child and my mother or aunts roasted chicken. If organic chickens are unavailable or too pricey, most supermarkets nowadays offer—at relatively modest prices—chickens that have been raised strictly on a diet of vegetables with no hormone additives. They may not be totally organic, but they are of good quality, as are chickens from kosher butchers.

I roast chicken in a sturdy, thick skillet of cast iron, heavy aluminum, or copper lined with stainless steel. I want the juice of the chicken to come out during cooking and crystallize in the bottom of the skillet. These glazed or solidified juices are deglazed by adding liquid to them at the end of cooking time to produce a wonderful, natural juice. In restaurants, the pots and pans are used many times each day, and food does not stick to them. However, at home, where pots and pans are used only occasionally, food tends to stick. If you are concerned that the chicken may stick, start by placing a small piece of parchment paper (about the size of a dollar bill) rubbed with butter in the pan, and place your chicken on its side on it. Avoid nonstick saucepans or skillets for roasting chicken, because the solidified juices tend to stick to the chicken rather than the pan, and there is nothing left in the bottom of the pan to create a juice.

As an apprentice, I learned to recognize when a chicken was cooked just by hearing it in the oven. We would say, *"le poulet chante,"* or "the chicken is singing." At the end of cooking, any juices that have seeped out of the bird have evaporated, and what is left is the fat of the chicken, frying in the bottom of the pan and sizzling happily—the bird is cooked!

I love a Boston lettuce salad with my roasted chicken. The fresh, nutty taste of this delicate green makes it a perfect accompaniment. I also like small boiled potatoes with my chicken, and if I can't find the Red Bliss or the mini Yukon Gold varieties, I use larger Yukon Golds. Waxy and firm, they hold their shape when cooked and have a wonderfully creamy texture and buttery taste.

My "perfect meal" is a good lesson for students of cooking to understand simplicity and quality, and for home cooks to understand how appealing and delicious plain fare can be when properly prepared.

ROAST CHICKEN | Preheat a convection oven to 400°F or a regular oven to 425°F. Reserve the chicken liver, and sprinkle the CHICKEN (ABOUT 3½ POUNDS) all over with SALT and FRESHLY GROUND BLACK PEPPER, and place it on its side in the roasting pan. (I start it on its side, because the legs take the longest to cook.) Cook for 20 minutes on one side, and then turn it and cook it for 20 minutes on the other side. Finally, finish it up on its back, basting occasionally until done. It takes about 1 hour in a convection oven to produce a chicken with a beautiful, crusty, brown exterior and juicy meat.

Near the end of the cooking time, sprinkle the LIVER with A DASH OF SALT AND PEPPER, and add it to the pan next to the chicken to cook for 3 to 4 minutes. Cut it in half, place each half on a toast—half for me and half for my wife—and enjoy with a glass of wine as a special bonus for the cook.

Place the cooked chicken breast side down on a platter, so the juice goes into the breasts and keeps them moist, and then keep warm in a 170°F oven until ready to serve. Do not cover with a piece of foil, or the chicken will steam lightly and the meat will have a reheated taste. (For some reason, this doesn't happen with roasted duck, but it does with chicken, pheasant, and turkey.) Pour the pan drippings, which should be clear and transparent, into a bowl. This nutty fat is perfect for sautéing potatoes, carrots, onions, and mushrooms. It gives the vegetables a rich taste, and it can withstand the high temperatures necessary for frying potatoes.

I like to add some of that clear chicken fat as well as some of the juice in my salad. To make the natural *jus* or juice, remove most of the fat from the pan, and add A COUPLE OF TABLESPOONS OF DRY,

FRUITY WHITE WINE and about ¾ CUP OF GOOD CHICKEN STOCK to the glaze. Bring to a boil, and cook for 1 to 2 minutes to melt the solidified juices, then strain. This is the best natural juice. At the Plaza Athénée in Paris, we used to add a couple of tablespoons of freshly made brown butter to that defatted juice to add complexity and richness. With the same intention, I like to stir 1 to 2 tablespoons of the clear fat back into the juice to add some richness and satiny texture.

I sometimes cut up the chicken with shears, bones and all, for the family, but for guests I usually carve the two breasts and legs to serve at the table, reserving the carcass for me to eat the following day. This is my perfect lunch for the day after. I pick at the carcass with a paring knife and eat it with my fingers along with a salad containing a lot of garlic, olive oil, and mustard. The chicken should be at room temperature.

As a variation or for a change, I sometimes sauté some finely chopped shallots, a bit of chopped garlic, and a little chopped parsley in a couple tablespoons of chicken fat for a minute or so, and then drizzle the mixture over the chicken pieces at serving time.

BOSTON LETTUCE SALAD | Look for 1 ROUNDED AND HEAVY HEAD OF LETTUCE, preferably from your garden or a friend's garden in the summer. Clean the lettuce properly: if the rib in the outside leaves is thick and a bit fibrous, cut on either side of it and use only the tender parts of the leaves. As one gets to the second and third layers of leaves, the ribs are more tender, and the leaves can be halved only. The smaller white leaves from the center of the head are used whole.

Wash the lettuce properly: submerge it in a lot of cool water, then lift it up from the water gently, taking care not to bruise the leaves by squeezing them in your hands. Dry in a salad spinner to remove all the water, so the dressing isn't diluted by it. It is not easy to serve a perfect salad: the greens should not be bruised, the dressing should have the right proportion of vinegar to oil, the salad should be cool but not ice-cold, and it should be dressed at the last moment so it doesn't wilt. Finally, it should have just enough dressing to lightly coat the leaves but not so much that it soaks into them.

For the dressing, I use the best OLIVE OIL with, sometimes, A LITTLE PEANUT OR WALNUT OIL, and A DASH OF RED WINE VINEGAR (I make my own), using a ratio of 4 parts oil to 1 part vinegar; I like my dressing mild. Add FRESHLY GROUND PEPPER AND GOOD SALT, like kosher or fleur de sel, and mix in a large salad bowl. Then stir in 1 OR 2 TABLESPOONS OF THE CLEAR CHICKEN FAT to "marry" the chicken and the salad. Add the greens, and toss at the last moment. As soon as it is tossed, sprinkle A COUPLE OF TABLESPOONS OF THE NATURAL JUICE from the chicken on the salad. It makes a wonderful, savory liaison.

BOILED POTATOES | Use 3 TO 4 SMALL POTATOES PER PERSON or cut larger ones into equal-size pieces and round off the cut edges with a knife, so they look like small potatoes of about equal size. This is important, since they should cook in the same amount of time. Cover the potatoes with COLD WATER, add A DASH OF SALT, bring the water to a boil, and boil the potatoes gently for about 25 minutes, or until they are tender throughout but not mushy. They are best cooked as close to the moment of serving as possible. As soon as they are cooked, drain off the water by holding the potatoes back with the lid of the pan, and put the pan back over medium heat for a minute or so to draw out any additional water in the potatoes. They should be soft and creamy. Finally, add A TABLESPOON OF UNSALTED BUTTER, toss, and serve with the roast chicken, its juices, and the salad.

a picnic is the perfect way to share food and wine with friends

FRIED CHICKEN SOUTHERN-STYLE WITH CORN AND CORN BREAD STICKS

YIELD: 4 SERVINGS

As far as I can remember, in all of my experience with the chickens of Bourg-en-Bresse, in Lyon, or in Paris I never prepared deep-fried chicken in France. I had to wait until I came to the United States to taste that great American dish. I had it first at Craig Claiborne's house in East Hampton on a dreary summer Sunday afternoon. Craig, a Southern boy from Sunflower, Mississippi, was teaching me some American classics, and he prepared it according to a recipe from his mother. I immediately loved it, as well as the hush puppies he served with it.

Later on, when I worked at Howard Johnson's as director of research in the test kitchen, I would research, sample, cook, and eat many fried chickens. Some were prepared with a crust of cracker meal and evaporated milk, some with milk, eggs, flour, cornmeal, and even instant flour, like Wondra, which provides a wonderfully crunchy crust, although it tends to separate from the chicken after cooking. I remember trying a recipe in a pressure cooker with wonderful results, because the pressure cooker lent moisture, steaming the chicken and making it juicy inside while at the same time creating a crisp crust. I have always made a variation of this recipe.

Traditionally, fried chicken is prepared with a chicken cut into eight pieces. The problem is that at my house everyone likes the dark meat better than the breast meat, so I sometimes make my fried chicken with eight thighs or four whole legs that I separate between the drumstick and thigh. The standard recipe at Howard Johnson's used evaporated milk, thicker than whole milk, to which a lot of flour adhered. Better still, I use buttermilk for taste and to tenderize the chicken. I use regular all-purpose flour to which I add one teaspoon of baking powder for each cup of flour. This homemade self-rising flour gives crunchiness and lightness to the coating.

We enjoy this fried chicken most during the summer. I do the frying outside, heating the oil in a pot on a burner next to my grill to keep my wife happy (although covering the cooking vessel helps prevent splattering). I serve my fried chicken with plain, boiled corn, which I buy at a local farm market. The husks should be green and the silk a golden color; press with the nail of your thumb to see how juicy the kernels are. I like white corn and yellow corn, as well as the variegated type.

My American friends are always surprised when I tell them that I used to eat corn when I was a child. I come from the region of France known for its chickens, fed mostly on corn. As kids we would eat corn, not as good as the corn in the United States, because we did not eat it green but fully mature. We would pick it from the fields and roast it on a wood fire until it became caramelized all around. The kernels were partially burned, tough, and starchy, but we loved them.

We also ate a soup called *gaudes* that is made with roasted corn flour and is slightly beige in color (see page 46 for a recipe). It cooked for what seemed like hours, in salted water, and was served in thick, deep soup plates half an hour or so before we sat at the table, so the top formed a skin, which became cracked, like a map. Under that skin, the soup stayed boiling hot, and we ate it with the addition of spoonfuls of cold milk. This was a taste of my youth that I was anxious for my wife to sample the first time she went to France, but she thought *gaudes* was pretty disgusting. So much for childhood taste memories.

I have always loved the taste of corn and make many recipes with it: I use it in purees, as caramelized kernels in custards, as well as in a great oyster and corn chowder. One of my favorite corn recipes is corn bread sticks, which are great with fried chicken. We used to make different types of corn bread at Howard Johnson's, and I still make some that is a bit drier than the corn bread I use in stuffing. Although in the southern United States corn bread is usually made with white cornmeal, I prefer it made with yellow cornmeal. I use buttermilk as well as whole milk in my corn bread, and I separate the eggs, beating the whites before adding them to the mixture. This makes the corn bread a bit lighter and fluffier.

I like to make my corn bread sticks in a cast-iron corn bread mold that someone gave me many years ago. I have seen molds exactly like mine in many cookware shops. For some unknown reason, it contains seven corn-shaped indentations for the batter, so my recipe is designed to make a total of seven sticks, each requiring about 1/3 cup of batter. If I end up with a little extra batter, I pour it into a little mold and cook it on the side.

I love these sticks with everything, and Gloria loves them best on their own with a lavish coating of butter. Served with fried chicken and corn, this simple summer meal is the best.

———————————— ❦ ————————————

FRIED CHICKEN | Cut a CHICKEN (ABOUT 3 POUNDS) into 8 pieces, place in a plastic bag, and add 1 CUP OF BUTTERMILK, 1 TEASPOON OF SALT, and at least 1 TEASPOON OF TABASCO. Close the bag tightly, and then move the chicken around in the bag so the pieces are coated with the buttermilk. Marinate the chicken for a couple of hours refrigerated, although it can marinate overnight with

great results, too. I have a large cast-iron skillet that is 2½ to 3 inches deep, large enough to accommodate all the chicken in one tight layer. If the pieces are spread out in too large a pot, you will need twice the amount of fat for frying. If you don't have a big cast-iron skillet, use an aluminum or nonstick saucepan of about the same size.

Chicken fries best in a mixture of lard and oil. ONE POUND OF LARD and a good 2 CUPS OF PEANUT OIL is what I use. Heat the mixture to about 325°F. Remove the chicken pieces from the buttermilk mixture carefully to retain the buttermilk coating, and then dredge them in about 1 CUP OF HOMEMADE SELF-RISING FLOUR (made of 1 cup all-purpose flour and 1 teaspoon baking powder), so they are thickly covered on all sides. Place the chicken skin side down in the hot oil. The oil should be deep enough so that it comes almost to the top of the chicken pieces.

The secret of perfect deep-fried chicken is to cover the pan tightly, which duplicates to some extent my experience with the pressure cooker at Howard Johnson's. Cooked this way for 15 to 20 minutes, the chicken will be wonderfully moist, juicy, and tender in the center with a crisp exterior. Using tongs, transfer the chicken pieces to a rack set over a cookie sheet so air can circulate underneath and the bottom doesn't get soggy, as it would if placed on paper towels.

Freshly fried chicken is the best, but if you must cook it ahead, keep it in a 170°F oven for an hour or so at most.

CORN | When ready to cook the corn, bring a pot containing about 3 QUARTS OF WATER to a boil. Drop 4 TO 6 SHUCKED EARS OF CORN into the pot, cover, and keep the heat on under it for a minute or so to bring the temperature up quickly, then turn off the heat and let the corn sit in the water for 5 to 10 minutes before serving. The corn never comes to a boil and is succulent, moist, and creamy. Gloria takes A SLICE OF BAGUETTE or a piece of country bread, swathes the soft center with UNSALTED BUTTER, and uses it to rub butter all over the corn before sprinkling it with a little COARSE TABLE SALT, kosher salt, or a coarse *fleur de sel,* which gives a nice crunch as you bite into the tender kernels. Don't forget to eat the butter-soaked bread.

CORN BREAD STICKS | YIELD: 7 STICKS

Mix together 1 CUP OF YELLOW CORNMEAL, ½ CUP OF ALL-PURPOSE FLOUR, ½ TEASPOON OF BAKING POWDER (although you could use baking soda, if you prefer, because of the acidity of the buttermilk), ¾ TEASPOON OF SALT, and 2 TABLESPOONS OF SUGAR. Add 6 TABLESPOONS OF MELTED UNSALTED BUTTER, ½ CUP OF WHOLE MILK, ½ CUP OF BUTTERMILK, and 2 EGG YOLKS (save the whites), and whisk until smooth. Preheat the oven to 425°F. Using 1 TABLESPOON CORN OR PEANUT OIL, generously grease the indentations in the mold, set the mold on a cookie sheet, and place in the oven for 5 minutes to heat it.

Meanwhile, beat the 2 EGG WHITES by hand or mixer for a minute at the most, just until they are frothy but don't hold a peak. Fold into the batter, and then spoon the batter into the hot mold. Return the filled mold, still on the cookie sheet, to the oven, and bake for 20 to 22 minutes. The corn bread should be puffy and beautifully brown, with a wonderful aroma. Let the mold cool on the cookie sheet for 3 or 4 minutes before unmolding the corn bread sticks. Serve.

Chicken with Morel Sauce and Rice

YIELD: 4 SERVINGS

There are tastes and smells in our taste memory that are never really duplicated, like the taste of the *poulet aux morilles* that my Tante Hélène prepared when I was a child. I remember, as though it was yesterday, smelling this dish cooking through an open window at her restaurant in Port, near Nantua, a small town between Lyon and Geneva. Until her death several years ago, she cooked on an old coal stove, starting it with paper and wood each morning and feeding it coal the whole day. It sat in the middle of a wonderfully large and cavernous kitchen, a dreamy, comforting place for the would-be cook that I was in my early teens. Today, her two daughters run another small restaurant in Bourg-en-Bresse.

Although Aunt Hélène was famous for her chicken with morels, she never used real morels, but *Gyromitra* mushrooms, which are false morels that are sometimes called brain mushrooms. Although most mycology books advise the mushroom picker to eat these with great caution, as they could be dangerous, I have eaten them all my life—and still do—without suffering any ill effects. Their intense taste, often overpowering to a child, is of tree bark, truffles, earth, and the forest. Since it is almost impossible to find this variety today, I recommend using dried morels, particularly the imported ones from Switzerland, France, or Italy. The *Gyromitra*, which is sold dried, has a deeper, spicier, more pungent taste than the morel. Yet some people may have a reaction to them, and it is certainly better not to take any chances. In my opinion, both the morel and the *Gyromitra* are better dried, and are less expensive dry than fresh. Fresh morels or any mushroom from the *Morchella* family should never be eaten raw. Drying morels and *Gyromitra* makes them much safer to eat and more intensely flavored, and the soaking water used to reconstitute them is a bonus. They should be well cooked—at least 20 minutes. Tante Hélène always told me that she soaked her *Gyromitra* in milk, then strained the milk and used it to make her basic thickened sauce. I have tried to soak my morels in milk, but the milk curdles each time. Maybe she was just kidding me—who knows!

A couple of springs ago, I went to see my daughter, Claudine, in Portland, Oregon, with my friend, Jean-Claude, and as she knows our passion for mushrooming, she had a mycologist named Lars, a friend of her husband, Rollie, take us mushrooming. Portland is "wild mushroom heaven," and it was morel time, but we found only three morels. To our great surprise and pleasure, however, we found more than forty pounds of *Gyromitra* mushrooms. Our mycologist friend, who sold mushrooms to local restaurants, told us, "Well, you can pick them up if you want—I eat some myself—but you can't sell them. No one will buy them, and it may be against the law to sell them in America, although I sell some to Canadians."

So we happily took the booty, spread it out on Claudine's deck to begin drying during our two-day visit, and then packed the mushrooms up and took them to San Francisco. We finished drying them there in the back kitchen oven at KQED, the PBS-TV station where I was taping a series and Jean-Claude was in charge of the back kitchen. We both have been eating and enjoying these since then. This chicken dish is prepared with *Gyromitra*, although dried morels would work well, too.

My mother's most famous specialty was chicken with cream sauce, which was similar to the dish made here, minus the mushrooms. When my aunt prepared her chicken with *Gyromitra* or when my mother cooked her chicken with cream sauce, they both served rice as a side dish. Therefore, I am serving rice with my chicken. I remember my mother

Chicken with morels and cream brings back childhood memories

using the small round rice from Camargue, in the South of France. It is similar to the Italian Arborio rice used for risotto, and it cooks in about the same amount of time. My mother liked her rice cooked until it was slightly gooey and sticky, and I still like it this way with my chicken and morels. My mother called her rice *riz au gras,* rice with fat, because she always used the rendered chicken fat to sauté onions for the rice.

When cooking a regular rice pilaf like this one, the liquid is added to the rice and it is cooked covered, eliminating evaporation of the liquid. Carolina-type rice calls for using twice as much liquid as rice. Arborio-type rice cooked the conventional way doesn't absorb as much liquid, and 1½ times as much liquid as rice is usually enough. However, for this recipe I am using double the ratio of liquid to rice and using a fair amount of onion because I like my rice slightly soft and sticky, so it really absorbs the taste of the sauce. The rice is a perfect companion to the chicken; it just needs to be fluffed with a fork for serving, and is always welcome with a fish in sauce or with any type of grilled or roasted meat.

CHICKEN WITH MOREL SAUCE | Wash about 1 CUP OF DRIED MORELS carefully under cool water, because there is dirt attached to the stem or foot, and then soak them in a fair amount of cool water for 3 to 4 hours, so they get reconstituted. As they soak, try to use your thumb to get into the little holes or crannies to remove all remaining dirt. When the mushrooms are soft, split them in half, especially the large ones, and wash the insides, where some insects may have taken up residence. Lift the mushrooms from the water and set on a plate. When the water settles, pour it gently into another receptacle, taking care to leave the sediment behind and discard it. (It's not necessary to pour the liquid through a paper towel, although you can do so.) Return the mushrooms to the soaking water. They are ready to be cooked.

A chicken serves four. Cut a 4-POUND CHICKEN in half, and then cut each half into leg and breast pieces. Cut the breast joint of the

When we cooked together, Mom said she was a seamstress and I was a couturier

shoulder to remove the wings, which are made up of three pieces. Separate the wing pieces, and set aside the wing tips and the strip of carcass from the back for stock. Remove the skin from all the chicken pieces except the wings. Cut the breast, now without the shoulder and wing tips, into two pieces. Separate the drumsticks from the thighs, and cut the knob at the end of the drumsticks. The chicken is now divided into four pieces of dark meat, four pieces of white meat, and four pieces from the wings, so there will be one piece of dark, white, and wing for each guest. My Aunt Hélène never removed the skin from the chicken, but in my opinion it improves the dish; the skin gets rubbery and gooey as the chicken boils in the stock, and furthermore, it significantly increases the amount of fat in the dish. I have found that when the dish is made with the skin, guests generally leave this skin on the side of their plates.

Use a heavy saucepan to "sweat" the chicken in butter. Melt a good PAT OF SWEET BUTTER in the saucepan while you sprinkle the chicken pieces with SALT AND PEPPER. Add the pieces to the pan, and sweat them in the butter—this means that the surface of the chicken pieces should turn beige in color but no thick crust should form on the meat. Add ½ CUP OF SLICED SHALLOTS, a nice SPRIG OF THYME, A COUPLE OF BAY LEAVES, and about 1 CUP EACH OF A GOOD CHICKEN STOCK and A DRY, ACIDIC, FRUITY WHITE WINE, like a Sauvignon Blanc. The liquid should not quite cover the chicken. Bring to a boil, cover, and reduce the heat, so the chicken cooks at a very gentle boil or light simmer, just under the boil, what we call *frémissant* in French, or "shivering." After 8 to 10 minutes of cooking, remove the white meat (Aunt Hélène cooked it the entire time because she left the skin on, but it was always a bit dry), place it on a platter, and cover to keep warm. Continue to cook the wings, thighs, and drumsticks for another 15 minutes, for a total of 25 minutes for the dark meat.

Meanwhile, remove the mushrooms from the soaking water, put them in a saucepan, and, again, carefully pour the soaking water over them to leave any remaining sediment behind. You should have enough water to cover the mushrooms by an inch or two. Bring to a boil, and cook gently for 30 to 35 minutes. A great deal of the water should have evaporated. Even though the mushrooms are cooked a long time, they retain their firm, slightly chewy texture.

When the chicken dark meat is cooked, lift it from the broth, and put it on the platter with the breast pieces. Strain the broth and return it to the pan. Add the morels with whatever amount of juice remains, and cook together until the liquid is reduced to about 1½ cups at most before you thicken it. Aunt Hélène always used a *beurre manié* (kneaded butter and flour in equal proportions) to thicken the broth, but I tend to favor POTATO STARCH OR ARROWROOT. Dissolve a little of the starch in cold water, and pour this slurry into the boiling liquid while stirring constantly. It thickens on contact, so use what you feel is necessary to achieve a light, creamy texture. Add some HEAVY CREAM, ABOUT ¾ CUP, bring to a boil, and boil for a few minutes. Then add the chicken and heat through just until hot without boiling. Taste, adjust with SALT AND PEPPER if needed, and serve as soon as possible.

RICE | Heat 3 TABLESPOONS OF RENDERED CHICKEN FAT OR 1 TABLESPOON EACH OF BUTTER AND OLIVE OIL in a saucepan, and sauté about a ¼ CUP MIXTURE OF ONION AND SHALLOT gently for a minute or two, until the onion starts getting transparent and soft without taking on any color. Add 1 CUP OF RICE, and stir until it is coated all over with the butter and oil. Add 2 CUPS OF GOOD CHICKEN STOCK and A GOOD DASH OF SALT AND PEPPER. Bring this mixture to a boil, then reduce the heat, cover the pan tightly, and cook the rice over very low heat for about 20 minutes. Fluff with a fork before serving.

Chicken with Rice (Arroz con Pollo)

 YIELD: 4 SERVINGS

Chicken and rice is a seminal dish for my wife, who was raised on *arroz con pollo*. Her mother (from Puerto Rico) or her father (from Cuba) would make one variation or another of this dish, and we have prepared it many different ways, changing Grandma's recipe quite a bit. She used to boil the chicken separately and cook her rice in the stock, adding vegetables to it. Sometimes we prepare it with the addition of chorizo, sometimes without.

This is one of the recipes we like the best for this dish. Gloria thinks that the best of part of the chickens we roast at home are the wings, so since these are available on their own at the market, I do this recipe with chicken wings. I buy wings without tips and cut them in half at the joint, but you can buy whole wings, remove and reserve the tips for stock, and either divide the other two pieces at the joint or leave them whole.

Gloria likes Thai rice, a short-grain variety, which is similar to Arborio rice. It gets a little sticky as it finishes cooking, but we like it. Another great rice for this dish is the brownish red long-grain rice called Wehani. Available in health food stores and some supermarkets, it is aromatic, chewy, and nutty.

I add some eggplant to my chicken and rice, again because Gloria loves it, and put in capers and olives to give a little acidity to the dish. We flavor the dish with achiote, the seed of the annatto tree, because that is surely what Gloria's family used, although I like to add saffron or cumin, preferably saffron for my taste. Achiote, available in small seeds as well as powder, doesn't have much flavor, but it lends a wonderfully golden color to the chicken and rice.

Arroz con pollo is a whole meal, which we accompany with an escarole or romaine salad, red wine, and a piece of cheese for dessert. The best part of this dish is the leftovers, which we enjoy the day after. If there is a wing or two remaining, we pull the meat from the bones and add it to the rice with a little seasoning. We add chicken stock to transform these leftovers into a delicious soup that we serve topped with grated Swiss cheese, or we make little rice pancakes or a galette (recipe follows) with however much rice is left, topping it with fried eggs.

Heat 1 TABLESPOON OF OLIVE OIL in a very large (12-inch) nonstick skillet, and arrange A DOZEN WING PIECES, one next to the other, in the pan. Cook over medium heat for 10 to 12 minutes, flipping the wings after 4 or 5 minutes, so they brown nicely on both sides. Sprinkle 1 TEASPOON OF ANNATTO OR ACHIOTE SEED into the oil around the chicken, and cook for 1 minute. The achiote will color the oil and get soft eventually. If added to the rice later, it tends to stay hard and doesn't release its color.

When the chicken wings are brown on both sides, add 1 CUP CHOPPED ONION and ½ CUP CHOPPED SCALLION to the pan, and mix well. Stir in 1 TEASPOON OF SAFFRON OR CUMIN, 1 TEASPOON OF DRIED OREGANO (preferably from Mexico), 1½ TABLESPOONS OF CHOPPED GARLIC, and 1½ CUPS OF THAI RICE. Stir well. Add 2½ CUPS OF WATER, A GOOD DASH OF SALT, 1 CAN (14½ OUNCES) OF DICED TOMATOES, 1½ CUPS OF PEELED, DICED (½-INCH) EGGPLANT, 1 HOT JALAPEÑO OR SERRANO CHILE or A GOOD DASH OF TABASCO, 3 TABLESPOONS OF CAPERS, and ½ CUP OF MANZANILLA OLIVES (small Spanish olives stuffed with red pepper). Stir the ingredients together. Bring to a boil, reduce the heat to low, and boil gently, covered, for about 30 minutes. Let rest and settle for 10 minutes before serving. Serve on hot plates with extra Tabasco on the side, if desired.

RICE GALETTE

For the galette, heat A COUPLE TABLESPOONS OF OLIVE OIL in a nonstick pan, and add all the LEFTOVER RICE, VEGETABLES, AND CHICKEN MEAT. Press this mixture into the skillet, so it is ¾-to-1-inch thick, and cook for 7 to 10 minutes, or until it's crusty underneath.

At this point, either flip the galette over and continue cooking for another 7 minutes or so, or slide it under the broiler to brown the top. To serve, invert onto a platter, and serve, if desired, with fried eggs on top and a liberal amount of Tabasco.

CHICKEN LIVER TIMBALE WITH TOMATO-OLIVE SAUCE

YIELD: 6 SERVINGS

This is a dish specific to the Bourg-en-Bresse area, where some of the best chickens in France are raised. Chicken liver timbales are usually made with what is called *foies blonds,* or "blond livers," which are very pale in color and considered to be richer and more delicate than conventional livers.

Both my mother and aunt made this dish, but the best version of all was made by my cousin Merret. She had a bistro/bar, called Le

Petit Bar, in an area of Lyon where the nightclubs were located, and the pimps and prostitutes would mingle there with the cops and the local workers. They would all play *belotte,* a French card game, or 421, a game of dice you play on the counter for drinks. It was a friendly, warm, and happy place. Merret had great style and a deep sense of taste. She was a superlative cook, and her chicken liver timbales, which she often served with the pike quenelles of Lyon, were nothing short of extraordinary. She always served the timbales with a sauce called *financière,* although it was not really a true *financière* sauce, which should have cockscombs, chicken kidneys, sweetbreads, truffles, olives, and mushrooms. In the Lyon area, however, this rough tomato sauce, made with chunks of tomato, mushrooms, garlic, onion, and green olives, is popular and is always called *financière.* I add wild mushrooms, like chanterelles, to my version when I am lucky enough to find some in the woods.

Although the chicken liver timbale can be prepared in individual molds, I like it made in a large timbale mold and served coated with the sauce for an impressive presentation. Merret would usually serve it as a main course, starting the meal with sausage and cured ham, and would follow the timbale with salad, cheeses, and a prune tart.

Clean and remove the sinews from 3 LARGE CHICKEN LIVERS, as light in color as possible, and put them in a blender, which is better for this procedure than a food processor. Add 3 SMALL CLOVES OF

Cousin Merret and my mother sailing on the "France" to attend our wedding in 1966

PEELED GARLIC and 1 CUP OF MILK, and blend for 1 minute or so, until the mixture is well liquefied. The livers should not be visible; and the mixture should be creamy.

Preheat the oven to 375°F. Add 5 LARGE EGGS, 1 CUP OF HEAVY CREAM, A GOOD DASH OF SALT AND FRESHLY GROUND BLACK PEPPER, and blend for a few seconds to incorporate. This should yield nearly 4 cups. Stir in 2 TABLESPOONS OF FINELY CHOPPED FRESH CHIVES, and transfer to a large buttered timbale mold. Place in a roasting pan, surround with warm water that comes about halfway up the outside of the mold, and bake for 1 hour, or until it is completely set inside. Check for doneness by inserting a toothpick or the point of a knife into the center. It should come out clean. Allow the timbale to sit for 15 or 20 minutes while you make the sauce.

For the sauce, drop about 1½ POUNDS OF TOMATOES (3 or 4 large ones) into boiling water for 10 or 15 seconds, and then peel, halve, and press them to remove the seeds. Cut the tomato flesh into 1-inch pieces. You should have 2½ to 3 cups.

In a saucepan, sauté 1 CUP OF CHOPPED ONION and ½ POUND OF MUSHROOMS in 2 TABLESPOONS OF OLIVE OIL for 2 or 3 minutes. Add about 2 TEASPOONS OF CHOPPED GARLIC. Cook for 1 minute, and then add the tomatoes and ½ CUP OF TOMATO JUICE. Bring to a boil, add A GOOD DASH OF SALT AND FRESHLY GROUND PEPPER, and boil for 2 to 3 minutes. Stir in 18 PITTED GREEN OLIVES. Bring the sauce to a boil, and taste again for salt and pepper.

At serving time, run a knife all around the warm timbale (if it has cooled, place the mold in warm water, and reheat on top of the stove). Unmold the timbale, and sponge up any surrounding liquid that has come out of it. (Alternatively, spoon the timbale out of the mold and onto warm plates.) Pour the sauce on top and around it, sprinkle with some CHOPPED FRESH CHIVES, and serve immediately.

CHATEAU SIRAN

1989 1989

GRAND CRU EXCEPTIONNEL
MARGAUX

APPELLATION MARGAUX CONTRÔLÉE

SOCIÉTÉ CIVILE DU CHATEAU SIRAN
LABARDE · 33460 MARGAUX · FRANCE
Ancienne propriété des comtes de Toulouse-Lautrec
12% ALC. by vol.   L. 89 S1   75 cl
PRODUCT OF FRANCE

MI346N BOUTEILLE A JACQU
BORDEAUX WINE   NET CONTENTS 750 ml.
CONTAINS SULFITES   ALC. 12 % BY VOL.
SHIPPED BY: N. RICHARD · BORDEAUX · FRANCE

DON a Epernay
en 1743
nagne
igine Contrôlée
Perignon
1990

1990
ST. FRANCIS
ESTATE BOTTLED

SONOMA VALLEY
MERLOT

ALC. 13.5% BY VOL.

CORPORATION   CALIFORNIA SELECTION

Château d'Yquem
Lur-Saluces
· 1986 ·

SAUTERNES
APPELLATION SAUTERNES CONTRO
MIS EN BOUTEILLE AU CHAT
LUR-SALUCES · SAUTERNES · FRANCE

KOBRAND
Wines   Spirits

IMPORTED BY KOBRAND CORPORATION NEW YOR

MIS EN BOUTEILLE AU CHATEAU

GRAND VIN
DE
CHATEAU LATOUR
PREMIER GRAND CRU CLASSE
PAUILLAC
1979
75 c/
APPELLATION PAUILLAC CONTROLEE

PRODUCE OF FRANCE
NET CONTENTS 750 ml.   BORDEAUX TABLE WINE
                                    ALCOHOL 11 TO 14 % BY VOL.
IMPORTED BY: ATLANTIC WINE GROUP, BOSTON, MASS.

ON COCKTAILS AND WINE

Wine is the beverage of choice at our house. Whether it is a white wine aperitif or served with meals, it's hard for Gloria or me to conceive of a meal without wine. We do like to have an expensive bottle of wine occasionally, but on the whole we are satisfied with simple wines from the Rhône Valley, Spain, California, or Chile. I love Sauvignon Blancs from New Zealand, as well as white Alsatian Rieslings, and champagne is always welcome and special as an aperitif or with our meals. Through the years, however, I have made a few cocktails that we enjoy occasionally.

KIR ❧ On hot summer days, we enjoy a kir, a drink named after the Bishop of Dijon. It is made with crème de cassis, a black currant liqueur, not a syrup of cassis but a distillation of the fruit with about 16 percent alcohol and an intense fruit taste. The better the quality of the crème de cassis, the better the quality of the kir. I never add lemon peel or ice to this drink, as is sometimes done in restaurants. The cassis is used sparingly, a teaspoon at most for a 5-ounce glass of chilled, fruity white wine, like a Sauvignon Blanc. In the Burgundy area of France, kir is made with a wine called *aligoté*, which is a varietal that makes an ordinary and acidic wine, and the reason that Bishop Kir started adding a little crème de cassis to cut down on the wine's acidity. Now kir has become a classic aperitif.

REVERSE MANHATTAN ❧ Julia Child used to make a cocktail that she called a reverse martini by adding a little gin to a glass of red vermouth, a drink I occasionally serve at my house as well. When my friend Jean-Claude and I came to the United States, we became some-what addicted to the Manhattan cocktail—the Howard Johnson's at 42nd and Broadway was serving it in small pitchers. There was enough to fill a Manhattan glass straight up, plus enough left in the pitcher for a refill. I ultimately worked out a drink that we call a reverse Manhattan, less potent than the regular Manhattan. Put ½ cup of small ice cubes in a rocks glass, add ½ cup of sweet red vermouth, a wedge of lime, squeezing it into the drink, and 2 good tablespoons of bourbon. We still serve reverse Manhattans, but I also love bourbon on its own and enjoy it occasionally on the rocks as an aperitif.

GLORIA'S COCKTAIL ❧ Sometimes I make another drink that I call Gloria's cocktail. Gloria usually has white wine as an aperitif or Campari and soda. On occasion, however, she enjoys her special cocktail made with honey, a bit of lemon juice, Canadian or American whiskey, and ice. Stir together 1 tablespoon of lemon juice and 1 tablespoon of honey in an old-fashioned glass until the honey dissolves. Add ¼ cup of whiskey, mix well, stir in ¾ cup of small ice cubes, and add a lemon peel for garnish.

TI PUNCH ❧ In the mid-1990s, when we spent vacations in Guadeloupe and Martinique, both French Caribbean islands, a treat for us was a white rum punch that is widely served there. Known locally as ti punch, short for *petit* punch, it has become another of our favorite aperitifs when we vacation in Mexico in the winter. I sweeten our ti punch with cane syrup, known as "jarabe" and available here in some specialty stores, but sugar can be substituted. I prefer this drink served over plenty of ice, although many locals like it straight. For one drink, pour 1 tablespoon of fresh lime juice and 2 tablespoons of cane syrup or 1 tablespoon of sugar into a short (old-fashioned) glass, and add ¼ cup of white rum. Stir until the sugar is dissolved, and then add 1 small lime wedge and ¾ cup of small ice cubes. Stir and serve.

MOJITO ❧ Gloria, whose father was Cuban, always wanted to return to Cuba, where she had lived briefly in 1959. We went for a few days a couple of years ago and were introduced to the Mojito in Hemingway's bar. We enjoy it often now during our winter vacation in Mexico. When I prepare this cocktail for a lot of people, I add a bit of sugar to a whole bunch of mint leaves in a food processor to speed up the process of making this drink. Conventionally, however, we prepare one or two Mojitos at a time in old-fashioned or rocks glasses. Into each glass, put about ¼ cup of loose mint leaves, and using a pestle or wooden spoon, crush the mint with 1 tablespoon of sugar until it gets pasty. Stir in 1 tablespoon of lime juice and ¼ cup of white rum, and mix well. Add about ¾ cup of small ice cubes and, optionally, a few tablespoons of club soda, stir, decorate with a little sprig of mint, and enjoy.

MULLED WINE / HOT GROG ❧ On a cold winter day or after skiing, I like hot wine. I heat a fruity red wine to just below a boil, combine it with a little lemon juice and sugar, stir, and serve. I prefer it plain, rather than with cinnamon or nutmeg. When Gloria is under the weather and feels a cold coming on, she wants me to prepare Hot Grog just the way my father used to make it. Combine 1 tablespoon of fresh lemon juice with 2 tablespoons of sugar in a coffee mug. Add ¼ cup of cognac, and mix well to dissolve the sugar. Add 1 cup of boiling water, mix well, and serve with a wedge of lemon in the cup. Hot Grog is guaranteed to get rid of your cold!

PIG'S RINSE ❧ Another drink that was served in bistros in Lyon when I was a child was the *rince cochon*, which means a "pig's rinse." This was supposedly excellent for hangovers. In a highball glass, mix 1 tablespoon of lemon syrup (readily available in France, but if not available here, mix 1 tablespoon lemon juice with 1 tablespoon sugar to create a syrup). Add to 5 ounces of dry white wine, fill up the glass with seltzer water (about 5 ounces), some small ice cubes, and serve.

SPICY RUM PUNCH ❧ This is a punch that I have made for large gatherings on numerous occasions through the years. I made it for my own wedding reception as well as for Claudine's christening and also for her wedding. This is the welcoming punch we served to guests as they arrived at the wedding reception. Yielding 70 to 80 servings, the recipe is made with white rum. However, I have been known to also add whatever leftovers of whiskey, cognac, or Grand Marnier I had in my liquor cabinet to no ill effect. The secret to this punch is the spicy, highly seasoned syrup, which can be made a month ahead.

There is a story to this punch, which Craig Claiborne published the recipe for in *The New York Times* in the 1970s. After that syrup cooks for about 30 minutes and becomes highly concentrated, it must be strained. It is the strained syrup that is mixed with rum and orange and grapefruit juices and eventually diluted with ice. In Craig's article, there was only one small omission. It did not mention that the syrup should be strained. I can imagine the frustration of people drinking the punch and dealing with peppercorns, cloves, anise seeds, pepper flakes, coriander seeds, and bay leaves that should have been removed in the straining process. The punch must have been a real mess.

For the syrup, peel the skin from 4 oranges and 4 lemons with a vegetable peeler, and put the peelings in a large saucepan. Extract the juice from the oranges and lemons, and add it to the saucepan with 4 cups of granulated sugar, 12 cloves, 1 teaspoon of ground nutmeg, 2 teaspoons of ground cinnamon, 2 teaspoons of anise seeds, 1 teaspoon of red pepper flakes, 2 teaspoons of black peppercorns, 2 tablespoons of coriander seeds, 10 bay leaves, ½ cup of pure vanilla extract, and 2½ quarts of water. Bring to a boil, reduce the heat to low, and boil gently,

happiness is sharing a glass of wine with a friend

uncovered, for 30 minutes. Strain through a fine strainer, and cool. You should have about 2 quarts.

When ready to finish the punch, combine the syrup in a large punch bowl or stockpot with 6 quarts of white rum, two 12-ounce cans frozen orange juice concentrate, two 12-ounce cans frozen grapefruit concentrate, and 1 quart fresh grapefruit juice. Mix well, transfer to

gallon jugs, cover, and refrigerate until serving time. For each serving, fill an old-fashioned glass with ice, and pour ½ cup of punch over the ice. Combine the punch and ice at least 20 or 30 minutes before serving, so the ice can melt and dilute the very potent punch. Stir well, decorate the glass, if you like, with a peel of lime, orange, or lemon, or with a sprig of mint, and serve to the happy couple.

Roasted Squab with Pea-and-Lettuce Stew

YIELD: 4 SERVINGS

If I want to please Gloria or surprise her for her birthday or any special occasion, all I have to do is cook squab; she adores it, and so do I. Squab is a young pigeon before it flies, and it is very tender. When we had our house in New York State, we used to leave the city on Friday nights and drive along Route 17 in New Jersey to get to upstate New York. I often stopped at a little farm on Route 17 that André Soltner had told me about. They sold fresh rabbits and squabs, the beautiful white Royal King, plump and fat.

I remember driving to our weekend home with Claudine when she was five or six years old and stopping at the farm to get a couple of squab for us for the weekend. The birds were alive in a cage, and after I paid the farmer he told us to go ahead and take them, but I had to do the killing. I smothered the squabs, as I had learned to do as a teenager, by holding the bird under the wings and pressing on each side to suffocate it. I put the squabs in a bag in the trunk of the car. I never enjoy killing animals, but I learned from farmers how to do it quickly, so the animal would not suffer. This is a normal process of nature, and a chef should be familiar with it. When we arrived in Hunter, I plucked and eviscerated the birds right away.

As a child, Claudine was quite interested in the whole process. When I skinned a rabbit, or killed a chicken or a duck, I would explain it to her, telling her it was not a process to derive pleasure from, but a part of life. I would tell her how it was done properly, and she was never horrified or unhappy about the killing of a frog or the skinning of a rabbit. I believe she somehow understood that it was not a gratuitous act, but a normal process performed gently and with compassion by the chef, the farmer, or the butcher.

That said, we do love squab at our house. I have occasionally prepared them in a nouvelle cuisine way, serving the breasts rare and

Daughter Claudine often cooked with me — she "made" it, therefore loved it. The tradition continues with granddaughter Shorey

braising the legs. However, I like squab best roasted whole, medium, juicy, and tender. Squab are usually about 1 pound each, and I roast one squab for two people as part of a three- or four-course dinner. I like fresh peas and Boston lettuce cooked together as a garnish. Since the squabs are served with the bones, this is the type of meal to enjoy with close friends or on your own, using your fingers and sucking on the bones, enjoying every morsel from the carcass.

mixture, and cook for another 5 minutes or so, about 30 minutes in all. By then, a great deal of fat should have come out. Place the squabs on a platter, and keep warm in a 160° oven.

Pour the fat from the roasting pan. You will notice that the basting mixture you used will have lent a beautiful dark color to the pan juice. Add ⅓ CUP OF GOOD CHICKEN STOCK to the mixture, bring to a strong boil to mix everything together, strain, and serve as natural pan juice or gravy. Cut the squabs in half, and serve half a squab per person with the pea-and-lettuce stew.

ROASTED SQUAB | For four people you need 2 SQUABS. I use a Chinese technique when I prepare squabs: I place them in a pot, cover them with water, bring the water to a simmer, and poach the birds gently for 8 to 10 minutes. This makes the skin very taut and presses the fat between the skin and flesh, similar to the technique used for Peking duck. You can do this part a day ahead and leave the squab uncovered in your refrigerator overnight. The ventilation will tend to dry the skin and make it a bit parchmentlike, similar to Peking duck.

Preheat the oven to 400°F. Combine about 1 TABLESPOON OF DARK SOY SAUCE, 1 TEASPOON OF MAPLE SYRUP, 1 TEASPOON OF CIDER VINEGAR, and A GOOD DASH OF TABASCO SAUCE. Brush the birds with this mixture, and sprinkle them on top and inside with a little SALT. Place them in a sturdy, thick aluminum pan, and place in the oven. The juice should crystallize but not burn in the bottom of the pan. After 6 to 8 minutes, baste again with the soy sauce mixture, and cook for another 6 to 8 minutes. By then the squabs will be browning beautifully. Turn them upside down, baste again with the remaining soy

PEA-AND-LETTUCE STEW | I buy peas in late spring at a little farm along the road near my home in Connecticut. The peas are still small in the pod at this time, and they are the best. As they get older and larger, they become starchy and are not as good. Be aware that 1½ POUNDS OF FRESH PEAS will yield about ¾ pound of shelled peas at the most. ONE SMALL BOSTON LETTUCE, washed and cut into 2 to 3 inch pieces, will give you about 3 cups, and you will also need 12 TO 16 PEELED, SMALL PEARL ONIONS.

Bring the onions to a boil in a saucepan with 1 CUP OF WATER OR CHICKEN STOCK, A GOOD DASH EACH OF SUGAR, SALT, AND PEPPER, and A TABLESPOON OR SO OF GOOD OLIVE OIL. Cook until the onions start to get tender, about 4 minutes, and then add the lettuce, mix it in, and continue cooking for another couple of minutes, until the lettuce is wilted. The recipe could be prepared a little ahead to this point. At serving time, add your peas, and cook for 3 or 4 minutes. Mix in a nice PAT OF BUTTER (1 or 2 tablespoons at most), a DASH OF SALT, FRESHLY GROUND BLACK PEPPER, AND SUGAR, if needed, and serve next to the squab on hot plates.

Roasted Squab with Pea-and-Lettuce Stew

Sautéed Duck with Sweet Potatoes and Kohlrabi

YIELD: 6 SERVINGS

We cook duck many ways at our house. Plain roasted duck is still a favorite, although I occasionally cook the breast rare and then cook the legs in fat to make a *confit*. One of the easiest and tastiest duck recipes is to sauté it on top of the stove. When it is halfway cooked, I add root vegetables that I grow in my garden—from parsnips to white or yellow turnips, sweet potatoes, and kohlrabi. Cut into large pieces and braised in duck fat, kohlrabi has a wonderfully sweet taste, slightly nutty, redolent of white turnips and cabbage. We serve the duck in pieces with the bones, because we love to suck on the bones right at the table. This is a dish to have *en famille* or with close friends.

The duck liver is added to the skillet for a couple of minutes at the end of the browning period. Sliced on toast and shared with my wife, I enjoy this cook's bonus with a glass of wine or an aperitif.

Cut a 5½-POUND DUCK into pieces. First, cut it in half, then cut each half into the leg and breast portions. Separate the wings at the shoulder joints, and cut each breast and each leg in half. You will have a dozen pieces with the neck and gizzard. Set the liver aside. Sprinkle the duck pieces and gizzard generously with salt. Remove any extra skin from around the neck or lumps of fat from inside the duck, and cut it into ½-inch pieces.

Place the duck pieces skin side down in two nonstick skillets, and sprinkle the pieces of duck skin and fat around them. They should not overlap. Cook over high heat for 20 to 25 minutes, partially covered, so it doesn't splatter too much. After 5 or 6 minutes, check the pieces by lifting them with tongs to see that the skin is browning nicely.

While the duck is browning, prepare the vegetables. I like RED GARNET SWEET POTATOES, and prefer to use small, narrow ones. Peel 2 OR 3 POTATOES, and cut them into 1½-inch chunks to have 2 pieces per person. Peel about 12 PEARL ONIONS and 2 OR 3 KOHLRABIES, each about 5 or 6 ounces, and cut into 2 or 3 pieces. Separate about 12 CLOVES OF GARLIC from the heads, leaving them UNPEELED, and have a SPRIG OF ROSEMARY to add for flavor.

When the duck has browned for 20 to 25 minutes, the pieces will have shrunken considerably, the skin will be beautifully brown and crystallized, and a great deal of fat will have accumulated around them. Transfer the duck pieces, still skin side down, to a larger saucepan, so they fit in one slightly overlapping layer, add the fat and crackling from the duck, arrange the vegetables on and around the duck pieces, and top with the rosemary. Sprinkle with SALT. The vegetables should be at least partially submerged in the fat. Bring to a strong boil over high heat, and then reduce the heat to medium or low, cover tightly to create steam inside, and cook for an additional 30 minutes. By then, the duck and the vegetables should be tender to the point of a knife.

Transfer the duck and vegetables to a platter. You should have about 1½ cups of fat, which can be reserved and refrigerated or frozen for use in sautéing potatoes or adding to pâtés or soups.

There should be a nice crystallization of cooking juices in the bottom of the pan. Deglaze the pan with about ¾ CUP OF CHICKEN STOCK OR WATER. Strain this mixture, and pour over the duck for a natural gravy. Sprinkle with some CHOPPED PARSLEY, and serve this hearty country dish with an earthy red wine, like a Cahors, Madiran, or a California Syrah.

ROAST RABBIT WITH MUSTARD CRUST

YIELD: 4 SERVINGS

I have a long history with the rabbit. When I was a boy, I remember my brother and I picking clover and morning glories along the sides of country roads to feed the rabbit my aunt was raising in a cage in the back of her house. Rabbit was a favorite Sunday stew, often in white wine sauce.

When Claudine was about five years old, our friend Pierre Larré brought us a rabbit that became a pet, and we couldn't consider eating it for dinner. His name was Jeannot Lapin, and he even became friends with our rottweiler, Pastis. One day Claudine came to me and asked, "When is he going to be big enough so we can eat him?" That was the end of it. I sent the rabbit back to Pierre and decided to have a distant relationship with any rabbit I planned to eat, preferably buying it ready-to-cook at a farm or market. Although I have killed many rabbits and know how to do it well and quickly, I certainly don't enjoy it.

When I make rabbit stew, I use older, larger rabbits than I do for roasting. But Gloria's and my favorite rabbit preparation is to simply sauté a small, young rabbit, about two pounds, and finish it in the oven with a crust of mustard and bread crumbs. To properly enjoy my roast rabbit, use your fingers. The bones are left in, so it is a dish to relish with family or close friends. The mustard and bread crumbs make a flavorful crust on top. A small rabbit roasts relatively quickly and will dry out if overcooked. I add small sausage balls to my recipe and a lot of onion, and sometimes I add mushrooms or potatoes. You should experiment to give the recipe a sense of your own style.

Cut A YOUNG RABBIT, 1¾ TO 2 POUNDS, into 6 pieces: 2 back legs; the saddle in 2 pieces; and the front part, consisting of the shoulders and rib cage, cut in half. Sprinkle the pieces generously with SALT AND PEPPER, and brown in a skillet in one layer, in 1 TABLESPOON EACH OF OLIVE OIL AND BUTTER, turning occasionally, for 12 to 15 minutes. The pieces should be nicely browned on all sides.

Prepare ½ POUND OF HOT ITALIAN SAUSAGE MIX, rolling it into balls about the size of walnuts. Peel and cut 1 LARGE ONION into 1-inch pieces (about 1½ cups). Transfer the rabbit pieces to a plate, and add the sausage balls and onion to the skillet in one layer. Place the rabbit pieces back on top of the sausage and onions in one layer in the skillet.

Preheat the oven to 400°F. Process cubes of day-old baguette or rustic bread in the bowl of a food processor to make 1 CUP OF COARSE BREAD CRUMBS. Mix the crumbs with 1 TABLESPOON OF OLIVE OIL, a DASH EACH OF SALT AND BLACK PEPPER, and 1 TABLESPOON OF CHOPPED CHIVES. Generously brush the top of the rabbit pieces with HOT DIJON MUSTARD, and pat on the bread crumb mixture.

Place in the oven and roast for 20 to 25 minutes, until the rabbit pieces are crusty and beautifully browned. Baste the pieces with the drippings, and let rest for a few minutes before serving.

Use a young tender rabbit for roasting

PORK AND BEANS STEW

One of the great recipes that Gloria has dished up from out of her past and makes for me occasionally is her pork and beans, somewhat Cuban and somewhat Puerto Rican. When my late brother, Roland, came to visit from France, Gloria made his two favorite things: her pork and beans served with rice and onions, and her cheesecake.

She makes pork and beans with red beans or black beans. She sometimes uses spare ribs, but my favorite version is made with country ribs (also called shoulder chops), the part of the pork chop containing some of the shoulder blade in the center, or sometimes boneless. The stew of rice and beans is loose, with a lot of juice, which is soaked up by the rice when they are eaten together.

When we use the cilantro from our garden in this dish, Gloria removes the leaves to use as a garnish, and she uses not only the rest of the

stems, but also cooks the roots with the beans. She washes the roots first and ties them up like a bouquet garni to make them easier to remove at the end of cooking. The roots lend a wonderful earthy flavor to the beans.

It is standard practice to soak dried beans before cooking them, but I never soak my beans. I wash them, picking out and discarding any stones or debris, and then start cooking them in cold water. In fact, when beans are soaked for as long as twenty-four hours, as is common practice, a lot of bubbles come to the top, an indication that the beans are fermenting. Dried beans from the supermarket are usually from the previous year's crop and do not need presoaking or should not be soaked for more than a couple of hours before cooking.

When I prepare pork and beans, I usually cook the meat and beans together, but Gloria prefers to cook her beans separately. Occasionally, she cooks them in the conventional way, but other times she cooks them in a pressure cooker. Depending on how old the beans are, cooked conventionally they sometimes cook in 1 hour, or they can take as long as 2½ hours. Cook them until they are tender.

Pour 1 POUND OF SORTED BLACK, RED, OR WHITE BEANS into a sieve, run under cold water, and put into a stockpot with 8 CUPS OF COLD WATER. Using kitchen twine, tie up A BUNCH OF CORIANDER ROOTS AND STEMS and A FEW BAY LEAVES to create a bouquet garni, and reserve the leaves (cilantro) for later use as a garnish. Add 1 TEASPOON OF HERBES DE PROVENCE OR ITALIAN SEASONING, and

Gloria's pork and beans stew makes me sing

1 TEASPOON OF SALT, and bring to a boil. Boil gently, covered, for 1½ hours or so, checking the pot occasionally, until the beans are just barely tender. Drain in a colander.

Heat 2 TABLESPOONS OF OLIVE OIL in a large saucepan, and add about 2½ POUNDS OF COUNTRY-STYLE OR SHOULDER PORK CHOPS (6 to 8 pieces). Sauté for 3 or 4 minutes on each side, until the meat is nicely browned. Add 2 CUPS OF COARSELY CHOPPED ONION, 1½ CUPS OF COARSELY CUT SCALLIONS, and about 2 TABLESPOONS OF CRUSHED AND COARSELY CHOPPED GARLIC. Mix well, add 1 TEA-SPOON OF SALT, a 1-POUND CAN OF DICED TOMATOES IN JUICE, 2 TABLESPOONS OF TOMATO PASTE, and if you want it very hot, add A CHOPPED JALAPEÑO, SERRANO, OR HABAÑERO CHILE. Bring to a boil, cover, and let simmer gently for about 1 hour, or until the meat is tender.

Combine the beans with the meat in the larger pot, stir gently, then bring the mixture to a boil over high heat. Reduce the heat, and simmer together, covered, for another 30 minutes. Remove and discard the herb package, taste for seasonings, and add more salt, pepper, Tabasco, or jalapeño, as needed. Serve garnished with CILANTRO LEAVES and PLAIN BOILED RICE.

BEAN SOUP

Pork and beans are just as good or better reheated as they are when fresh. Sometimes we turn the leftovers into bean soup. Remove any remaining bones from the meat, and put it in a saucepan with the remaining stew and rice. Process with an immersion blender until the mixture is partially pureed but still somewhat chunky. Bring to a boil, adding more water if it is too thick. Season, and serve garnished with CHOPPED CILANTRO LEAVES, 5 OR 6 SLICES OF BANANA PER PERSON, A LITTLE CHOPPED ONION, A DRIZZLE OF OLIVE OIL, and a FEW DASHES OF TABASCO.

PORK ROAST WITH PIG'S FEET, RUTABAGA, AND CHESTNUTS

YIELD: 6 SERVINGS

To celebrate the fall season and its vegetables, my aunt used to braise rutabagas, big yellow turnips, and chestnuts around a pork roast. Following her example, I include rutabagas and chestnuts with my pork roast too, adding them to the roast during its last hour of cooking. I also add pig's feet, which lend richness and texture to the dish.

One of the best, juiciest pork roasts is from the shoulder, with the shoulder bone attached. It is sometimes called Boston butt. Although it is fattier than other cuts, a great amount of the fat is removed at the end of cooking. Another good cut, sometimes called a porterhouse roast, is from the end of the loin near the hip. It has a fillet on one side of the bone and the loin on the other. I like to give my pork roast a spicy Asian taste, so I rub it with five-spice powder before cooking. It is important to cook the roast very slowly to keep it moist and tender. Any leftovers are delicious in sandwiches the day after. Sliced and served on country bread spread with strong Dijon mustard and extra ground pepper, it makes a great lunch.

We love pig's feet at our house—my wife more than anyone else. She would gladly leave the pork roast to the guests and eat just the pig's feet, which greatly enhance the flavor of the sauce from the roast, making it silky and rich. The feet get soft when cooked and the larger bones fall out of the meat. I let the guests deal with these small bones.

Rutabaga has an assertive taste that people either like or object to strongly. If you prefer milder-tasting vegetables, substitute kohlrabi or regular white turnips. And there is nothing like the smell of roasting chestnuts. It is one of the smells I loved as a child, and it is the smell I most associate with New York City that first winter after I came to America.

I find the combination of ingredients in this hearty dish a comforting respite on a cool autumn or cold winter night.

RUTABAGA | Cut 1 OR 2 LARGE RUTABAGAS into pieces about the size of a golf ball with the skin and all. Then trim the skin off with a knife to make the pieces all about the same size. Cover with cold water in a saucepan, bring to a strong boil, boil for 1 minute, drain, and set aside.

CHESTNUTS | Buy about 1½ POUNDS of the fattest CHESTNUTS you can find, and make certain that they do not have any tiny wormholes. Three to five chestnuts per person is sufficient, and 20 large chestnuts weigh about 1 pound.

Using the point of a sharp paring knife and guiding it with your thumb, make an incision in the chestnut skin and cut all the way around the chestnut, turning the nut as you cut. When the chestnut is exposed to high heat in the oven, the skin will lift up, making it easy to remove from the flesh.

Preheat the oven to 425°F. Scatter 10 to 15 chestnuts on a cookie sheet, and roast for 12 to 15 minutes. The skin will begin lifting and separating from the flesh. Remove the chestnuts from the oven, and put in another batch to cook while you peel the first batch—burning your fingers is part of the ritual. Underneath the thick shell is a softer brown skin. Remove both skins with the help of a little knife, if needed. Some of the chestnuts stay whole and some break, but it doesn't matter, as these are served in a sauce.

Another way to loosen the shells of chestnuts is to microwave them. Cut a small slit in each chestnut, spread the chestnuts out on a microwaveable plate, and microwave them full blast for about 2½ minutes. Let cool

the smell of roasting chestnuts during my first winter in New York

for a few minutes, and then peel while still hot. Cut through the skin with a knife, and remove it and the brown skin underneath. Both skins come off quite easily, and the chestnut is moist inside.

PORK ROAST AND PIG'S FEET | Cut 2 OR 3 CLOVES OF GARLIC into two or three wedge-shaped pieces. Punch holes 1 inch deep into a 5-POUND PORK ROAST with the point of a paring knife, and insert the garlic wedges. Sprinkle the roast with SALT, and rub it with about 2 TEASPOONS OF FIVE-SPICE POWDER.

Heat 1 TABLESPOON OF OIL in a big cast-iron pot that you can bring directly to the table, and brown the roast on all sides over medium heat for a good 15 minutes. When the roast is browned, add 2 PIG'S FEET, halved (about 2 pounds) and $1\frac{1}{2}$ CUPS OF WATER. Bring to a boil, cover, reduce the heat to very low (as low as your stove goes), and cook very gently for 3 hours. At this point, the pork should be fork tender.

Transfer the roast and pig's feet to a plate, and tilting the pot a little to one side so the cooking juices collect there, scoop out and discard as much fat as you can from the surface. You will notice that most of the big bones have come out of the pig's feet. Remove these bones, cut the pig's feet into two or three pieces, and return them to the pot along with the pork roast, rutabagas, and chestnuts. Put the pot back on the stove, cover, and continue cooking slowly for 1 hour longer. Everything should be quite tender.

Bring the pot to the table, cut the roast into nice slices, and serve on hot plates with the pig's feet, rutabaga, and chestnuts. Follow with a salad, and finish the meal with fruit or a little cheese and plenty of robust red wine, like a Cahors or a Syrah.

Tripe with Polenta and Spicy Tomato Sauce

YIELD: 6 SERVINGS

Claudine loves tripe, and always has, even when she was a child. I cook it for her a couple of times every year. The honeycomb, the lining of the second stomach of a cow or steer, is the best of the different types of tripe, and is usually the only tripe available in the United States. In France there are three other types available at the market: the *panse,* or first stomach, the *feuillet,* which resembles the leaves of a book, and the *caillette,* where rennet is produced. All of these varieties are called tripe in France as well, but the Lyonnaise call it *gras-double.*

For several years, my friend Jean-Claude would raise a steer each year at his home in the Catskill Mountains, and I would join him in the fall for the slaughtering of the animal. We spent one day removing the skin, boning the steer, removing the different tripe, and cleaning them up. It was a great deal of work, but a lot of fun, too, and at that time, we had all four types of tripe at our disposal to use in our tripe dishes.

Lamb tripe and intestines, also prized in France, are not readily available in the United States. The guts from veal are used in France to make a famous sausage called *andouillette,* which Gloria loves and always eats sautéed with shallots and white wine, the conventional way that it is served in bistros around Lyon. The best-known preparation of tripe in France is *"à la mode of Caen,"* which refers to a town on the way to Normandy from Paris. For this dish, the tripe is braised slowly for a long time with pig's feet or beef feet added, along with white wine, garlic, onion, carrots, and leeks. It is finished with Calvados or applejack. While I make it this way occasionally, Gloria prefers this recipe, which is lighter, simpler, more akin to what is served in the little Lyonnaise restaurants, and more in the Italian style.

I like tripe pretty spicy, and use a little Chinese garlic-chili paste and a bit of soy, which gives a slightly deeper color to the sauce. At the last moment, I like to add black olives; they add color, a bit of crunch, and a different taste that marries well with it. I love to serve tripe on polenta.

In this recipe, I cook the honeycomb by itself in water for a long time at low temperature, so that it is tender, soft, and moist, and then I cut the honeycomb and continue on with the sauce and make the polenta just before serving. There are two other methods of cooking tripe in the Lyon area that my mother and aunt always featured in their restaurants, and which I include here. The first is *gras-double Lyonnaise.* The second method is called *tablier de sapeur,* which literally means "soldier's (or fireman's) apron." It was made famous by a great Lyonnaise cook named Léa at her restaurant, La Voute, in Lyon. I remember my mother cooking this at Sally Darr's La Tulipe restaurant in New York in the 1980s.

TRIPE WITH SPICY TOMATO SAUCE | Put 2½ POUNDS OF TRIPE in a pot of water, bring the temperature to 190 to 200°F (under a boil). Cover and place in a 225°F oven, which maintains the liquid just under the boil, and cook for about 3½ hours. This can be done a day or two ahead, and the honeycomb doesn't shrink much. In this recipe, using about 2½ pounds of honeycomb, it is about the same weight after it is cooked.

To make the sauce, put 1¼ CUPS OF OLIVE OIL OR PEANUT OIL in a saucepan with 1½ CUPS OF COARSELY CHOPPED ONION, 1 CUP OF COARSELY CHOPPED CARROT, ABOUT ¾ CUP OF COARSELY MINCED SCALLION, ¾ CUP OF COARSELY CHOPPED CELERY, 2 TABLESPOONS OF COARSELY CHOPPED GARLIC, and 1 TEASPOON HERBES DE PROVENCE. Cook slowly for about 10 minutes over medium to low heat, until the

vegetables start browning. Add ONE 28-OUNCE CAN (ABOUT 3$\frac{1}{2}$ CUPS) OF DICED TOMATOES, 1 CUP OF WHITE WINE, 2 TABLESPOONS OF GARLIC-CHILI PASTE (Chinese or Thai), 1 TABLESPOON OF TOMATO PASTE, and 2 TABLESPOONS OF DARK SOY SAUCE. Bring to a boil, boil for a couple of minutes, and then add the tripe, cut into 1$\frac{1}{2}$ to 2 inch pieces. Bring the mixture to a boil, reduce the heat, and boil gently, covered, for about 30 minutes. The recipe can be prepared ahead to this point.

Taste for seasonings; you will certainly need more salt, but probably not more pepper. Make the polenta just before serving. At the last moment, add 5 OR 6 OIL-CURED BLACK OLIVES PER PERSON, or reserve these for sprinkling on the plated dish at serving time.

To serve: Spoon the polenta into soup plates or onto large dinner plates. Make a hole in the center and spread it out to create a border of polenta. Spoon the tripe mixture into the center, sprinkle on a few oil-cured olives, if desired, and a little FRESH PARSLEY OR CHIVES, and serve. We particularly enjoy this earthy dish in the winter, and it is excellent with a light, fruity red wine of the Lyon area, usually made with Gamay grapes, like Beaujolais.

POLENTA | Bring 4 CUPS OF WATER, 2 TABLESPOONS OF OLIVE OIL, SALT, AND PEPPER to a boil in a saucepan. Gently sprinkle 1 CUP YELLOW CORNMEAL into the seasoned water, and mix it in with a whisk. Bring the mixture back to a boil and cook for 3 or 4 minutes, or until thick and creamy. Add $\frac{1}{4}$ CUP OF GRATED PARMESAN CHEESE, and mix it in. If made ahead, the polenta may thicken, so add a little water, and mix it in to bring it back to a creamy, moist consistency.

GRAS-DOUBLE LYONNAISE

After cooking the tripe in water as directed in the first recipe, drain and cut it into $\frac{1}{2}$-inch strips. For 4 cups of tripe, sauté 3 CUPS OF THINLY SLICED ONIONS in $\frac{1}{4}$ CUP OF OLIVE OIL (it is often sautéed in lard, but I prefer the oil) until they are a pale golden color. Add the tripe, and cook over high heat, until the tripe is a light gold color, and then add a good DASH OF SALT AND PEPPER and 3 TABLESPOONS OF PERSILLADE (PARSLEY AND GARLIC CHOPPED TOGETHER). Finally, add a good $\frac{1}{3}$ CUP OF WHITE WINE to deglaze at the end, OR A COUPLE TABLESPOONS OF WINE VINEGAR. Serve on very hot plates, with boiled potatoes, if you like.

TABLIER DE SAPEUR

After cooking the tripe in water as directed in the first recipe, drain and place it flat on a cookie sheet. Put another cookie sheet on top and then a weight, so that when the honeycomb is cold, it is very flat. Cut the cold tripe into rectangles about 4 inches by 8 inches, and marinate the pieces in A LITTLE WHITE WINE mixed with A LOT OF HOT MUSTARD. When ready to cook, dip the pieces in BEATEN EGGS, and then in FRESH BREAD CRUMBS. Sauté in PEANUT OIL for 4 to 5 minutes a side, until nicely browned and crisp. Serve with Tangy Herb Mayonnaise (page 194) or a cold tartar sauce and a good Beaujolais, like a Morgon.

CRISPY SWEETBREADS

Sweetbreads from veal are my favorite of the variety meats. Gloria's two favorite offal are calves' brains and pig's feet, both of which she ranks above sweetbreads. When I came to the United States many years ago, sweetbreads were extremely inexpensive because no one bought them. Unfortunately, times have changed, and sweetbreads are quite expensive now.

There are two types of sweetbreads: the long, narrow strip in the throat, which is the thymus gland, and a larger, rounder gland near the heart, which is the pancreas gland. Both are good, though I tend to prefer the larger one, which is more solid and in one piece, so it is easier to slice into it. You can have your sweetbreads in pâtés, braised slowly in the oven, or in puff pastry. In this recipe, they are sliced and sautéed. Regardless of how you plan to serve sweetbreads, they must be soaked in cold water first. I often do this overnight, but the water should be changed a few times, as it gets reddish in color. Sweetbreads should be white after soaking, which improves their taste and appearance.

In most of my cooking life, I have blanched sweetbreads and pressed them under a weight before proceeding with a recipe. All of my books reflect this. Some chefs blanch sweetbreads for a minute or so, others for 15 minutes. Blanching eliminates the sometimes offending odor of raw offal, and keeping them under a weight makes them more compact and uniform in texture.

But for this recipe, I slice raw, unblanched sweetbreads into ½-inch slices and sauté them with excellent results. You can dredge the slices in one of the following: fine, dry bread crumbs, regular flour, Wondra flour, or roasted corn flour (masa harina, see page 46). Each of these gives a slightly different coating and crispness to the sweetbreads. A favorite classic preparation is to brush the sweetbreads with melted butter before coating them with bread crumbs, so the crumbs will adhere well.

I serve sweetbreads on top of corn or other vegetables in season, and make a little dressing with fresh tomato, onion, capers, oil, and lemon juice to spoon over them. The dressing shouldn't be spooned on until the last minute, because you don't want to lose the crispness of the sliced sweetbreads. The dressing can also be served on the side.

———————————— ⚜ ————————————

Soak 1 OR 2 PIECES (ABOUT 1¼ POUNDS TOTAL) OF VEAL SWEET-BREADS overnight or for at least 6 hours, changing the water occasionally, until they are white. Remove any skin, and pull out any sinews from the outside. Cut into ½-inch slices, about 2 slices per person, and set aside.

For the corn, remove the kernels from about 5 EARS OF SWEET CORN, which should yield about 3 cups. Sauté the kernels in 3 TABLESPOONS OF BUTTER for about 2 minutes over high heat, just enough for the starch to set, making the corn very sweet. Add SALT, PEPPER, and A SPRINKLING OF MINCED CHIVES, mix, and set aside. You can always rewarm the corn in a regular oven or a microwave oven at serving time.

For the dressing, combine in a glass bowl ¾ CUP OF DICED (½-INCH) SEEDED TOMATO, 1 SCANT TEASPOON OF FINELY CHOPPED GARLIC, 2 TABLESPOONS OF FINELY CHOPPED ONION, 1 TABLE-SPOON OF DRAINED CAPERS, 2 TABLESPOONS OF GOOD OLIVE OIL, 1 TEASPOON OF LEMON JUICE, SALT, PEPPER, and 1 TABLESPOON OF CHOPPED PARSLEY. Set aside.

When ready to sauté your sweetbreads, salt and pepper the slices. Melt 2 TABLESPOONS OF BUTTER in a microwave oven, and dip the sweetbread slices into about 2 CUPS OF FINE DRIED BREAD CRUMBS, making sure that they are well coated on both sides. (I dry leftover bread, preferably from a country-style loaf or baguette, in a 180°F oven, and then process it in a food processor to a make a fine meal.)

Heat 2 TABLESPOONS OF OIL and 1 TABLESPOON OF BUTTER in a large nonstick skillet (or two smaller skillets). Add the sweetbread slices, and cook over high heat for about 4 minutes on each side, or until each side is nicely browned and crisp.

Divide the warm corn kernels among four dinner plates, and form them into "nests." Arrange 2 slices of sweetbreads in the center of the nest on each plate. Spoon the dressing around the sweetbreads or on top of them, as you prefer, and serve immediately.

POT-AU-FEU

YIELD: 6 TO 8 SERVINGS   PICTURED ON PAGE 16

Pot-au-feu, literally "pot on the fire," is certainly the classic Sunday meal for French families, especially in the colder months of the year. Everyone loves a good pot-au-feu, and it is usually a whole meal in itself, because the stock is made with beef and bones and, sometimes, veal. In the Bresse area, we also add chicken to the dish, and, sometimes, chicken gizzards, which are available at my market, as well. The potent stock, served as a soup on the side, should be defatted and eaten with toasted country bread and Gruyère cheese. Sometimes people add pasta or rice to the broth, but I like to do this the day after with the leftovers.

Use a piece of flatiron from the beef shoulder, which is very gelatinous, or short ribs. At my market, I am fortunate to find beef tail, which lends a wonderfully moist, creamy, and gelatinous taste to the pot-au-feu. The pieces of beef tail should be eaten with the fingers to be thoroughly enjoyed. The boiled beef is served on its own with an array of different vegetables cooked in the stock during the last hour of cooking. Use leeks, white turnips, carrots, celery, a parsnip, a big onion studded with cloves, and a bouquet garni for flavoring. I avoid cabbage, which tends to overpower the other flavors. The meat and vegetables are served with strong French mustard, coarse salt or *fleur de sel*, which is sprinkled on the meat as you eat it, cornichons (small, sour gherkins), and a light horseradish sauce, made with a béchamel, whipped cream, or sour cream (I use whipped cream in this recipe).

Arranged on a big platter, the pot-au-feu meat and vegetables are served at the table, and the broth is served in bowls with bread and cheese. In the country, where I came from, the farmer would do *chabrot*, which means that when diners finish their bowl of bouillon, they pour half a glass of red wine into the warm empty bowl, swirl it around, and drink the wine. My father used to mix some of the red wine directly into his bouillon. The pot-au-feu is often followed with more red wine, cheeses, and some fruit or, occasionally, a fruit tart. This is the ideal Sunday meal.

There are several sub-recipes with the pot-au-feu. The first is marrow toast, where slices of marrow are broiled on baguette toasts, and eaten hot, sprinkled with *fleur de sel* and a dash of pepper. This is one of the high points of the pot-au-feu for my wife, who loves marrow. Another dish derived from pot-au-feu is a soup I make the following day. I coarsely cut whatever vegetables are left, combine them with the remaining bouillon, bring to a boil, and add some vermicelli pasta.

Finally, you can slice whatever meat is left over, and either sauté it in a skillet with a lot of onion (in Lyon we sauté the onion in lard or peanut oil), and finish with a little sprinkling of red wine vinegar at the end, along with salt, freshly ground pepper, and chopped parsley. Alternatively, prepare a beef salad with the leftover meat, and serve it with a green salad for a great lunch.

POT-AU-FEU | Buy 5 POUNDS OF BEEF MARROW BONES, 3 POUNDS OF BEEF TAIL, 2 TO 2½ POUNDS OF FLATIRON BEEF from the shoulder blade, OR SHORT RIBS (with or without the bones), and 1 POUND OF CHICKEN GIZZARDS.

Trim off and discard as much surface fat from the meat as possible, and put the meat and gizzards in a large stockpot with about 8 QUARTS OF COLD WATER. Brink to a boil over high heat, which will take 45 minutes to 1 hour. You will see a lot of gray scum come to the surface. Using a skimmer, scoop it out along with any residual fat.

After 30 minutes of gentle boiling and skimming, add 2 TEA-SPOONS OF SALT, 1 LARGE ONION STUDDED WITH 8 TO 10 CLOVES, a bouquet garni consisting of a BUNCH OF PARSLEY STEMS, 2 OR 3 BAY LEAVES, 1 OR 2 BRANCHES OF FRESH THYME tied together, and 3 RIBS OF CELERY. Position the lid so that about two-thirds of the pan is covered and one-third is open. Covering the pot completely makes the liquid cloudy. Control your heat so that the mixture literally "shivers" on top, maintaining a very, very low boil. Cook over low heat for 2½ to 3 hours. At that point, everything should be really tender.

Remove all the solids with a skimmer, and pull the meat from the bones if using short ribs with bones. Put the meat on the side in a gratin dish, spoon a ladleful of the liquid over it, cover, and set aside for later. Remove the marrow from the bones; it should fall easily from inside the bones. Set aside to serve on toast.

Return all the bones to the stock, and cook for another hour. Strain the liquid through a fine strainer; you should have 3 to 4 quarts. Clean the pot, then return the liquid to the pot, bring to a boil, and remove as much fat as possible. No more than 45 minutes to 1 hour before serving, tie 4 LARGE LEEKS (1 TO 1½ POUNDS), cleaned and with most of the light green leaves left on, into a bunch, and add to the pot. Add 2 PEELED PARSNIPS (½ POUND), 2 MEDIUM-TO-LARGE PEELED WHITE TURNIPS, and 6 TO 8 PEELED CARROTS, and bring to a boil. Reduce the heat, and boil gently, uncovered, for 30 to 35 minutes, until everything is tender.

Arrange thin slices of the reserved marrow on baguette toasts, and place these under a hot broiler for 1 to 1½ minutes, until the marrow is bubbling and very hot. Serve right away, while very hot, with coarse salt and a little freshly ground black pepper.

To serve pot-au-feu: Spoon the bouillon into really hot bowls, and serve with baguette slices that have been toasted in a 400°F oven for about 10 minutes, until nicely browned.

While eating the soup, reheat the beef with a little of the liquid in a microwave oven until piping hot. Arrange the hot vegetables around the meat, and serve on very hot soup plates. Add a couple of tail bones to each plate with a little additional meat and some vegetables. Enjoy with CORNICHONS, MUSTARD, COARSE SALT, and the HORSE-RADISH SAUCE.

HORSERADISH SAUCE | Whip 1 CUP OF HEAVY CREAM for 1 minute or so, until it is creamy, thick, and just barely holding a peak. Add 4 OR 5 TABLESPOONS OF GRATED HORSERADISH, SALT, BLACK PEPPER, and 1 TEASPOON RED WINE VINEGAR. Stir; it will thicken.

BEEF SOUP

The following day, if there is any fat on the STOCK, remove and discard it. To the stock, add whatever VEGETABLES are left, very coarsely chopped, bring to a boil, add a little VERMICELLI, or another very thin pasta. When the pasta is tender, serve the soup with GRATED SWISS OR PARMESAN CHEESE.

BEEF SALAD

Slice whatever BEEF is left, reheat with A FEW SPOONFULS OF BOUIL-LON in a microwave oven for a minute or so, until lukewarm, and add SOME DICED RIB CELERY, CHOPPED MILD ONION, CHOPPED GAR-LIC, SALT, PEPPER, and PARSLEY. Combine with a lot of HOT FRENCH MUSTARD, OLIVE OIL, and A LITTLE DASH OF RED WINE VINEGAR. Mix and serve over SLICED TOMATOES or SALAD GREENS.

GRILLED SPICY LEG OF LAMB

A leg of lamb is always impressive for serving whole on a buffet or at the table. Often I bone a leg of lamb, butterfly it, season it with herbes de Provence, salt, and pepper, and grill it flat for a few minutes before finishing it in the oven. When I cooked leg of lamb in restaurants, I would separate all the muscles of the leg, using the bottom round and shank, which are a bit tougher, for a stew, curry, or brochette, and grill the other larger muscles, like the top round, top knuckle, and sirloin. This technique made it easier to serve individual patrons throughout the evening in a restaurant situation. At home, I still like to cook a whole leg of lamb as a showpiece and carve it at the table.

Domestic lamb is the best, but often supermarkets offer only Australian or New Zealand lamb. These are good, especially if you remove the top fat. They are young lambs, which because of climatic conditions have a more assertive taste than domestic lamb. However, the strong taste is always in the fat, and for the leg of lamb I am preparing here, I remove essentially all the surface fat. There should be very little fat remaining on the top, short of the skin on the shank area, where there is basically no fat, only skin. Sometimes leg of lamb comes with the pelvis bone still attached, while sometimes it comes without the pelvis bone, which is the way I prefer it. Remove it, or have it removed if your leg of lamb comes with it to make carving easier.

I marinate the lamb for a long time, at least overnight, in a spicy and assertive mixture and sear it on the grill to get that grilled, smoky taste. To finish the lamb, I place it in a low oven, about 275°F, to finish cooking. During that slow cooking, the meat has a chance to rest, becoming pink from beginning to end and releasing some of its juice, which can be served with it.

For my marinade, I use hoisin sauce (a sweet Chinese bean sauce classically served with Peking duck), balsamic vinegar, lots of chopped garlic, soy sauce, and Tabasco sauce to make a very spicy coating that can also be used on ribs or pork tenderloin in the same manner.

For a small whole LEG OF LAMB weighing ABOUT 4½ POUNDS with hip pelvis bone removed, trim most of the fat from the top, especially from the hip area, where there is a thicker layer. There should be about 12 ounces of fat on a leg this size, although there may be more on domestic lamb. Leave the skin intact on the lower part of the leg and shank area.

In a bowl, mix together ⅓ CUP OF HOISIN SAUCE, 2 TABLESPOONS OF BALSAMIC VINEGAR, 2 TABLESPOONS OF CHOPPED GARLIC, 2 TABLESPOONS OF SOY SAUCE, and 1 TABLESPOON OF TABASCO SAUCE. Place the trimmed leg of lamb in a large plastic bag, pour the marinade over it on all sides, and tie the bag tightly. Refrigerate the lamb and let it marinate overnight.

A few minutes before you want to cook the lamb leg, heat a gas or wood charcoal grill, and preheat your oven to about 275°F. If using a charcoal grill, make sure you use wood briquettes, not charcoal briquettes, which are made from a petroleum derivative. Also, make certain that the grill is cleaned thoroughly and the wood briquettes are white hot before you put the leg of lamb on the grill. Clean off most of the marinade from the leg, and set it aside in a roasting pan for later use. Grill the lamb for about 10 minutes, turning it so it is nicely browned all over, and then put it on top of the marinade in the roasting pan with ¾ CUP OF WATER.

Place the lamb in the oven, and cook for about 1 hour. Turn the oven off, and let the lamb rest there until serving time. Adjust the time if the leg is bigger or if you like lamb medium rather than rare.

Veal Roast with Shiitakes in Tarragon Cream Sauce

YIELD: 6 SERVINGS

I love veal and prepare it occasionally at home—although not as often as I used to, because it is not as available as it used to be at the market. A moist veal roast is the perfect Sunday meal and reminds me of the family cooking I enjoyed when I was small.

There are so many ways to cook veal. Part of the back leg, top round, and bottom round are particularly good for scaloppine. Because these cuts are very lean and a bit drier, they should be cooked quickly. For me, veal chops are the best part of the animal. They are quite expensive, unfortunately, so I only enjoy them grilled for special occasions. Fillet of veal is great sautéed, but when I make a roast or a stew, I use the shoulder. The top blade or flatiron in the shoulder is a good cut, as is the chuck, which is a continuation of the rack toward the neck. I also love osso buco, from the veal shank. The meat is gelatinous, moist, and not stringy at all, and when cooked for a long time the gelatin melts in it and the texture becomes creamy and unctuous. Conventionally, osso buco is a slice of the shank with the bone in the center and the meat around it.

For my roast, I like the shank left whole, boned, tied, and braised slowly. It makes a very tender, moist roast, which I cook with shiitake mushrooms. Dried shiitakes have more taste than fresh ones, particularly winter shiitakes, which take longer to grow and are meatier and more full-flavored than regular shiitakes. The cap is thicker, whitish, with brown or black lines across it. A bit more expensive but much better than regular dried shiitakes, it tastes almost like meat at the end of the long cooking time.

Cook the roast gently for a long time in the oven, and finish it with some cream and tarragon for a special dinner, although it can be enjoyed with the natural juices as well.

Put 10 TO 12 DRIED WINTER SHIITAKES, depending on size, in A QUART OF WATER with a weight on top to keep them under water, and rehydrate them for about an hour. Drain, remove the stems, and reserve them for stock; they are too tough to be used in the roast.

Preheat the oven to 275°F. If the shank came with the bone, bone it out and tie it together. The oven-ready VEAL SHANK ROAST should weigh about 3 POUNDS. Melt 2 TABLESPOONS OF BUTTER in a large, sturdy saucepan with a cover. SALT AND PEPPER the roast generously, and place it the hot butter. Brown the meat over medium to high heat for about 12 minutes, turning it occasionally, until it is browned on all sides

Add 1 CUP OF COARSELY CHOPPED ONION and 1 TABLESPOON OF COARSELY CHOPPED GARLIC, and mix well. Add a bouquet garni (2 BAY LEAVES, 1 LARGE SPRIG OF THYME, and A LITTLE BUNCH OF PARSLEY STEMS, all tied together with a string) along with the shiitakes, 1 CUP OF WHITE VERMOUTH, and another DASH OF SALT AND PEPPER. Bring to a boil, cover, and roast in the oven for 3 hours, or until the meat is fork tender.

At serving time, remove the string from around the roast, and place it on a warm serving platter. Reduce the juice in the pan to about 1/2 cup or so, add 3/4 CUP OF HEAVY CREAM, bring the mixture back to a boil, and cook over medium to high heat for 2 to 3 minutes to reduce it until it just coats a spoon. Add 1 TABLESPOON OF FRESH TARRAGON, taste for salt and pepper, and add A SQUEEZE OF LEMON JUICE. Cut the roast, and serve with the sauce and shiitakes.

CORNED BEEF WITH POTATOES, ONIONS, AND CABBAGE

YIELD: 4 SERVINGS

I have always loved corned beef, even the canned version I tasted in France at the end of the Second World War, when we occasionally got American canned foods. Needless to say, it was far from the real corned beef that I came to love in New York.

The first time that my brother Roland came to New York I took him to the Stage Delicatessen to try their famous corned beef sandwich, made with fatty corned beef. He couldn't believe how large and how good it was, and he simply adored it. I took him another day for a lunch of corned beef hash with a fried egg on top, and he loved that as well. I always think of him when I cook corned beef.

I am also very fond of the Reuben sandwich that we made at Howard Johnson's, and it's a favorite with Gloria and Norma Galehouse, my assistant, for lunch at the house. I mound pastrami or corned beef on pumpernickel or rye bread, and add slices of a good imported Gruyère or Emmenthaler cheese, and sauerkraut. I like a lot of corned beef, not too lean and thinly sliced. I make Russian dressing, using a mixture of mayonnaise, a bit of ketchup, a little horseradish, Worcestershire sauce, and Tabasco. With the dressing, Swiss cheese, and sauerkraut all surrounding the corned beef in the middle, this great sandwich is sautéed in a nonstick skillet in a little oil and butter for four to five minutes a side, partially covered, until the whole center gets hot and the cheese melts. Cut in half and served with a beer, it is one of my best lunches.

At least once during the winter, often around St. Patrick's Day, we cook corned beef in the classic way, with onions, potatoes, and cabbage. I add these vegetables to the corned beef at the end of the cooking time, so they retain their vibrant color and they don't overcook. I always try to buy the point cut of corned beef. This is the side of the brisket that is thicker and has more fat than the cut called the flat end, which is thin, narrow, and too lean for my taste. These come vacuum-packed with curing liquid inside the package.

After the corned beef dinner comes the corned beef hash, which I enjoy for breakfast, lunch, or dinner. I like to make my hash with Red Bliss, Yukon Gold, or Yellow Finn potatoes, boiling them in the skins until tender and then peeling the skins off. We served this dish at Howard Johnson's, and in the spirit of how we used to prepare it there, I still chop my potatoes for the hash with the sharp-edged end of an empty can opened at both ends.

Put the unopened vacuum-packed point cut piece of CORNED BEEF (ABOUT 3 POUNDS) into a pot with water to cover that has been heated to about 180°F. Keeping the water temperature at about the same level, cook the beef for 3 hours. (Sometimes the bag cracks in the water and some of the juice comes out, but it doesn't really matter.)

After 3 hours of cooking, remove the corned beef from the bag and put it back in the pot with 4 PEELED POTATOES, 4 MEDIUM PEELED ONIONS, A SMALL LEEK, and A CABBAGE (ABOUT 2½ POUNDS) cut into six wedges. (When preparing just the corned beef, cook it in the bag the entire time.) Continue to cook for an additional 45 minutes to an hour. At that point, the corned beef will have an internal temperature of 170 to 180°. Cut the corned beef against the grain into thin slices, and serve on warm plates with the vegetables and a little of the cooking liquid.

CORNED BEEF HASH WITH EGGS

For about ¾ POUND (2½ TO 3 CUPS) OF COARSELY CHOPPED LEFT-
OVER CORNED BEEF, you will need ABOUT 1 POUND, OR 3 CUPS OF
COARSELY CHOPPED COOKED POTATOES. If you have leftover potatoes
from the corned beef dinner, use them, or boil unpeeled whole potatoes
in water to cover for about 30 minutes, drain, and when cool enough to
handle, peel and cut very coarsely. Mix with the chopped corned beef.

Put 1 CUP OF CHOPPED ONION in a skillet with 2 TABLESPOONS
OF PEANUT OIL and about ¼ CUP OF WATER, and sauté the onion
until soft but not brown. (Onions tend to brown quickly in hot oil.
Adding a little water to the skillet at the beginning helps prevent this.
After 4 or 5 minutes, the water will have evaporated and you will hear
the onions sizzling in the oil.)

Add these onions to the mixture of corned beef and potatoes
along with 2 TEASPOONS OF CHOPPED GARLIC, 3 TABLESPOONS OF
CHIVES, a fair amount of FRESHLY GROUND BLACK PEPPER, and A
LITTLE SALT, the amount depending on the saltiness of the corned
beef. This mixture can be formed into four patties, or you can put the
whole mixture into a nonstick skillet and sauté it for a total of about
15 minutes, browning it on one side and then flipping it over and
browning it on the other side. At Howard Johnson's we used to form the
hash in the pan so it would take on the elongated shape of an omelet. It
was a nice way of doing it, and we served it with a fried egg on top.

To cook individual hash patties, heat 1½ TABLESPOONS OF OIL
in a nonstick skillet, and place four patties side by side in the skillet.
Cook them over medium heat for 5 or 6 minutes until nicely browned on

one side, pressing with a spatula to flatten the patties in the pan. Then
turn over gently and press down again, so the surface of the underside
crusts, and when they have browned a few minutes, make an indentation
in the center of each patty, and break an EGG into it. Add A DASH OF
SALT AND FRESHLY GROUND PEPPER on top. Cover, and cook for
about 1½ minutes, so the eggs get beautifully cooked on top from the
steam, but the yolk is still quite soft in the center.

Lift the patties out with a spatula, slide onto plates, and serve.
I like my corned beef hash with a little Tabasco on top and a salad
accompaniment.

Grilled Rib-Eye Steak with Tarragon Butter and Haricots Verts with Shallots

YIELD: 4 SERVINGS

Carème, the greatest chef of the nineteenth century, said that beef was the soul of cooking, and I am always ready for a good steak. Years ago, I sautéed my steaks, but now I like grilled steaks better, and there is no beef that compares with the beef we have in America. I come from a part of France near the Charolais, where the beef is considered exceptional, but it doesn't compare to American beef in quality, tenderness, and juiciness.

My mother adores steak and could eat one every day, and when I visit her in France, I often take a strip loin that I cut into steaks and freeze for her. She likes her steak *bleu*, or very rare. She sautés her steak in a skillet for about 45 seconds on each side, and it is still totally cold and raw in the center. I couldn't eat it this way, but this is how she loves it, and that is how I make steak for her.

When I want to cook a steak large enough to serve about four people, I choose the rib eye. It has a little more fat than the loin, and the flavor is better. A large one-rib steak will weigh 2 to 2¼ pounds and be two inches thick, which is plenty to serve four. I make a tarragon butter to serve with this rather than a béarnaise made with an emulsion of egg yolks, melted butter, shallots, vinegar, and tarragon. The simple tarragon butter is just as good. One of the secrets of the tarragon butter is to blanch the tarragon in boiling water for a few seconds, drain it, and cool it before blending it with the soft butter. If it is not blanched, the tarragon tends to change color, becoming more brownish than green and tasting slightly bitter.

It is important to allow beef to rest before carving. When beef starts cooking, the meat contracts, and its juices are pushed toward the center. A roast beef carved right out of the oven will have a center that is flabby, barely lukewarm, and practically raw, while one or two inches of the outside edge is gray and looks overcooked. While resting, the meat relaxes and the liquid from the center flows through the meat and starts accumulating in the outer inch and in the pan. After resting, the meat will be pink throughout. Even a grilled steak should rest for a couple of minutes before serving.

A good garnish is haricots verts, tiny string beans that are common in France and are available here in specialty markets. Happily for me, Bishop's farm market in nearby Guilford has haricots verts that they grow themselves. Sautéed with butter and sliced shallots, these beans are the perfect garnish for my steak.

TARRAGON BUTTER | Use about ⅓ CUP OF FRESH TARRAGON LEAVES, lightly packed. Drop the leaves into boiling water for about 15 seconds, then lift from the water with a slotted spoon, cool under cold water, and pat dry with paper towels. Put into the bowl of a blender or food processor and puree with ½ STICK (4 TABLESPOONS) OF SOFT UNSALTED BUTTER, 2 TABLESPOONS OF OLIVE OIL, and a good DASH OF SALT AND FRESHLY GROUND BLACK PEPPER. Set aside.

STEAK | Salt and pepper a 2 TO 2¼ POUND BONELESS RIB-EYE STEAK just before grilling (if salted too far ahead, the juices will start running out). Rub it on both sides with a DASH OF PEANUT OR OLIVE OIL. Place on a very hot, clean grill, and cook for about 2 minutes, then turn the steak over to mark it on the other side, and cook for 2 to 3 minutes. You will notice it is marked on both sides now. Turn again, and

pivot the steak 90 degrees on the grill so that the new marking lines go the opposite direction from the original lines, creating a grid pattern on the surface of the meat. Cook for 2 or 3 minutes more, then turn again, and position it on the grill so the second side is similarly marked like a grid. Do not cook the steak too long on one side. It is better to turn it three times altogether—from the first side to the second side, back to the first side, and then back to the second side to finish cooking, so both sides are equally marked and crusty. The rare part is exactly in the center. If the steak is big enough, you might also like to stand it on edge on the grill to brown the side. A 2-pound steak should cook in 10 to 12 minutes for rare to medium rare. Transfer the steak to a warm oven (150-160°F) and let rest for 15 minutes before slicing. While the steak is resting, prepare the beans.

To serve, cut the steak on the bias into thin slices, and arrange several slices on each of four warm dinner plates. Top each serving with a dollop of soft tarragon butter, so the butter melts over the meat. (Extra tarragon butter can be rolled up in plastic wrap or pressed into a ramekin and frozen for later use.) Serve the beans around the steak.

HARICOTS VERTS | Break off the tips of 1 POUND OF HARICOTS VERTS, drop them into boiling salted water, and boil over high heat for about 5 minutes, or until they are tender but still firm. Drain, and refresh immediately under ice-cold water to stop the cooking.

At serving time, sauté about ½ CUP OF SLICED SHALLOTS in 1 TABLESPOON EACH OF SALTED BUTTER AND OLIVE OIL for about 40 seconds. Add the haricots verts, SALT, and PEPPER, and sauté for a couple of minutes, or until the beans are hot.

Beef Stew in Red Wine Sauce

YIELD: 4 SERVINGS

For many Americans, the quintessential French stew is *boeuf bourguignonne* or beef Burgundy, beef cooked in Burgundy red wine (although it is often made with other wines instead of real Burgundy). In my aunt's and my mother's restaurants, the stew was featured regularly and was made from the tougher, cheaper, fattier cuts of beef, which had to be braised a long time to get tender and stay moist. In classic restaurants, chuck was often used. The beef was browned and the juices deglazed with red wine and brown stock or reduced brown stock (demi-glace), and the stew was finished with *lardons* (browned pieces of diced bacon), mushrooms, and tiny boiled onions.

For my beef stew, I like to use a special piece of the shoulder called a flatiron, sometimes called a chicken steak, blade steak, or under-blade steak. This long, narrow piece from the center of the shoulder is extremely lean and has gelatinous sinew in the center. It is excellent sautéed or grilled for steak. The meat is very tender and moist, and it makes an ideal stew. This stew is also very good made with chuck, which is the continuation of the rib eye into the shoulder.

Instead of cutting the meat into small cubes, I cut it into large chunks, serving a couple of pieces per person. I do not use stock, demi-glace, or even water. I make my stew strictly with red wine, and my preference goes toward a fairly robust, heavy wine in the style of the southern part of the Rhône Valley, like a Carignan, or an Australian or American wine, like a Syrah or Zinfandel. After I brown the meat on top of the stove, I add the liquid and finish it up in the oven for about 1½ hours, so it cooks equally all around. It is best made and served in a beautiful cast-iron pan.

For the garnish, I use small, round, flat cipollini onions, flavorful but expensive; whole mushrooms, like small creminis; *lardons* made with pancetta; and baby carrots, which are not conventionally part of beef Burgundy. This rich winey beef stew is always a hit with my chef friends.

Buy about 2 POUNDS OF BEEF FROM THE FLATIRON PART OF THE SHOULDER, and remove the skin or sinew from the top. This is about half of a whole flatiron, depending on the size. Alternatively, use lean beef chuck in the same manner. Cut it into 8 pieces.

Preheat the oven to 350°F. Melt 1 TABLESPOON EACH OF BUTTER AND OIL in a nice cast-iron pan attractive enough for the table. Arrange the pieces in one layer in the skillet, and sprinkle them with SALT AND PEPPER. Cook on top of the stove over medium-high heat for about 8 minutes, browning the meat on all sides. Add 1 CUP OF

FINELY CHOPPED ONION, and 1 TABLESPOON OF FINELY CHOPPED GARLIC. Cook for another 2 minutes, stir to mix, and add 1 TABLESPOON OF FLOUR. Mix in well, so the flour doesn't form lumps, and stir in 1 BOTTLE (3 cups) of RED WINE. Add 2 BAY LEAVES, a nice BRANCH OF FRESH THYME, SALT, AND PEPPER, and bring to a boil, Stir well and cover, remove from heat.

Place in the oven and cook for about 1½ hours. The meat should be soft and tender and the liquid properly reduced. The recipe can be prepared to this point up to a day ahead and the garnish added at the last moment.

For the garnishes, peel 12 TO 15 SMALL-TO-MEDIUM CIPOLLINI OR PEARL ONIONS, wash 12 TO 15 SMALL-TO-MEDIUM CREMINI (BABY BELLA) MUSHROOMS, and peel 12 TO 15 BABY CARROTS.

For the *lardons,* you will need a piece of PANCETTA weighing about 5 OUNCES. Bring the pancetta and 2 CUPS OF WATER to a boil in a saucepan, cook for about 30 minutes, until practically cooked. Remove, and when cool enough to handle, cut the pancetta into ½-inch slices and then cut the slices into 1-inch-wide *lardons.* You should have about 1 cup.

Combine the *lardons,* carrots, mushrooms, and onions in a skillet with 1 TABLESPOON OF OLIVE OIL, ¼ CUP OF WATER, a good DASH EACH OF SUGAR, SALT, AND PEPPER. Bring to a boil, and cook, covered, for about 5 minutes. At this point, there should be practically no water left. Uncover, and continue cooking over high heat, sautéing until the vegetables are nicely browned on all sides, about 4 minutes.

When ready to serve the stew (directly from the pot, or on a large platter), mix some of the vegetables into the stew and sprinkle the remainder on top as a garnish. Add a little FRESH PARSLEY, and serve immediately. Enjoy the stew with glasses of the same wine you used in cooking this dish.

THE FOOD CRITIC

"Watch out! He is here!" With these five seemingly innocuous little words, the waiter disperses confusion through the entire restaurant. Disorder reigns in the dining room and tumbles through the kitchen. It is Waterloo! HE (or SHE) is the food critic, a personage imbued with such great power that by merely expressing his opinion, he can raise a restaurant to the pinnacle or reduce it to bankruptcy. And, whether the motive is to praise a restaurant or to confront mediocrity, the critic has to be reckoned with because he exercises a governing influence over the restaurant scene.

The first ancestor of the professional food critic is undoubtedly Alexandre-Balthasar-Laurent Grimod de La Reynière (1758–1838), a nineteenth-century "gastronome." A newspaper drama editor, he was the first modern cook/critic to make a living discussing restaurants and food. He was very thin and could eat several meals a day without putting on any weight, a characteristic shared by Archestratus, the Greek poet and traveling gourmand, whose experiences were later immortalized in the *Deipnosophist* (*Dinner of the Wise*) by Athenaeus. La Reynière created the "tasting jury," the forerunner of the academies of food critics of later times. This jury would meet at the Rocher de Cancale, a famous Paris restaurant of the time, and people would bring products from all the towns to get the certificate of approval or disapproval from these first professional tasters.

During his heyday, La Reynière was accused of bias and bribe but remains the founder of gastronomic journalism. His most important book, *L'Almanach des gourmands* (*The Gourmets' Almanac*), was issued yearly from 1803 to 1812. He was witty and, in addition to criticizing the restaurants, included a lot of anecdotes in his writing, and his comments were interesting enough for people to take notice and patronize the restaurants he discussed. He also published the *Manuel des amphytrions* (*Manual for Hosts*), wherein he laid down the rules on the new style of serving meals, advocating the method of serving a whole meal dish by dish in the Russian style (one of the first to do so). This new style was, he said, "a refinement of the art of living well. It is the way to eat hot, long, and copiously, since each dish is then a single center that is the focus of all appetites." He was a satirist, inventing a culinary rhetoric that is still used by gastronomy today. This professional gourmand, an arbiter of taste, did much for the development of cooking in the nineteenth century. However, many people look down on a person who makes a living from criticism.

Balzac, the famous gourmand and great writer of the nineteenth century, jeers at the critic for making and unmaking names without being able to make one for himself and, according to Grimm, the critic is subordinate, complex, and unconsciously envious of the creation he criticizes. In *Hugging the Shore*, John Updike defines the writing of criticism, as opposed to the writing of fiction and poetry, as ". . . what hugging the shore is to sailing the open sea." In the eighteenth century, Rousseau went so far as to say that criticism is a pleasure of depraved old men, and Voltaire emphasized the small, wicked, and morbid aspect of criticism, which he considered a state of mind rather than a profession. Those are harsh statements against the poor old critic!

How does one go about criticizing a restaurant? Should one be passionate? Partial? Objective? Analytic? Any of these approaches is acceptable, providing the common denominator is knowledge, honesty, and passion. Some people pretend that the less one knows about the food when evaluating it, the better. The premise here is that if there is no knowledge, the palate is virgin and thus ready to respond to a stimulus in a virtuous, undefiled, and objective manner. This is erroneous, however. The process of criticism is usually based on comparing the object to be criticized to an ideal model, so the more knowledge and more exposure food critics have, the larger their taste memory, and the deeper the

the best and so demand piquancy and stimulation. They may disregard blunders and lack of skill for the sake of the mighty gods of novelty and originality and tend to be too critical of the classic and standard.

If in music or painting, the quality of a work is judged by an aesthetic perception, in cooking criticism should be based on the most important element, which is taste; the aesthetic quality of a dish is valid only if the dish is first good to eat. Good reviewers appreciate this fact and respect tradition as well as novelty. They are capable of evaluating a dish on its own merit, even if it is not their favorite kind of food.

One way to judge a restaurant is to warn the chef and the owner that a critic is coming to challenge this restaurant to do its best. This is fine if one wants to evaluate the chef at the best performance he can give. It is certain that the restaurant will do its best and rise to the occasion, but will it do the same for everyone? In a food establishment, the worst enemies of the chef are routine and monotony, which generate boredom—the mortal opponent of good cooking—and in the daily routine of a restaurant, the chef must always be aware of the "challenge of monotony." The honesty and professionalism of a kitchen should be judged by what it serves day after day, customer after customer. If the quality is good and stable, then one knows there is a sense of aesthetics behind the stove. It is better, therefore, for food critics to remain anonymous to get the proper experience when visiting a restaurant. The establishment should be visited at least twice and probably three times if the reviewer is uncertain about his findings or if the restaurant is complex enough to warrant such attendance.

It is difficult for a chef to be criticized by someone unable to create what he criticizes. However, I have met several food reviewers whose taste buds were more acute and who were more knowledgeable than many chefs who take the limit of their tastes to be the limit of all tastes. There is always someone who can taste better, deeper, and

subtlety of their palate, the better equipped they are to analyze and discriminate between good and bad.

However, when criticism is pushed to the extreme of objectivism, it results in a kind of Platonistic critic, who looks only for an ideal set by standards and rules. This critic will be skeptical of novelty and turned off by bold innovation. A knowledgeable and talented critic, although scrupulous and picky, will never forget to enjoy the certain characteristics of food that defy rigorous explanation. Of course at the other extreme are the impressionistic critics, bored with conformity and standard foods. Their taste buds are dulled from too much exposure to

farther than you can, and it is certainly a lesson in humility to realize that fact. Yet it is impossible to separate critics from their culture, from their special position, from their background, and even from the fads and criteria of the moment. Critics who are too cautious content themselves with sorting out or underlining the problems of a restaurant in relation to what they think is perfection, but positive critics go one step further and generate enough stimulation to stir the criticized into changing, improving, and sustaining enthusiasm.

Although critics, especially good ones, are respected, they are rarely liked. Criticism is a bittersweet occupation, and to quote the words of an unknown writer, a critic is ". . . like a file that polishes what it bites." More than once I have gone to restaurants with bad reviewers who are imperious, conspicuous, and have come to judge and destroy rather than to assist. These people rejoice in power, are categorical in their decisions, and always right. These critics are skeptical of anything they don't know, and are often condescending to the staff. They love to show off, with wine as well as food. They are the type of critics who are feared, but who are mocked behind their backs and are detested. These are bad critics.

However, I remember going to restaurants with Craig Claiborne when he was the food reviewer for *The New York Times*, and I would consider him the quintessential good critic. He always called ahead and reserved a table under an assumed name. He arrived on time and would walk quietly with his guests to his table. Making a diversified selection from the menu, he would order his food and wines swiftly. He always noted the service afforded others around him and observed what patrons at nearby tables were eating and drinking. When he discussed the different dishes with his guests at the table, he was more listening than flaunting his knowledge. He was always open, understanding, giving attention to excuses, and always positive and helpful. Because he truly loved food and the restaurant business, he was sad when disappointed by the food or the service, but he could also be severe and indignant when confronted with fakery and excess. More than anything, he was always positive and spoke with hope rather than trying to destroy. Although Craig always judged a restaurant in relation to other restaurants, standards, and prices, and he listened to his friends, he relied primarily on his own palate. He always tried a restaurant several times before passing final judgment on it. Embarrassed by praise and turned off by flattery, he was inconspicuous and very happy not to be recognized. He was respected, esteemed, and listened to. He was a good food critic.

It is obvious that food criticism has to be subjective to a point, but you cannot escape yourself and your background, culture, and taste buds. But these personal feelings should be balanced by a very thorough knowledge of food and restaurant mechanics for the criticism to be valid. If I were to visit a dozen 3-star Michelin restaurants, which are recognized to have impeccable food, service, and décor, I would probably rate a few as extraordinary, a few as very good, and a couple that I feel do not deserve the highest rating. I would choose the extraordinary ones because their food and presentation happen to coincide exactly with my taste buds and sense of aesthetics. My choice would be purely a narcissistic reflection of my own taste, and someone else may choose differently. Up to a point, our taste is egocentric, because one cannot circumvent one's taste buds.

The bias of the critic should lean toward his readers, even though his point of view doesn't necessarily correspond to the multiple palates of his readers. The role of the critic is to educate his readers, and the raison d'être for criticism is to help readers choose a restaurant and help the restaurant to correct mediocre food and faulty service or reward it for great food and great service.

Anonymous criticism is preferred, as it reflects the situation of the ordinary diner who comes to a restaurant daily or weekly. Even the most honest, straightforward, and objective critics, when known by the restaurateur and the public, are under great pressure. Feared and admired, they are more respected when they go into a restaurant; they are catered to, fussed over, and, consciously as well as unconsciously, in time become used to that extra attention. This is an insidious process that falsifies their judgment. Therefore, anonymity remains the best approach, from the point of view of the patron as well as the restaurant and the critic.

In my opinion, what is even better than the anonymity of one food critic is a consensus by a small group of food experts, anonymous in the style of the *Michelin* guide in France. There are many advantages to this. First, a group, rather than one individual has a broader knowledge base. Experts can be selected who specialize in one particular type of cooking—Asian, French, Italian, etc. Just as it is impossible for one person to have a thorough knowledge of all types of cooking, it is also impossible for one person to keep up with the developments in each of the different cuisines. The different experts could be chosen from among known people in the food industry. Being anonymous, they could criticize their peers and even friends.

It is almost impossible for the palate of one person not to get jaded by being overexposed to good, great, and less great restaurants on a daily basis and sometimes more than once a day. The critic may easily fall into the habit of criticizing cooks for lack of imagination, even though the food itself is expertly prepared, because unusual combinations excite his palate and divert him from the boredom of standard, although excellent, food. Using a group of experts, the workload would be divided, insuring that each food reviewer is not so overworked that his palate becomes bored and bland. With a lighter schedule, an individual reviewer could go to a restaurant with the same positive anticipation as any diner who looks forward to eating out occasionally. The restaurant, knowing that it had been judged by a group of experts rather than one,

would be more likely to accept the criticism than it would that of one person, who might be resentful or vengeful toward a particular restaurant. It would eliminate the idea of a personal vendetta.

The food world would undoubtedly speculate about the identity of the unknown expert, but this would only generate ink and excitement and would not, in any way, be negative in the context of good criticism. Furthermore, when the food critic changes at *The New York Times*, the criticism remains the same and is still awaited every Friday with the same excitement.

The anonymity of the experts would ensure that there would be no possibility of bribery on the part of the restaurant, chef, or others. To assure that an expert would, at all costs, try to preserve his anonymity, a rule would be established at the outset that any expert whose identity is revealed must resign from his job.

Whether working alone or as one of a group of experts, all critics have a responsibility to expand their knowledge about their trade and to be able to understand, explain, and judge better. Yet, for those lucky enough to be born with a discriminating palate, and possessing an open mind and a thorough knowledge in all matters of food, there is good work to be done. A cold, prickly shower can be invigorating occasionally and have a positive effect. In the same manner, by gently nudging, criticism can improve and change things for the better.

To finish, listen to Sainte-Beuve, the famous nineteenth-century critic, who defined his job as ". . . the pleasure of getting acquainted with minds without dominating them." The relationship between the critic and the criticized is a give-and-take situation where each party can learn from the other. The food critic should enjoy and gain knowledge from the experience, and the restaurateur should accept and use the criticism to better his business. The net result would benefit the patrons.

Side Dishes

In this chapter you will find vegetable, potato, pasta, and rice dishes, as well as salads and spreads. The salads—from TOMATO AND ZUCCHINI SALAD to DANDELION SALAD to RED CABBAGE WITH ANCHÖIADE DRESSING—we sometimes enjoy as first courses, especially when Gloria and I eat alone. The decision to include them in this chapter is arbitrary, and although many of these dishes are presented as accompaniments to a main course, they should be served as you see fit within the context of a menu. TAPENADE and FROMAGE FORT are dishes that we also serve as snacks along with cocktails at large gatherings. The RISOTTO WITH TOMATO BROUILLADE is great with grilled meat or fish but also makes a terrific first course. Again, feel free to use these dishes to suit your needs, serving them as a first course, appetizer, or side dish.

Asparagus with Hazelnut Sauce and Croutons, recipe on page 202

FROMAGE FORT

When I think about my father, I can still see the old earthenware crock that he used for marinating his *fromage fort*, or "strong cheese." Now, my wife usually makes this at the house. I'm sure that our friends are tired of it, because when Gloria makes it she makes a big batch and freezes it in half-cup ramekins. It freezes well, and defrosted under refrigeration can be served on toast with drinks. Alternatively, we slide the ramekin into the lower part of a very hot oven or under the broiler for five or six minutes for a bubbly, crusty, and fragrant appetizer or salad garnish.

Making *fromage fort* is the ultimate way of using your leftover cheese. When my father used to make it every month or so, he would go through our *garde manger* (we didn't have a refrigerator at the time), which was a wooden container that he had made (after all, he was a cabinetmaker) with a very fine screen in the top and bottom. This was hung in the cellar in summer and outside the main door in the winter. He would search through our leftover cheese in this container, often finding pieces of very hard, strong, smelly goat cheese. He would scratch the top of the cheese with his knife to see if there was mold on it, which he would remove before placing the cheese in his crock. On top of this he would place pieces of Camembert or Brie, again after removing and discarding any moldy parts. He would then add pieces of Swiss, blue cheese, and fresher goat cheese. He would cover these with leek broth (my mother was always making soup, and her standard soup was leek and potato, so there was never a problem finding a ladleful of that broth), white wine, and two or three cloves of crushed garlic.

These ingredients would marinate in a cold place in the cellar for 1 to 1½ weeks, sometimes longer. He might add additional ingredients to the mix until, eventually, it was smelly enough and soft enough for him—the cheese would soften again with the added liquid—and then he would crush it with a large fork into a puree and add salt and pepper, if need be.

He liked it really strong. Often we would eat it plain on toast. Sometimes, though, he would spread a thick coating of it on a slab of country bread, and balancing the bread gingerly on the tines of a fork, he would hold it close to heat in our cast-iron stove, so that within one or two minutes, the cheese would start bubbling and browning on top. This was his own personal salamander or grill, since we didn't have a broiler at the time and this is how he would grill the *tartines* of *fromage fort*.

The recipe we now use regularly for strong cheese is probably a pale imitation of what my father used to do, but it is quite good, convenient, and since we use a food processor, it takes seconds to make. Once every month or so, my wife picks up whatever leftover cheese we have in our refrigerator cheese drawer, from Brie to cheddar to Swiss to blue to goat to mozzarella cheese. She trims off any mold or thick crust, and puts the cheese in the food processor. If it turns out that she has too much dry cheese and not enough soft cheese, she adds some cream cheese or even a few tablespoons of cottage cheese along with the other ingredients.

Put about ½ POUND OF CHEESE in the bowl of a food processor, add A COUPLE CLOVES OF GARLIC, ABOUT ¼ CUP OF DRY WHITE WINE, and a big grinding of BLACK PEPPER. Salt is usually not needed, but taste the mixture, and add some if it is needed. Process for 30 seconds or so, until the mixture is creamy but not too soft, and then pack it, into small containers. The *fromage fort* is ready to use now, either as a generous cold spread for bread, or you can run the coated bread under the broiler for a few minutes to melt the cheese, brown it, and make it wonderfully fragrant.

TAPENADE

YIELD: ENOUGH FOR 40 TO 50 TOASTS OR BAGEL CHIPS

In the south of France, tapenade is often called the "butter of Provence." It is usually available at most bistros and restaurants south of Valence. I have used tapenade as a coating on top of fish before sautéing it, so the tapenade becomes a dark shell and flavors the fish. I have used it to season salads and added it to sauces, like fresh tomato sauce. I've also mixed it into the drippings of roast chicken to create a wonderful juice. But the raison d'être of tapenade is as a spread on toast with drinks, and this is the classic accompaniment for drinks in the south of France, whether it is enjoyed with a glass of cold rosé or a glass of pastis, like Ricard or Pernod, the licorice-flavored aperitifs.

Although it originated in the south of France, tapenade is served all over France nowadays. There are many recipes for it, but conventionally it is a puree of olives, capers, and anchovies. Some people add garlic, some don't; I have had tapenade with almonds, sometimes smooth and sometimes coarse. The word "tapenade" comes from the Provençal name *tapano,* which means capers, so capers seem to have been an ingredient from the beginning. It is great for a picnic, spread on little toasts from a baguette, so the base is crunchy, but my favorite tapenade base is bagel chips, which are crunchy, thin, and perfect with this great concoction.

For my tapenade, I take a slightly different path, adding some dried figs. It seems like a natural combination; figs grow next to olive trees, and they add a little sweetness and an exotic taste to the mixture. I also like to add a few mint leaves occasionally. Their cooling and perfumed attributes give a special accent to the dish.

I like my tapenade to be fairly coarse, rather than the conventional smooth puree. Chop it by hand or in a food processor using the pulse button, starting and stopping it several times to achieve a uniform chunky and coarse texture. I like oil-cured black olives or kalamata, and I often use a mixture of both. If the olives are not pitted, I do that first: lay an olive flat on the table, and press on it with your thumb or the blade of a knife to crack it open. Once it is cracked, the pit is easily removed.

Use about 1½ CUPS OF PITTED OLIVES. Put the olives in the bowl of a food processor with 2 TABLESPOONS OF CAPERS, 2 SMALL CLOVES OF PEELED, CRUSHED GARLIC, about 8 ANCHOVIES IN OIL, 3 SMALL QUARTERED DRIED FIGS, 7 OR 8 MINT LEAVES, and ½ TEASPOON OF FRESHLY GROUND BLACK PEPPER. Add ¼ CUP OF THE BEST POSSIBLE EXTRA-VIRGIN OLIVE OIL. Pulse 15 or 20 times, or until you have achieved the texture you want. Taste again, and add salt, if needed, although the tapenade is usually already salty enough from the olives and capers. Refrigerate until serving time.

Serve cool, but not ice cold, with BAGEL CHIPS and a glass of chilled rosé or pastis. You will think you are in Aix-en-Provence. I like a few slices of *saucisson,* a dry French salami, with my tapenade and wine. I prefer my *saucisson* to be fairly coarse in texture, cut into not-too-thin slices, and arranged around the plate containing the tapenade.

tapenade is the ideal accompaniment to aperitif

Tangy Herb Mayonnaise

I first made this piquant sauce to serve with sweetbreads (see pages 166–167), but it is also good with poached fish and cold cuts.

It's important that you properly hard cook the egg for this recipe, not an easy task. If eggs are boiled too rapidly, the albumen in them toughens, producing a rubbery white, and if they aren't cooled properly after cooking, the exterior of the yolk turns green, and the eggs develop that sulfur or "rotten egg" smell.

Cook 1 EGG very gently in boiling water to cover for 9 or 10 minutes, and then fill the pan with cold water and ice, and let the egg cool completely before peeling off the shell.

Cut the hard-cooked egg into slices on an egg slicer, and then lift the whole egg carefully, pivot it 90 degrees in the slicer, and cut through it again to make small sticks. Alternatively, cut the egg into matchstick size pieces. Put the egg sticks in a bowl, and stir in 2 TABLESPOONS OF CHOPPED ONION, 1 TABLESPOON OF DRAINED CAPERS, 4 COARSELY CUT ANCHOVIES IN OIL, 1 TABLESPOON OF HOT MUSTARD, 1 TABLE-SPOON OF CHOPPED TARRAGON, 1 TABLESPOON OF CHOPPED CHIVES, ¼ TEASPOON OF TABASCO SAUCE, and 1 CUP OF MAYONNAISE. Refrigerate until serving time.

Against all traditions, a dandelion salad in Lyon will likely be served on a lukewarm plate with a glass of cool Beaujolais and a chunk of crusty baguette! Warm salad with cold wine breaks the rules. I like to finish this meal with a ripe Camembert or a piece of bleu cheese. The bleu de Gex, a cheese from my area of France, is not creamy, but semi-hard, with a deep, moldy, mushroomlike taste. Serve it with more Beaujolais.

Pick through the greens in your sink to remove wilted leaves and dirt, and wash them in a lot of cool to tepid water, which removes more sand than cold water. Lift the greens out of the water and wash again once or twice, or until you can run your finger along the bottom of the bowl you are using as a cleaning receptacle and not feel any dirt or sand. Then dry the greens in a salad spinner, so there is no water left to dilute the dressing. You should have about 10 TO 12 CUPS (LOOSE) OF CLEAN SALAD GREENS. If you have picked more, keep them for another occasion. At this point, the greens can be put in a plastic bag and will keep, ready to be served, in the refrigerator for five or six days.

Lower 2 OR 3 EGGS into boiling water in a small saucepan, and bring the water back to a very light, gentle simmer (if you boil the eggs too fast, it toughens the albumen in the whites, making them rubbery). After 8 minutes (I like them slightly wet in the center of the yolk), remove the pan from the heat, drain off the water, and then shake the eggs against the sides of the pan to crack the shells. Fill the pan with ice and water to cool the eggs quickly. One of the secrets to eliminating the green coloration from around the yolk and the resulting smell of sulfur is to cool eggs in ice water long enough so the sulfur dissipates in the water .

Place a 6-OUNCE PIECE OF PANCETTA in a saucepan, cover with cold water, bring to a light simmer, and cook for about 30 minutes. Drain, cut into ½-inch slices, and then cut the slices into 1-inch pieces or *lardons* (to have 1 to 1¼ cups). Cook slowly in about 2 TABLESPOONS OF PEANUT OIL in a skillet for 5 to 8 minutes, until the pieces are lightly browned on all sides. The cooking oil and whatever juices come out of the pancetta are used hot in the salad dressing.

Preheat the oven to 400°F. Cut CUBES ABOUT 1½ INCHES SQUARE FROM A DAY-OLD BAGUETTE OR COUNTRY BREAD to have about 6 croutons per serving. Scatter on an aluminum foil–lined cookie sheet, sprinkle with PEANUT OIL, rub them together so they are well coated with the oil, and bake until nicely browned, 8 to 10 minutes.

Anchovy fillets are a standard addition to my dandelion salad. When I can get anchovies in salt, I desalt them, and then separate the fillets from the central bone and keep them in olive oil. The standard little cans of flat anchovy fillets in olive oil are also fine to use. Use the oil from the can in your salad dressing.

For the dressing: With a large chef's knife, crush the ANCHOVY FILLETS (FROM A 2-OUNCE CAN) into a paste, mix with 1 TABLESPOON OF CHOPPED GARLIC, and put this mixture in a big salad bowl with 2 TABLESPOONS OF RED WINE VINEGAR, A GOOD DASH OF SALT, and a liberal amount of FRESHLY GROUND BLACK PEPPER.

Add the just-cooked *lardons*, along with their fat, to the dressing. Stir, and add EXTRA OLIVE OIL so that you have about four times more oil (ABOUT ½ CUP) than vinegar. Next, add the dandelion greens, mix well with the dressing, and taste for salt and pepper. Sprinkle the croutons on top, toss lightly, and scoop the salad onto lukewarm plates. Add a few wedges of egg to each serving, and enjoy with crunchy baguettes and a glass of cool Beaujolais.

TOMATO AND ZUCCHINI SALAD

YIELD: 8 SERVINGS

Tomato salad is almost a daily treat for me when tomatoes finally ripen on the vine, which usually doesn't happen in Connecticut until the beginning of the second week in August. When this occurs, I go into my garden and pick a tomato, sprinkle a little coarse salt on top, and eat it right away, still lukewarm from the sun. Nothing could be better.

When tomatoes are in season, we eat them in a variety of forms. I love them stuffed, and use leftover chicken, any type of roast, even cold cuts as stuffing, chopping the meat and mixing it with a little bread or leftover rice or potatoes, sometimes an egg, and lots of fresh herbs from the garden. I bake my stuffed tomatoes until the tops caramelize. We also enjoy fresh raw tomato salad with pasta, just dicing the tomatoes and seasoning them with salt, pepper, and olive oil before tossing them with freshly cooked pasta and topping the dish with basil.

A very simple traditional French dish that is exceptional when made with fresh seasonal tomatoes, tomatoes Provençal is a summer must for us. We halve tomatoes crosswise, and cook them cut side down in a very hot oiled skillet until seared. Then arranged cut side up in a gratin dish, the tomato halves are topped with a *persillade* (parsley and garlic chopped together), salt, freshly ground black pepper, and olive oil, and baked for a few minutes, until soft and hot.

We probably prepare tomato salad more than any other dish with our homegrown tomatoes. I grow a lot of heirloom tomatoes. Some are bright red, some yellow, some striated. Sometimes we serve the tomatoes on their own, sometimes with red onions, sometimes with basil, sometimes with both onions and basil, and sometimes with zucchini, which is available at the same time from the garden. Julienned and cured with salt, zucchini is great on its own with a dash of oil and lemon juice, but in this recipe we make it part of the tomato salad. I like my dressing mild, and use about four to five times more oil than vinegar.

Cut A LARGE, FIRM ZUCCHINI crosswise into 3-inch chunks, then stand the chunks on end, and cut them lengthwise into ½-inch slices, stopping when you reach the seeds and discarding that seedy center. Stack these slices, and cut into zucchini sticks. You will have about 2 cups of julienned zucchini. Season with about ¼ TEASPOON OF SALT, toss it with the zucchini, and set aside. Within 10 or 15 minutes, the zucchini becomes wet and softens somewhat.

Use 2 OR 3 LARGE, FLESHY TOMATOES that contain a minimum of seeds. Cut the tomatoes crosswise, parallel to the stem, into ½-inch-thick slices (I like fairly thick tomato slices), and arrange them flat or slightly overlapping on a platter. Top with a good CUP OF VERY THINLY SLICED RED ONION. Onions come out of the garden at about the same time as tomatoes, and I particularly like the long torpedo red onions, which are mild when fresh. Sprinkle liberally with SALT AND FRESHLY GROUND BLACK PEPPER.

Drain the zucchini of any excess liquid, and sprinkle it on top of the tomatoes and onions. Before serving, douse the salad generously with the BEST POSSIBLE OLIVE OIL and A LITTLE RED WINE VINEGAR.

Make your own vinegar with leftover wines, it is easy and superb

HOMEMADE VINEGAR

I make my own vinegar in a crock at home from a "mother" of vinegar. This "mother" is an acetobacter or bacteria that usually floats around in the air and forms on its own. If this doesn't happen in your crock after a couple of weeks, however, you can make vinegar by combining some good wine (use wine left over in glasses after a dinner party) in a crock with a little unpasteurized good-quality red wine vinegar to start the process. Cover the crock with a piece of cheesecloth, and place a bay leaf on top of the cheesecloth to keep the flies away (this is a tip from my wife, Gloria). After a couple of weeks, a skin will form on top of the liquid; this is the work of the bacteria that will transform the wine into vinegar. The deep color of the red wine becomes lighter, and a very strong, fruity smell of vinegar can be detected.

Keep adding wine to the crock of vinegar. The "mother" will duplicate itself in pancake-like layers, and you can give one to a friend to start his or her own vinegar crock. After a couple of months, push the "mother" aside, and you will see that the liquid is crystal clear underneath.

Ladle the vinegar gently into a very fine strainer, and then fill empty wine bottles with this clear liquid. Push a few sprigs of tarragon into one of the bottles and fresh thyme or sage into another. I label my bottles to remind me of the flavoring. Tarragon is the most common flavoring for red wine vinegar.

I use this vinegar year-round right out of the bottle. Cut a small wedge about ¼ inch deep the length of a wine cork on each side, and push the cork back into the bottle. When you need vinegar, grab the bottle, and shake it into a salad bowl. The vinegar pours out in a nice stream through the two wedges on the sides of the cork, and it is easy to control the flow.

Red Cabbage Salad with Anchoïade Dressing

Anchoïade, from the word "anchovies," which in French is *anchois,* is a puree of anchovies in oil and garlic with the addition of olive oil. This is a classic mixture used in the south of France. A similar dip, served warm in Provence, is called a *bagna cauda,* which literally means a "hot sauce" in Provence and is served surrounded by raw vegetables, like carrots, fava beans, and asparagus. People dip the vegetables into the *bagna cauda* before eating them.

Anchoïade is also served as a dressing for salads, and I love this one made with red cabbage. It can be prepared ahead, and the cabbage, either red or green, doesn't need to be blanched. It will wilt a little after a couple of hours, but will stay very crunchy and keep in the refrigerator for a few days.

I have served this cabbage *anchoiade* on its own as part of an assortment of hors d'oeuvre, as a bed for a piece of grilled fish, and with omelets. It's versatile and highly flavored, but is not recommended for people who object to the taste of garlic.

For this salad, I use a SMALL, TIGHT HEAD OF RED CABBAGE, ABOUT 1½ POUNDS. After halving it and removing the core, cut it like coleslaw into ¼-inch pieces with a sharp knife or hand slicer (mandoline). You should have about 10 cups of shredded cabbage, which is what you need for this recipe, along with A 2-OUNCE CAN OF ANCHOVY FILLETS IN OIL, and about 5 CLOVES OF PEELED GARLIC.

With the blade of a knife placed flat on the garlic cloves, crush them by smacking down and forward on the blade. Pile the anchovies on top, sprinkle with salt, and continue crushing. The salt will act as an abrasive, like sandpaper, turning the mixture into a puree. Transfer the puree to a large bowl, add SALT AND A LOT OF FRESHLY GROUND PEPPER, 1 TABLESPOON OF RED WINE VINEGAR, A GOOD ⅓ CUP OF YOUR BEST OLIVE OIL, and mix well.

Add the cabbage to the *anchoïade,* and toss well. After about 20 minutes the mixture will soften a bit. Mix again, and taste for seasoning. Add more salt and pepper if needed; it takes a fair amount for this dish to be properly seasoned. If there is too much liquid coming out of it, pour some of it off. It is best eaten two or three hours after it is prepared.

The *anchoïade* sauce can also be prepared in a food processor, but often the processor emulsifies it too much, and it becomes thick, like a mayonnaise. This is good when it is served as a sauce with grilled fish or cold meat, but it is not the proper consistency for the cabbage salad, because that thick sauce will stick to the coleslaw. If the mixture is somewhat broken, it will mix well into the cabbage, making it shiny and glossy, without any thick sauce really sticking to it.

Cabbage and anchoïade is your standard French coleslaw

ASPARAGUS WITH HAZELNUT SAUCE AND CROUTONS

YIELD: 4 SERVINGS   PICTURED ON PAGE 188

Big fat stalks of asparagus mean spring to me, along with dandelion salad, rhubarb, fresh trout, and strawberries. I like my asparagus thick and with very tight heads, like the buds of a rose. It is a mistake to believe that small asparagus are young specimens that are more tender than the fat stalks. When I used to pick asparagus from Claude's garden, some emerged from the ground fat and some thin. So thin asparagus spears are not necessarily young; fat ones with tight heads are the most tender.

As a young kid and cook in France, I was accustomed to white asparagus, especially the Argenteuil type. Green asparagus, the most common variety in the United States, was unusual and special to us. White asparagus has a slightly bitter taste and requires longer cooking; the stalks don't take well to being undercooked because they are fibrous. Purple or violet asparagus, less common and more expensive, often comes from Italy.

I remember that my brother and I would hunt for wild asparagus next to the Rhône River in Neyron. The stalks were thin and narrow, and they had a really strong taste. We cut them down about ten to twelve inches from the top. Not long ago, I found some of these in Madison, Connecticut, around Hammonasset Beach. Wild asparagus has a wonderful taste—more pungent and more assertive than cultivated varieties.

Even when I worked in Paris as a young man, asparagus was considered a rich, expensive dish, and was costly, especially the first crop of the spring season. It was cooked to order, and nine out of ten times served with a hollandaise, or sometimes with *sauce choron,* which is a hollandaise with tomato and tarragon added, or a *beurre moussant,* which is melted butter emulsified with a little water or lemon juice.

When I was a kid, my favorite asparagus dish was in the Belgian style, with cooked asparagus wrapped in slices of ham—wonderful boiled *jambon de Paris,* with a mild cure—and these were coated with a white sauce, topped with Gruyère, and gratinéed under a hot broiler. It is a wonderful dish, but if you want a purer taste of asparagus, you will probably want to prepare it in a simpler way.

I prefer to buy my asparagus loose at the market, so I can select fat spears with tight heads. To store them, I take a wet paper towel and stand them up in a container with a little water in it. This keeps them nice and fresh in the refrigerator for a couple of days, if need be. There are ten to twelve large spears per pound. The lower third of the spears are fibrous, so I peel that section, so the entire spear is edible and tender. Putting the spears flat on the table, peel them with a good vegetable peeler, rotating the spears as you go. All in all, I like the fat green asparagus stalks the best and I like the spears cooked so they are a bit firm—not very soft, as I used to have them prepared as a child, and not too crunchy, as they are served in many restaurants.

At home, more often than not, we eat asparagus lukewarm with a vinaigrette made with a great deal of Dijon-style mustard, olive oil, and, sometimes, a little walnut oil. As a kid, I would spoon some of that strong vinaigrette onto my plate, and then incline the plate toward me, propping it underneath with a knife, so the vinaigrette collected in a pool. Then, holding the asparagus spears in my fingers, I would dip them one by one into the sauce and eat them.

In this more elegant recipe, I prepare a *noisette* (hazelnut) sauce, which is a hollandaise made with butter that has been cooked until it turns a light brown color. Whatever moisture is in the butter starts foaming during the cooking. Then the moisture evaporates, the butter clarifies, and eventually turns a hazelnut color, becoming a *beurre noisette*, so called because the butter tastes like roasted hazelnuts when cooked this way. The top of the asparagus is sprinkled with coarse toasted bread crumbs. These crunchy crumbs are great for topping salads and soups. Sometimes I sprinkle a little herbes de Provence or curry on the cubes before putting them into the oven.

To make the croutons: Preheat the oven to 400°F. Cut a COUNTRY BREAD OR BAGUETTE (ABOUT 8 OUNCES) into 1-inch cubes, and toss them with A LITTLE HAZELNUT OR PEANUT OIL to moisten the bread a little. Sprinkle on a little SALT, spread the bread cubes onto a cookie sheet, and brown them for 10 to 12 minutes. Cool until lukewarm, and then put into a plastic bag and pound with a skillet or meat pounder to break the cubes into large, uneven crumbs. Sprinkle with COARSELY GROUND BLACK PEPPER. Set aside.

Using a vegetable peeler, peel the bottom third of 16 TO 20 LARGE ASPARAGUS SPEARS, ABOUT 1½ POUNDS. Do not peel too high on the stalks; they are not fibrous at this level, and you will remove the beautiful green color from the upper portion of the spears.

To cook the asparagus: Pour 1 TO 1½ CUPS OF WATER into a large skillet, preferably stainless steel or nonstick. Add A DASH OF SALT, and when the water boils, add the asparagus in one or two layers.

Bring back to the boil, and cover, so the spears come back to a boil very quickly. After 4 or 5 minutes, the asparagus should be tender but still firm. Remove the lid, drain off the water, and spread the spears on a tray to cool if not serving right away, so they cool quickly and retain their beautiful color. I don't like to rinse asparagus under cold water, as it waters down the taste. Yet, if I cook a large quantity, I cool it down briefly under cold water and drain while still warm, so any remaining moisture evaporates.

It is easy and quick to make the hazelnut sauce in a blender. Melt 1 STICK (8 TABLESPOONS) OF THE BEST QUALITY SWEET BUTTER in a saucepan. As it cooks, it will foam a little, and then the foam will disappear and the solids will stick a little to the bottom of the pan, creating a darkish coating. The butter will turn a rich, very light brown color with a pleasant hazelnut taste. Let the butter cool for 5 minutes before using because if it is too hot it may curdle the yolks. Put TWO EGG YOLKS and 1 TABLESPOON OF WATER in a blender, turn the blender on, and with it running, pour the butter into it in a slow, steady stream. Add about 2 TEASPOONS OF LEMON JUICE, A DASH OF SALT, and A LITTLE CAYENNE PEPPER, and process for a few more seconds. The mixture should be smooth, creamy, and have a delicious flavor.

To serve: reheat the asparagus (if necessary) in a microwave oven for about a minute, or place in a conventional oven for a few minutes at 180°F to warm it. Sprinkle the reserved croutons on top, and serve right away with the hazelnut sauce. It is said that the sulfur in asparagus gives a metallic taste to wine, especially red wine, but it takes more than that to prevent me from enjoying wine with this dish.

CAULIFLOWER GRATIN

YIELD: 6 SERVINGS

Whatever the season, a gratin is always welcome at my table. This goes back to when I was a child, and gratins were always a prominent part of the menus at my mother's and my aunt's restaurants. Gratin means "crust" in French, and we use the expression *"le gratin"* to mean the upper crust of society. Prepared in a shallow dish, gratins always have a crust on top.

Gratins I am particularly fond of include my sister-in-law's gratin of eggs, consisting of hard-cooked eggs in a cream sauce with a lot of onion, and cheese on top, and my mother's zucchini gratin, made from pureed cooked zucchini, a dash of flour, eggs, milk, and cheese. She made similar gratins with mushrooms, eggplant, and spinach and featured them on her menu throughout the year. In the classic Swiss chard gratin, the green chard leaves are pureed and spooned into a gratin dish with its cooked ribs, a bit of cream, and Gruyère cheese on top. For the cardoon gratin, a Lyonnaise specialty, cardoon ribs are cooked like artichoke bottoms in a *blanc*—a mixture of flour, water, lemon juice, and salt—until tender and white, and then they are spread out in a gratin dish, usually enhanced with the natural juice of a roast, like beef or veal, and often poached beef marrow is added. Swiss cheese is sprinkled on top.

One of my all-time favorites is the cauliflower gratin. I love cauliflower in any form, and this recipe is great for a party because it can be done ahead, ready to go into the oven at the last moment.

Choose cauliflower that is as white as possible. It should be very firm, without any brown or yellow spots, and the flowerets should be tight. Remove any surrounding green leaves from 1 LARGE, WHOLE HEAD OF CAULIFLOWER, ABOUT 2 POUNDS, and cook it stem side down in 1½ CUPS OF WATER in a stainless-steel saucepan, covered, for about 10 minutes, or until it is tender to the point of a knife. (Sometimes I serve it poached like this with a little olive oil, salt, and pepper on top.)

Make the béchamel sauce. Melt 3 TABLESPOONS OF UNSALTED BUTTER in a saucepan, and add 3 TABLESPOONS OF FLOUR. Mix well with a whisk, cook for 10 or 15 seconds, and then add 2 CUPS OF HALF-AND-HALF and A GOOD DASH OF SALT AND PEPPER. Bring to a boil, whisking occasionally, making certain that you push down on the handle of the whisk to force the tip into the corners of the pan, so that the mixture doesn't stick there. Boil gently for 30 seconds, remove from the heat, and set aside.

Butter a 6-cup gratin dish. Cut the cauliflower into flowerets, and arrange them in one layer in the dish, pressing them a little with your hand to distribute them evenly. Slice the core, and add it as well. Sprinkle with SALT AND FRESHLY GROUND PEPPER, and top with about ¼ CUP GRATED SWISS CHEESE. Use the best Emmenthaler, Gruyère, Comté, or Jarlsberg your market offers. Pour the sauce evenly over the cauliflower, moving the vegetable pieces a little to let the béchamel flow between. Add ½ CUP OF GRATED SWISS CHEESE, sprinkling it evenly on top, so the cauliflower is nicely covered all over. Finally, sprinkle on 2 TABLESPOONS OF GRATED PARMESAN CHEESE. The gratin can be prepared ahead to this point, covered, and refrigerated for cooking later.

If cooking the gratin while the ingredients are still hot, bake in a 400°F oven for 20 to 25 minutes. If the dish is cold to start, cook for 35 to 40 minutes to get it piping hot. It should be beautifully crusted on top with a wonderful aroma. Bring it to the table, and let rest a good 10 minutes before serving. Make certain to spoon out some of the crusty cheese with all the servings.

ZUCCHINI FLOWER FRITTERS

YIELD: 12 FRITTERS

I love to make fritters with produce from my garden, and one of my favorites is made with zucchini blossoms. When flowers appear in the zucchini plants in your garden, you will notice that some of the stems are thick and round, the indication of a future zucchini. Right next to these, however, you will likely see flowers on long, thin stems; these are the male flowers, and they will never produce zucchini. Pick these two-to-three-inch-long male flowers, which are usually more numerous than the female. During the popularity of nouvelle cuisine, zucchini flowers were stuffed with meat or shellfish and steamed, poached, or sautéed. It's still nice to do those preparations occasionally, but making little fritters with these mild, slightly sweet flowers is a seasonal treat for me. They are made quickly and are ideal for serving with drinks or as a garnish for fish or meat. I just step into the garden, pick a dozen or so zucchini flowers, come back inside, and within 10 minutes we have fritters. Open the flowers to check for and remove any insects. I leave the flowers whole and do not wash or dry them.

For a dozen fritters, mix ½ CUP OF FLOUR and ¼ TEASPOON OF BAKING POWDER in a small bowl. Add ½ CUP OF CLUB SODA. Mix well with a whisk; the batter should be thick and smooth. Add another ¼ CUP OF CLUB SODA, and whisk it in to make the batter very light. (If all the club soda is added at the beginning, the mixture might get lumpy.) Put a large nonstick skillet over high heat on top of the stove, and add A COUPLE OF TABLESPOONS OF PEANUT OR VEGETABLE OIL.

Press A ZUCCHINI FLOWER into the batter, so it is covered with batter on both sides, and place in the hot oil. Repeat, adding enough flowers to fit in one layer in the skillet (probably 6 to 8 at a time). Cook the fritters over high heat, for a total of about 6 minutes, 3 minutes per side, until they are very crisp. When you turn the fritters after the first 3 minutes of cooking, you will notice that batter inside the fritters makes them bubble out. Using your spatula, press down on the fritters, so they become flat in the pan. This will make them crisper. Turn the fritters a few times during the cooking, so they are beautifully brown and crisp on both sides.

Lift the fritters one by one from the pan, and place on a wire rack set over a layer of paper towels. Do not drain the fritters on paper towels, as is conventionally done. The bottoms will become soggy. (I learned this technique from Korean cooks, who are great at frying.) Repeat the process with the remaining flowers and batter. Prepared like this, they won't really absorb much of the cooking oil in the skillet, so you may have enough oil left in the skillet to fry the second batch. Sprinkle SALT on both sides of the hot fritters, and serve.

these flower fritters are great with drinks

mushrooming is a rite of Summer

Marinated Summer Mushrooms

YIELD: 8 TO 10 SERVINGS

I use mushrooms as garnishes for roasts, in quiche, in timbales, as well as in gratins, and sautéed in cream sauce. More often than not, however, I cook different types of mushrooms in a recipe I call Marinated Summer Mushrooms.

Although mushrooms begin to grow in the early spring while there is still snow on the ground, and continue growing until temperatures dip to freezing in late fall, summer and fall are really the most exciting times for mushrooming. This quest may take me to the fields, the woods, or near the river. I go by myself, with my dog, and if I'm fortunate, Gloria, Jean-Claude, or Jean-Michel will join me.

Mushrooming has been a tradition in my family since I was a kid. My father and mother would pick up mostly field mushrooms, which is the wild variety of the white domestic mushrooms you find at the supermarket, *Agaricus campestris* or *Agaricus arvensis,* sometimes called "horse mushrooms," which grow particularly in pastures where farm animals graze. We just sautéed them a little in butter and, since they render a lot of water, thickened them lightly with flour and added a little cream. These have a very delicious, nutty, intense taste. The "wood" mushrooms we gathered were limited to chanterelles, which are sometimes called *"girolles"* in France. Occasionally, we would find cèpes, which is a *Boletus* variety.

Since I was five or six I remember going mushrooming with my father, brother, and mother, and often having a picnic for lunch. In France, farmers would often post signs cautioning people to watch out for the bull, because there were cows in the field. More often than not there was no bull, but it was the farmers' way to keep mushroom pickers out of their fields.

Before moving to Connecticut in 1976, we spent time in upstate New York, near Hunter Mountain, where we fixed up an old, abandoned house that became our weekend destination. We skied during the winter, fished for trout during the summer and fall, but one of our favorite pastimes was hunting for mushrooms. Mushrooms are plentiful there. Often I would do this with other chefs who had homes in the area, like Jean-Claude, André Soltner, or Michel Keller. When I moved to Connecticut, I made a new friend, Gerry Miller, a shaman, artist, and a bona fide mycologist. It is always a pleasure and a learning experience for me to go mushroom hunting with Gerry. There are more than five thousand species of mushrooms, and at least four hundred types of tube mushrooms (where the underside looks like a sponge) in northeastern America, where the *Boletus* (porcini in Italian, cèpes in French) is the most known and appreciated. There are many poisonous mushrooms, as well as some slightly toxic, some very poisonous, and some deadly, usually all in the *Amanita* genus, Never pick up mushrooms and eat them. Start foraging with a mycological society or with someone who really knows mushrooms.

It is not a good idea for wild mushrooms to be eaten raw or undercooked. Even known mushrooms, like morels, can be toxic when eaten raw, and many species require more than flash cooking. So, to avoid problems, I cook my wild mushrooms for at least 20 minutes. When a mushroom is firm, such as *Boletus edulis* or chanterelle, it can cook for one hour and still be firm and crunchy. Soft mushrooms, like "Slippery Jack," another type of *Boletus,* or the yellow *Boletus,* will get soft after a few minutes of cooking and will remain soft and slimy, so these are better used for making a stock or soup that will be emulsified.

It sounds pedantic to use Latin names for mushrooms, but I have found it comforting and necessary. There are many classic and common names for mushroom varieties in France, but these names tend to change from region to region. The situation is the same in America; there are the true names or mycological names for mushrooms, and several common names, which tend to differ from state to state. When you know the Latin etymology, it is easier to identify mushrooms.

In mushroom books, the listings do not always specify whether the mushroom is edible or not. Some species considered edible in Europe are not considered so in the United States, and some are even deemed edible on the East Coast but not on the West Coast, and vice versa. It is vital that you forage with people who truly know mushrooms.

I pick about forty types of mushrooms, starting in the spring with morels, somewhat elusive, as well as *Gyromitra*. I discuss this variety, often described as poisonous, in the Chicken with Morel Sauce recipe, page 138. The St. George's mushroom is another species that comes early in the spring. From the middle of June, depending on how much rain we've had, mushrooms burst forth all over until the end of fall. These are the best months. There are all kinds of *Boletus* that we pick: *Boletus affinis, Boletus separans, Boletus frostii, Boletus bicolor,* and the "old man of the wood" are all part of the same genus. Even the *Boletus luridus* or *erythropus,* which are red or yellow underneath and turn blue when cut, are varieties that Claude and I have eaten for years without any ill effects, although many mushroom guides would not advise it.

In addition to the *Boletus*, summer is time for the *Lactarius*, which seeps a latex-type sticky liquid that looks like milk. We pick up the red *Russula*, with a red stem, as well as the virescent with its green cracked top, often found in summer markets in France. Summer is always great for chanterelles. We get the big thick yellow ones, known as *cibarius*, and the *lutescens*, the tiny red and yellow ones, and, of course, the so-called black Orpheus, called *"trompette de mort,"* or "horn of death" in France, one of the best mushrooms that we gather.

The *rosé* mushrooms of my youth come into the fields in full summer, some small and the large ones that we used to call *"boule de neige"* (snowball), which is the "horse mushroom," basically what a portobello would be in the wild. The tiny, delicious "fairy ring" mushroom grows into a ring, and is known as *Marasmius oreades*. Very choice except for its tough stem, it is best around a veal roast. The tall "parasol mushroom," a *Lepiota*, and the "pig's trotter" ("sheep's feet" in France), which is *Hydnum repandum*, with little needles under the cap, are part of the summer's bounty, along with *Cortinarius*, and *Clavaria amethystina*, a mushroom the color of amethyst. All the colors of the rainbow can be found in field mushrooms.

One of the most prized mushrooms of early fall is the "hen of the woods," *Polyporus frondosus*, which the Native Americans considered the greatest of mushrooms. They felt it protected them against cancer and other illnesses. These parasite mushrooms can grow on trees into enormous clumps. Every year Jean-Claude collects 30 to 40 pounds of mushrooms from one tree, all divided among 8 to 10 large clumps. The "chicken of the woods" (*Polyporus sulphureus*), with its bright red-orange cap, glows at night when very young. The "oyster mushroom," also a parasite, is found on tree stumps, and late fall is the season for the "honey mushroom" (*Armillaria mellea*), as well as the "shaggy mane," (*Coprinus comatus*), very delicate, with a rich-flavored taste.

During a good year, I have gathered up to 100 pounds of assorted mushrooms. I wash them carefully, and when I have a lot, I arrange them in a roasting pan and put them into a 400°F oven for 1 to 1½ hours, or until all the water comes out. At that point, the mushrooms have lost a great deal of their volume. I pack them very tightly in plastic bags (compacting them into balls), with a bit of their juice and freeze them. When I defrost them during the winter, I use the juice for soups or sauces, and the mushrooms are ready to be sautéed for a few minutes or used otherwise in stews or soups.

I sometimes dry mushrooms in a microwave oven, or outside on a barbecue fire, which is a great way to dry them, because the smoke of woods like oak, hickory, or maple penetrates the mushrooms and makes their flavor very intense. Once mushrooms are frozen, they keep indefinitely.

For eight to ten people for a picnic, you will need about 2 POUNDS OF MISCELLANEOUS WILD MUSHROOMS. Using different varieties gives amazing color and complex taste and texture to my marinated mushroom dish. Wash the mushrooms at the last moment before cooking, and cut the big ones in pieces. Place in a large nonreactive pan.

Peel and cut A LARGE (10-OUNCE) MILD ONION into 12 wedges, separate the pieces, and place in the pan with the mushrooms. Add at least 3 TABLESPOONS OF SLICED GARLIC and a bouquet garni, made with A LITTLE BUNCH OF PARSLEY, some FRESH THYME, and A COUPLE OF BAY LEAVES tied together. Add A TEASPOON OF FRESHLY GROUND BLACK PEPPER and A TEASPOON OF WHOLE CORIANDER SEED to the pot. A good CUP OF SHARP WHITE WINE is very good with this, or if the wine is too soft (less acidic), add 2 TABLESPOONS OF RED WINE VINEGAR. Add ⅓ CUP OF GOOD OLIVE OIL, along with plenty of SALT. Bring the mixture to a strong boil, cover, reduce the heat, and continue boiling for 25 to 30 minutes. Let cool, and serve with FRESH PARSLEY sprinkled on top, and maybe a little EXTRA-VIRGIN OLIVE OIL.

The marinated mushrooms can be eaten as soon as they are cooked and will keep at least one week in the refrigerator. Serve as an hors d'oeuvre or as a garnish for meat or fish. The same recipe can be made with regular white domestic mushrooms or cremini mushrooms.

GRATIN DAUPHINOIS

YIELD: 6 SERVINGS

A seminal dish for me is *gratin dauphinois*, which consists of thinly sliced potatoes that are combined with milk, cream, garlic, salt, and pepper, brought to a boil on top of the stove, and transformed into a glorious golden gratin with a cheese crust.

The gratins I enjoyed as a child came from my two aunts, my cousin Merret, and my mother. All of these formidable women prepared *gratin dauphinois,* with various taste results, but I loved different things about most of them: the simplicity of my mother's; the richness of my Aunt Hélène's; the finesse of Merret's. But it was the gratin from Tante Aimée, from Valence, that was my favorite—I am not sure why. She would serve it with veal roast, which was perfect with it.

Dauphinois defines an area of France around Grenoble, the town at the bottom of the Alps. This gratin is a specialty of the area, and it is considered an abomination to put cheese on top. Yet, in other parts of France, Lyon for example, people do top the potatoes with cheese. My mother always put Gruyère on top and made the dish entirely with milk. In many of the Michelin 3-star restaurants—from Troisgros, near Grenoble, to Bocuse in Lyon—it is usually prepared with heavy cream rather than milk, and no cheese. Subsequently, it glazes beautifully. My mother's gratin would not have glazed as well, so she topped it with grated Swiss cheese for the look as well as for the taste.

I have had *gratin dauphinois* with eggs in it, and with precooked potatoes, neither to my liking. I do not like it prepared just with heavy cream—it is much too rich—or just with milk, which makes it too lean. I recommend a mixture of milk and cream; about 2½ cups of milk for 1 cup of heavy cream gives a beautiful result. In this recipe, I use half-and-half, which works out to be about the same ratio you would achieve if you used part milk and part cream.

The good thing about *gratin dauphinois* is that leftovers are great the day after. When I was a kid, there was often a big *gratin dauphinois* my mother prepared for special family dinners. Since we had no refrigerator, the leftover gratin was kept in the cellar overnight with a towel on top to keep the flies away. The following day, it was a special lunch for my father. The leftover gratin had to be at room temperature and served with a salad of curly endive tossed with a dressing of garlic, mustard, salt, pepper, red wine vinegar, and peanut oil. I have come to love my gratins the day after as much as my father did. The room-temperature *dauphinois* is served on the same plate with the cool (but not cold) salad and a glass of Côtes du Rhône or Zinfandel. Lunch usually finishes with a piece of goat cheese or a wedge of Reblochon cheese, from the Savoie.

The potatoes are very important in the *gratin dauphinois*. Boiling potatoes, like Red Bliss, are my favorite choice for this dish. It is essential to peel the potatoes, rinse them under cool water, and then cover them with water. This much can be done the day before and the potatoes refrigerated in the water. Be certain they are totally submerged in the water, as any areas not submerged will discolor.

It is anathema to slice the potatoes ahead and wash the slices. When potato slices are washed, they release some of their starch, which is needed for the texture of the *gratin dauphinois*, and the gratin doesn't have the glossy, silky texture that it should have. If you are very proficient with a knife, cut the peeled and washed potatoes thinly into

With a Gratin dauphinois I could be a vegetarian

slices about ⅛-inch thick. If not, use a food processor with a slicing blade or a mandoline to slice the potatoes.

This dish is excellent with roast chicken, roasted veal, or grilled leg of lamb. Make certain that you save enough to enjoy the following day with garlicky salad for lunch, just like my father did and just like I do each time I prepare *gratin dauphinois*.

For six people, slice about 2 POUNDS OF PEELED POTATOES, and put them in a large saucepan (do not wash the slices). Add about 1 QUART OF HALF-AND-HALF, 1½ TEASPOONS OF FINELY CHOPPED GARLIC, a good amount of GROUND BLACK PEPPERCORNS (although Julia would have preferred white!), and SALT. Mix together, and bring the mixture to a boil on top of the stove. Make sure to stir it well with a wooden spatula to separate the slices of potato, which tend to stick together. As the mixture comes to a boil, scrape the bottom of the saucepan to prevent the potatoes from sticking to it. When it gets close to the boil, the mixture will thicken and get creamy.

Let the potatoes bubble for a minute or so, and then pour them into a 6 to 8 cup buttered gratin dish. Sprinkle about ½ CUP OF FINELY GRATED SWISS CHEESE (Gruyère, Jarlsberg, or Emmenthaler) and 1 TABLESPOON OF GRATED PARMESAN CHEESE on top. Plan to bake the gratin far enough in advance so that it can sit for a while before serving, as it is too hot and bubbly when it emerges from the oven to be served right away.

Preheat the oven to 400°F. Bake the gratin for about 1 hour. It should be beautifully glazed when ready. Let rest and cool for about 30 minutes before serving. If not ready to serve at this point, keep, uncovered, in a 160 to 170°F oven until serving time.

Mashed Potatoes

Mashed potatoes are frequent fare on French family tables. Most of the time they are simply coarsely mashed with butter and milk. They are ubiquitous in restaurants, from the unpretentious, inexpensive ones to the very expensive 3-stars, with slight differences from one restaurant to another and each telling you they make the best version.

In Paris many years ago, a specific process was used to mash potatoes quickly. The drained potatoes were placed in one layer on a *tamis,* a flat sieve shaped like a drum and very taut. On that very fine screen, we used a big, round, heavy pestle, called a "mushroom," made of hard wood to rapidly push the potatoes through the sieve. It was important that the "mushroom" pound straight down on the potatoes in a fast up-and-down motion rather than smear them back and forth, which would have made the potatoes stringy, rubbery, or "cordy." Smearing potatoes was a capital sin!

My favorite mashed potatoes are a mix from my Paris restaurant training and from my family tradition of home cooking. Peel the potatoes (I like Yukon Gold or Yellow Finn) and cut each into two or three chunks, depending on size. Rinse under cold water, place in a pan with enough cold water to cover and a good dash of salt. Add peeled garlic—one clove for each pound of potatoes—which is what my Aunt Aimée always did. This garlic, mashed with the potatoes after cooking, lends a very faint, delicate taste of garlic to the dish.

Tatan Aimée's mashed potatoes were the best

I always make extra mashed potatoes, so that I have enough to prepare a favorite leftover recipe that Gloria loves. It is called *pommes mont d'or,* or golden hill potatoes. Made with leftover mashed potatoes, eggs, and grated Swiss and Parmesan cheeses, it puffs in the oven, like a soufflé-gratin.

———————————————— ❊ ————————————————

Boil 1½ POUNDS OF POTATOES gently for about 30 minutes, until they are really tender, and then drain them right away and mash them. Spoon the drained, cooked potatoes into a ricer, which duplicates exactly the same movement as the *tamis,* and press down on it rapidly, so the potatoes are pushed right through. Return the mashed potatoes to the saucepan, place them over medium heat on top of the stove and, stirring occasionally with a sturdy wooden spatula to keep them from sticking, dry them out for a minute or so. Then, add about ¾ STICK (6 TABLE-SPOONS) OF SWEET BUTTER of the best quality to the mixture.

Remove the pan from the heat and work the mixture with the wooden spatula until the butter is well incorporated. Return to stovetop and, over low heat, mix in ½ CUP OR MORE OF HOT MILK, depending on how soft you like your mashed potatoes, and SALT AND PEPPER to taste. By now, the mixture will be soft and creamy. Next, using a sturdy whisk, whip the potatoes into a *pomme mousseline,* or mousselike mixture, a light, creamy, smooth, and silky puree. Taste for salt, and, finally, spoon the potatoes into a bowl and place in the top of a double boiler. Smooth the top surface of the potatoes, and pour on A FEW TABLESPOONS OF HOT MILK to moisten the top and prevent the potatoes from discoloring or forming a crust. The milk will eventually soak in to the potatoes and can be stirred in thoroughly at serving time. The potatoes can be kept warm over simmering water for an hour or so. Alternatively, set the potatoes aside in a bowl, and reheat in a microwave oven at the last moment.

GOLDEN HILL POTATOES ❊ (POMMES MONT D'OR)

For about 2½ CUPS OF COLD MASHED POTATOES beat 3 EGGS, and stir them in to the potatoes along with 1 CUP OF GRATED SWISS CHEESE. Butter a gratin dish, spread the potato mixture evenly in the dish, and sprinkle A LITTLE PARMESAN CHEESE on top. Keep refrigerated until ready to use.

Preheat the oven to 400°F. Bake for 35 to 45 minutes to have a "golden hill" of beautifully crusted, golden potatoes raised almost like a soufflé. This makes a great accompaniment to roasted poultry, steak, or a lamb chop.

RISOTTO WITH TOMATO BROUILLADE

If I had to choose one starch—which I hope I will never have to—it would probably be either potatoes or pasta, with potatoes having a slight edge. My wife would certainly choose rice in any form—from rice soup to rice with chicken to rice fritters to rice pudding.

Gloria particularly likes risotto, and I often prepare it for the two of us when I don't have anything planned for dinner. In summer, I often combine rice with herbs and tomato and another great favorite of hers, eggs, and make a tomato *brouillade*, a coarse scrambled-egg dish specific to Provence. This consists of a lot of fresh tomatoes sautéed briefly, finished with eggs, and served on Boston lettuce leaves with a sprinkling of olive oil. This is a great lunch dish, and *brouillade* is best served lukewarm or at room temperature.

At some point, I decided to mix my risotto with the tomato *brouillade* to make the ultimate comfort dish. When I make risotto, I use small roundish rice from Italy or the south of France, although the dish works well made with Thai rice, too. In restaurants, risotto is often partially made ahead. The rice is cooked covered until it absorbs about half the liquid needed for the risotto. Then, when the dish is ordered, more liquid—chicken stock, vegetable stock, fish stock, or water—is added a little at a time to finish the risotto in the classic way.

Risotto absorbs an enormous amount of liquid because when adding small portions of liquid to hot rice, uncovered, while stirring it, much of the liquid evaporates. When the rice is covered, there is no evaporation, and so much less liquid is needed. In my recipe, I first cook equal amounts of the rice and chicken stock, covered, until the stock is absorbed by the rice. Then I finish the risotto by adding small amounts of stock at a time and cooking the rice, uncovered, until it is done. My risotto can be served on its own, as can the tomato *brouillade*, but here they are combined for a luscious, creamy outcome.

For risotto serving four people, cook ½ CUP OF CHOPPED ONION in 2 TABLESPOONS OF OLIVE OIL in a skillet for a minute or so over high heat, just until the onion begins to take on a little bit of color. Add 1¼ CUPS OF SMALL ROUND-GRAINED RICE (RISOTTO-TYPE), 1¼ CUPS OF CHICKEN STOCK, and A GOOD DASH OF SALT AND PEPPER. Cover, and boil gently for 7 or 8 minutes, or until the mixture is dry again. You can continue with the recipe here, or you can set the rice aside at this point and finish it just before serving. If continuing to cook it now, start the tomatoes while the rice cooks.

For the *brouillade* you will need about 2 CUPS OF CUBED TOMA-TOES. Halve 1 or 2 ripe tomatoes (depending on size), squeeze out the seeds, and cut the flesh into 1-inch pieces. Heat about 2 TABLESPOONS

Gloria loves risotto and tomato brouillade for lunch with a green salad

OF OLIVE OIL in a skillet over medium-high heat. Add about ⅓ CUP OF CHOPPED ONION to the oil, cook for 30 seconds or so, and then add the tomato cubes, 1 TEASPOON OF CHOPPED GARLIC, and SALT AND PEPPER to taste. Cook gently for 7 to 8 minutes, uncovered, so the juice evaporates and the taste becomes concentrated. The recipe can be made ahead to this point. Meanwhile, beat 4 EGGS in a bowl with SALT AND PEPPER, and set aside.

To continue preparing the rice, add about ⅓ CUP OF CHICKEN STOCK, stir it in, and cook over medium to high heat, uncovered, for a few minutes, stirring occasionally, until the liquid is absorbed. Add ADDITIONAL STOCK, about ⅓ CUP AT A TIME, until you have added A TOTAL OF ABOUT 2½ CUPS OF LIQUID. This will take another 10 minutes or so after the initial 8 minutes of cooking. I like my rice slightly al dente but not raw in the center at the end of the cooking time. Taste, and add salt and pepper, if needed. Add 2 TABLESPOONS OF UNSALTED BUTTER, 3 TABLESPOONS OF GRATED PARMESAN CHEESE, and mix well to make the risotto creamy and moist. If a little more liquid is required, add it.

To finish the *brouillade:* With the tomato sauce still over the heat and hot, add the eggs to it, and stir gently with a spatula or wooden spoon until the eggs have coagulated nicely and are still quite moist. Add 2 TABLESPOONS OF CHOPPED CHIVES to the egg mixture.

Have four hot plates ready, either soup plates or dinner plates. Divide the risotto among the plates, making a nest in the center. Spoon the *brouillade* into the middle of the rice on the plates. Sprinkle each serving with about ⅓ CUP OF PITTED, DICED, OIL-CURED BLACK OLIVES, and serve immediately.

GRATIN OF PASTA

YIELD: 4 SERVINGS

Lyon has been the center of the silk industry for many centuries, beginning in the sixteenth century when the Italians lived in the place that is now "old Lyon" in France. Old Lyon is an extraordinary place now, an antique city with tiny streets not suitable for cars, and great churches dating back to the tenth and eleventh centuries. There are hundreds of small, authentic *bouchons* (bistros) that daily serve chitterling sausages, *cervelas* (hot salami) with potato salad, tripe, steak with french fries, and gratins of macaroni similar to our macaroni and cheese. This is the ordinary fare of Lyon, and you will find these gratins in establishments ranging from the 3-star restaurant of Bocuse to the most humble café. The gratins always contain Gruyère cheese. Sometimes there will be greens—spinach or Swiss chard—mixed into the pasta, and often diced ham, and there may even be a sprinkling of tomato throughout. There are variations from one bistro to the next throughout Lyon.

The pasta is always cooked ahead, then drained and cooled off under cold water to stop the cooking. Of course, if you plan to prepare a gratin and your guests are already there, you can cook the pasta, drain it, and assemble the dish immediately. Since the whole mixture is hot, it will take much less time to cook than if the pasta is prepared ahead and cooled. Conventionally, the pasta is combined just before baking with a light cream sauce made with milk, as my mother made hers.

For four people, you should have about 2 CUPS OF PENNE. This will make a fairly large gratin. Cook the penne, covered, in about 2 1/2 QUARTS OF SALTED BOILING WATER for about 15 minutes, or according to the package instructions for al dente pasta, since cooking time differs from brand to brand and from domestic to imported pastas. At this point, the penne should be cooked but still firm to the bite. You should have about 4 cups of pasta. Drain in a colander, and then rinse under cold water. Drain again, and transfer to a buttered 6-cup gratin dish. Sprinkle the penne with SALT, FRESHLY GROUND BLACK PEPPER, 2 TABLESPOONS OF MINCED CHIVES, and 2 TEASPOONS OF OLIVE OIL. Mix well.

When ready to bake the gratin, preheat the broiler. Grate 1 CUP (on the large hole side of a box grater) OF SWISS CHEESE (Jarlsberg, Emmenthaler, or either of these mixed with a little mozzarella and cheddar, if you like). Mix with 3 TABLESPOONS OF GRATED PARMESAN CHEESE and 1 TEASPOON OF PAPRIKA.

Make a light white sauce: Melt 2 TABLESPOONS OF BUTTER in a saucepan, and add 1 1/2 TABLESPOONS OF FLOUR. Cook over medium to high heat for about 30 seconds, mixing with a whisk. Add 2 1/2 CUPS OF MILK, mix well, and bring to a boil, whisking occasionally. Add SALT AND PEPPER.

Pour the sauce over the pasta in the dish, and sprinkle the grated cheese mixture on top. Place the gratin under the hot broiler about 6 inches from the heat source, and cook for 6 to 8 minutes if the sauce is hot when poured over the pasta, or 12 to 15 minutes if the sauce is cold when combined with the pasta. The gratin is ready when the sauce is bubbling and the cheese on top is golden brown and crusty. Serve right away.

HOME COOKING VERSUS
Restaurant Cooking

Sometimes I would gladly give up dinner at a starred restaurant for real home-cooked food; other times I crave the excitement and sophistication provided by a great restaurant. Although a French saying asserts that *"On ne mange bien que chez soi,"* or "we eat well only at home," travel guides like the Michelin maintain that the greatest food is found in starred restaurants.

It is evident that there are differences between home cooking and restaurant cooking, and the great cooks—whether home cooks or professionals—are those who are aware of these dissimilarities and shape their cooking accordingly. Home cooks want to please their families and are usually attached to a few recipes, often passed verbally from generation to generation. Professional cooks learn dishes and techniques that may or may not be part of their background and recipes that may not coincide with their sense of taste. These recipes are sometimes varied based on the whims of the customers and the habits of the restaurants where they work. Restaurant cooks have to be more objective in their point of view and learn how to detach themselves from the food.

First and foremost, good home cooks want to please their families while staying within a given budget. They have to make dishes with tastes familiar to the family and usually drawn from a specific region with well-defined traditions. They can't be too adventurous, and if so, only occasionally. They recognize the dishes that are well suited to the home kitchen and realize that many requiring elaborate decoration, for example, should be left to professionals. Likewise, good restaurant chefs know that slow-simmering, stewlike concoctions with natural juices lend themselves better to the attentive care of the home kitchen than to the professional kitchen, where the emphasis is on greater variety and creativity.

There are obvious differences in equipment. Restaurant kitchens have large refrigeration systems with walk-in iceboxes that enable the chef to have on hand a great diversity of products organized to be used in many different ways. A professional kitchen has machines that slice, chop, and puree ingredients with a speed and proficiency not attainable with conventional food processors or blenders. Powerful vacuum-packing machines and special vessels with temperatures controlled to a single degree allow the chef to cook dishes *sous-vide,* or "under vacuum," slowly in a water bath with accuracy not attainable in the home kitchen. Commercial steam-injected ovens cook food under pressure in minutes, and restaurant stoves have a BTU several times greater than that provided by a home stove. Restaurant grills are so powerful that you can grill a thin fillet of fish without it sticking to the grill, as it usually does on even the best-designed home grill. To illustrate further, making blackened fish entails placing fish in an extremely hot skillet, thus generating a lot of smoke. Although this is feasible with the exhaust systems in commercial kitchens, the same procedure would probably blacken the normal kitchen along with the fish. Likewise, deep-frying in fryers with highly controlled temperatures and automatically filtered oil will yield better results and is great in a professional kitchen, but is not advisable in an apartment or home kitchen, where the resulting smell can be most offensive. In addition, used cooking oil doesn't keep well, and the home cook, who may not want to deep-fry every day, must discard oil that becomes rancid before it is needed again.

Expensive ingredients, like truffles, foie gras, and walnut oil, do not fare well either in the hands of home cooks, who may need them only once and must store the remainder. Conversely, dealing in volume, professional cooks use these ingredients often and can create dishes to utilize these ingredients.

Professional chefs usually have several purveyors supplying them with exotic new ingredients every season of the year. Home cooks, on the other hand, probably have to make do with what the neighborhood market or farm stand has to offer. Having an outlet for different kinds of meat, professional chefs order larger cuts—a leg of veal, for example—and divide them. They use the bones and trimmings for stock, grind the trimmings for pâtés, and reserve the better segments for scaloppini or roasts. Home cooks must settle for the limited variety and smaller cuts available at the supermarket or from a local butcher.

Repetition of techniques and recipes enables the professionals to find faster and better ways to prepare a dish than is possible for those who make the dish only occasionally. Professional cooks can touch a roast with their finger, for example, and, depending on its springiness, know whether it is rare, medium, or well done. Anyone cooking ten or fifteen racks of lamb each night can, after a few days, determine the "doneness" of the meat just by touching it. "Practice makes perfect," and home cooks don't have the opportunity to practice enough. The repetition of preparing a dish again and again gives professionals an in-depth knowledge of that dish and enables them to try small variations until a perfect result is achieved.

Relying on a team of coworkers, the chef obtains brioche from the pastry chef, cleaned fish fillets from the butcher, *velouté* from the sauce cook, and cleaned vegetables from his apprentices when preparing a complex dish, like a *coulibiac* of salmon. Continuous exposure

Some recipes are always prepared more successfully at home

to food and the exchange of ideas with coworkers deepens one's understanding as does watching and learning from fellow cooks.

Yet the technical knowledge of restaurant chefs doesn't necessarily equate with sensitivity and a flair for taste. Even though the repetition of their tasks enables them to work quickly and have a fairly good comprehension of food in general, many chefs don't have the sensitivity, "touch," or the taste buds to make them anything but ordinary cooks. Home cooks don't have to contend with the quantities of food that professional cooks must deal with and the boredom associated with making the same dish over and over again. Home cooks prepare only food that they like to eat or want to prepare for someone else.

Even though the professional has a greater variety of ingredients to choose from, they aren't always of the best quality, except in superlative restaurants, and often must be bought in quantity for use in several future meals. The home cook can choose with great attention each ingredient needed for a particular meal. Some home cooks who live in the country have their own gardens or have access to farm markets, enabling them to use the freshest possible ingredients—freshly picked corn, perhaps—for that evening's dinner, while it is difficult for the professional to match this. Therefore, although the professional may be able to create dishes of greater complexity, the home cook—using top-quality products at their flavor peak—can focus on producing simple, perfect dishes.

Because of the time and attention a home cook can devote to one dish for four to six guests, some recipes are always prepared more successfully at home. Cooking a veal roast slowly in a cast-iron Dutch oven, where a dish can be gently braised, basted, then served in its natural juices, is extremely difficult to do in a restaurant kitchen.

There is close contact with all aspects of a meal for the home cook. When one person is responsible for the entire process of choosing, buying, cooking, and serving the food, there is an unbroken continuity that often accounts for a consistent, harmonious meal, with one point of view. The home cook who goes to the market with one specific meal in mind can make selections based on freshness, availability, and price but also in accordance with the kitchen equipment. With only one oven, four burners, and a limited number of serving pieces, the home cook must calculate the menu carefully to conform to these limitations.

The same limitations apply to labor. Timing is essential. There is usually only one person in the home kitchen preparing the meal, and if the cook is to eat with the guests, one must plan accordingly. The entire meal has to be orchestrated and viewed as a whole. The table must be set, the flowers arranged, the wine opened, and the bread sliced. Conversely, a professional chef handles one specific area of the kitchen, concentrating on a few dishes and repeating these over and over again without considering the meal as a whole. The meal prepared in the home kitchen represents a more personal expression of what one person can cook since he or she has probably worked alone on every aspect of the dinner, down to the selection of the china and silver to be used on the table.

Certain dishes, especially those with several accompanying garnishes, are more easily prepared in a restaurant, however. There is more

The Joy of cooking is present in the home cook as well as the restaurant cook

emphasis on decoration, as many people can work on the same plate, making designs in the sauce and arranging ingredients in an intricate fashion around the plate. Trying this at home would be counterproductive. If it takes several cooks a few minutes to garnish one plate in a restaurant, it will take the home cook working alone five to six times longer to do so at home. By the time individual plates are prepared and served to six guests, the food is cold. Even a professional chef's attempts to duplicate a meal at home in the same way that it is prepared at the restaurant often backfire. It is more likely that the home cook will be most successful when serving the main dish bourgeois-style, arranging the food appetizingly on a large platter and encouraging guests to help themselves.

Yet the love of cooking and the joy of giving are present in both the good home cook and the good professional cook. I've had the pleasure of dining many times in the home of André Soltner, the great professional chef/owner of the famed Lutèce restaurant until he sold it in 1994. He cooks in a different way at home—closer, perhaps, to the cooking of his Alsatian mother. He understands the limitations of both spheres of cooking and abides by them.

Both types of cooking are satisfying at their best, and both are dependent on ingredients. Farmers who raise stock and grow vegetables can make do without cooks, but the reverse is not true. Farmers are essential providers, but cooks are only transformers. Yet Levi-Strauss says that the process of cooking is "the process by which nature is transformed into culture," and cooks are certainly important in the cultural makeup of a country. Furthermore, the ultimate goal of the professional as well as the home cook is the same: to please. As Brillat-Savarin says in one of his famous aphorisms, "To invite friends to dine at home is to make oneself responsible for their well-being for as long as they are under our roofs."

Desserts and Other Sweets

This chapter includes some of the favorite sweets served at my house, although Gloria and I rarely have dessert as part of an everyday meal. We usually finish our meals with a piece of cheese and, sometimes, fruit. Jam is included in this chapter, as well as PÂTE DE FRUITS, which are concentrated fruit-jelly morsels that are famous throughout France, and CARAMELS, which I am addicted to and keep in my refrigerator or freezer for serving as a kind of after-dinner petit four. BUGNES are special to my childhood, as they are served in Lyon on Fat Tuesday each year. The CHEESE, FRUIT, AND NUT PLATTER is really our classic dessert in summer, when fruit is at its best, and we enjoy it with roasted nuts. The crêpes, or PANNEQUETS, are in the old style, large and stuffed here with a strawberry-rhubarb nectar for a great dessert, and also used as the base for trout caviar, which makes a superb first course and shows the versatility of the crêpe. Classic desserts, like the APPLE TART WITH HAZELNUT FRANGIPANE or CHOCOLATE TARTLETS, are served at my house when we have guests and want to extend our menu and make it more elegant and festive.

Chocolate Tartlet with Candied Grapefruit Peel, recipe on page 236

BERRY POTPOURRI

What could be more summery than a mixture of ripe berries at peak taste, smell, and color? This is the ideal dessert for a big party; it is fast to make, and everyone loves it, especially if you serve the fruit with a moist and buttery piece of homemade pound cake and some crème fraîche.

I always try to go to local markets to buy berries. Instead of mixing them with sugar, I combine them with seedless raspberry jam or apricot preserves, a little lemon juice, and a julienne of lemon peel. In my garden I have spearmint, English mint, and peppermint, and I like to add some to my berries to lend fragrance, flavor, and coolness to the dessert.

The fresher and riper the berries, the better the result. Do not use frozen fruit, because all the juices are released as it thaws and the fruit becomes soft and mushy. I use frozen berries when I make a coulis, a puree, or a sherbet, however, because frozen berries have often been picked and frozen at their peak and are sometimes more flavorful than the fresh ones.

The raspberries should have a deep red color and the strawberries should be bright red, with no green near the stems or tips, an indication that they are not ripe. Your nose will tell you whether your strawberries and raspberries are ripe and at peak. As for blueberries, taste them and sort through them, discarding pieces of leaves and stems or spoiled berries.

Buy 1 PINT EACH OF BLUEBERRIES, RASPBERRIES, AND STRAWBERRIES, and, if available, ½ PINT OF BLACKBERRIES OR BOYSENBERRIES. Sort the berries, and if they are dirty, wash them before you remove the hulls, so the water doesn't get inside the berries. If the strawberries are large, cut them into 4 or 6 pieces, but leave small berries whole. Remove a DOZEN STRIPS OF LEMON ZEST with a vegetable peeler, stack them up together, and cut them into a fine julienne. Sprinkle into the bowl you will use for serving the berries.

Add ONE 12-OUNCE JAR OF SEEDLESS RASPBERRY JAM to the bowl, and whisk in 2 OR 3 TABLESPOONS OF LEMON JUICE. Make A COUPLE OF TABLESPOONS OF MINT CHIFFONADE by stacking up an assortment of mint leaves, rolling them together, and cutting them into fine shredded pieces. Add to the bowl, mix well, and then add the strawberries and blueberries (the firmer fruit) first. Toss, and at the last moment add the raspberries and blackberries, and toss again gently to avoid crushing the berries. Serve with A SLICE OF MOIST POUND CAKE (page 250) and A TABLESPOON OF SOUR CREAM, WHIPPED CREAM, OR CRÈME FRAÎCHE.

Berries are the soul of Summer

Pannequets (Crêpes) with Strawberry-Rhubarb Nectar

When Claudine was small, I often made crêpes for her, which she loved with sweet as well as savory fillings. When she went to boarding school, she would sometimes come home over the weekend with a friend, and they would get up in the morning, sit at the kitchen counter, and ask me to make crêpes, which we sometimes call by their older name, *pannequets,* especially when they contain a filling. Crêpes can be made very quickly. The first thing I would do is to put a nonstick skillet containing a pat of butter on the stove. By the time the butter had melted, I had time to grab a handful of flour and put it in a bowl, break an egg on top, stir, and whisk in some milk and a dash each of sugar and salt. I would then whisk the melted butter from the skillet into my batter and start my first crêpe. As the hot crêpes came out of the pan, I would pass them to the girls, and they would select from an assortment of homemade jams—apricot, strawberry, and sometimes peach, plum, or cherry—to spread on them, fold, and eat while warm.

I like to make large crêpes, cooking them in at least an 8-inch nonstick skillet, so one or two per person is more than enough. Crêpes are very versatile; they can be used as a vehicle for any leftover chicken or fish with a cream sauce, with the filled crêpes rolled up into a kind of cannoli and baked in a gratin dish. Crêpes also can be shredded and added to soup, used to line a soufflé dish for a crêpe soufflé, or as a base for serving with your best caviar. They can be made ahead and frozen, although I don't advocate this, since they take a long while to defrost and only a few minutes to make from scratch.

I mostly use crêpes as a dessert, preparing them here for serving with rhubarb and strawberries and a dusting of confectioners' sugar on top. Serve these with sour cream or yogurt. My market sells a Greek yogurt made with whole milk that is as good as sour cream.

I have rhubarb in my garden in the spring, and I often cook it with strawberries. Use red rhubarb with thick stems. Remember that the leaves of rhubarb are poisonous, so be sure these are removed. Buy strawberries that are not too big, and cut off the stem end, taking a little more if the berry is green, but keep the berries whole. This rhubarb and strawberry stew can also be served on its own with a cookie, a piece of sponge cake, or a slice of brioche.

I also make crêpes to serve as a savory with delicious trout caviar that we get from the Sunburst Trout Company in North Carolina. Their caviar is of the highest quality, with small, crunchy, nutty eggs, and we spread it on crêpes that we serve with sour cream and a little chopped chives on top. It makes a first-class first course.

For the sugar syrup, combine 1 CUP OF SUGAR and 1 CUP OF WATER in a saucepan wide enough (about 8 inches) so the fruit will not be piled too thickly as it cooks. Bring to a boil, and continue boiling until the mixture reaches the softball stage at about 240°F. This will take 8 to 10 minutes.

During this time, prepare the fruit. You will need about 1 POUND OF RHUBARB, 4 thick, bright red ribs or so, depending on the size, cut into 1-inch slices. Hull about ½ POUND OF SMALL STRAWBERRIES, about 12 in all. When the sugar-water mixture is at 240°F, drop in the

all children love crêpes stuffed with jam

rhubarb. Stir gently with a spatula, let come back just to a boil, and boil for 1 minute. Add the berries, and mix them in gently. Return the syrup to a boil, then cover and set off the heat immediately. The fruit will soften and sink into the syrup. When lukewarm, transfer to a bowl, and refrigerate. It is ready to be served.

For 8 large crêpes, measure out ½ CUP OF ALL-PURPOSE FLOUR, and put it in the bowl of a food processor with 2 EGGS, 1 TABLESPOON OF GRAPESEED, PEANUT, OR CANOLA OIL, 1 TEASPOON OF SUGAR, A DASH OF SALT, ¾ CUP OF MILK, and 1 TABLESPOON OF DARK RUM. Process for 8 to 10 seconds, until smooth. The yield will be 1⅔ cup of batter.

Using an 8-inch nonstick skillet, melt 1 GENEROUS TEASPOON OF UNSALTED BUTTER over medium to high heat. When it is sizzling, add 3 tablespoons to ¼ cup of batter to the pan and tilt the pan to spread it around as quickly as you can. It should not be too thin. Cook for about 1 minute, until brown and lacy around the edges. Flip the crêpe, or turn it over with your fingers and a fork, and cook it on the other side for about 1 minute. It should be well browned with a crunchy, buttery edge. One or two crêpes per person is certainly enough, and they can be served slightly warm (if necessary, warm them in the microwave) or at room temperature.

For each serving, gently crush 2 crêpes lightly in your hands to form a loose ball resembling a wrinkled handkerchief, and place in the center of a dessert plate. Sprinkle a little CONFECTIONERS' SUGAR on top, and surround the crêpe "ball" with small spoonfuls of strawberry-rhubarb nectar interspersed with DABS OF YOGURT. Pass additional nectar at the table.

Alternatively, arrange two overlapping crêpes on each dessert plate, and spoon some of the fruit from the nectar into the center of the crêpes. Fold in the edges of the crêpes to enclose the filling. Dust with powdered sugar, and spoon a little mound of yogurt alongside. Pass additional nectar at the table for spooning over the crêpes.

CRÊPES WITH TROUT CAVIAR

Prepare the crêpes as directed in the first recipe. Warm up a crêpe, place it on a plate, and push it gently in the middle, so it is slightly wrinkled. Spread with a good 2 TABLESPOONS OF SOUR CREAM and cover as lavishly as you can with TROUT CAVIAR OR BLACK CAVIAR (osetra, sevruga, or beluga). Sprinkle with CHOPPED MILD ONION AND FRESH CHIVES, and serve immediately.

Apple Tart with Hazelnut Frangipane

The quintessential dessert that my mother prepared at her restaurant and at home was an apple tart. There are many recipes for this classic dessert, some made with the simplest dough and some with puff pastry, sweet dough, or even bread dough. My mother's special recipe was made with flour, baking powder, a little butter, and lard. She would add water to this mixture, and the dough was so soft that she spread it out with her hands into her apple tart mold and arranged quartered apples on top. Because of the baking powder, the dough would rise a little between the apples, making a soft dough on top that was brown underneath, a cross between a brioche and a standard dough. She served this plain, seasoned only with the butter and sugar she sprinkled on top of the tart before she baked it.

I like very thin butter dough, made by mixing very cold butter with flour for a minimum amount of time, so there are still fairly large pieces of butter visible in the dough. The secret of this dough, whether it is made by hand or in a food processor, is to make it quickly and roll it immediately into a thin circle or oval.

In this recipe, I spread a frangipane on the dough before adding the apples. Consisting of hazelnuts, sugar, an egg, and a bit of butter, this creamy mixture coats the dough. My favorite apples, available in the fall at my market, are Russet apples, but any apple that you like can be used. Finally, the baked apple tart is glazed with my own apricot preserves, which contain chunks of fruit.

For the dough, mix about 1¼ CUPS OF ALL-PURPOSE FLOUR with A STICK (8 TABLESPOONS) OF VERY COLD UNSALTED BUTTER cut into thin slices, about 1 TEASPOON OF SUGAR, and A DASH OF SALT. Work this quickly with your fingertips for 15 or 20 seconds, until the butter is in pieces about the size of dried beans. Add about 2 TABLESPOONS OF COLD WATER, stir it into the mixture for a few seconds, and then gather up the dough onto a sheet of plastic wrap, and press it into a flat disk shape.

Line a cookie sheet or jelly roll pan with a silicon pad. Roll the dough out on a lightly floured surface into a rectangle about 15 inches long by 10 inches wide, with rough edges. Roll the dough up partially on your rolling pin, and then unroll it directly onto the lined pan.

Preheat the oven to 375°F. For the frangipane, roast ¾ TO 1 CUP OF SHELLED HAZELNUTS on a cookie sheet for 7 to 8 minutes. Transfer the nuts to a food processor, add ¼ CUP OF SUGAR, 1 EGG, A GOOD TABLESPOON OF SWEET BUTTER, and a little DASH OF VANILLA EXTRACT. Process until a creamy paste forms. Spread the frangipane on the dough, stopping about 1½ inches from the outer edge on all sides.

Peel 4 LARGE RUSSET APPLES (A COUPLE OF POUNDS), remove the cores, and cut them into thin (about ½ inch) slices. Arrange them attractively in a slightly overlapping pattern, like the tiles of a roof, on the pastry dough, so that the apples cover the frangipane underneath. Fold the edge of the dough back over the apples to make a 1 to 1½ inch border of dough. Increase the oven temperature to 400°F.

Sprinkle 2 OR 3 TABLESPOONS OF SUGAR over the apples, letting a little of the sugar fall on the dough border to help crystallize the dough. Break 2 TABLESPOONS OF SWEET BUTTER into pieces, and scatter them over the tart. Bake for 1 hour. The dough should be nicely crystallized all over. If the dough cracks a little during baking and the juices run onto the tray, slide a little piece of aluminum foil under the affected area to keep the juices from burning on the tray.

Remove the finished tart from the oven, and cool on a rack until lukewarm. Dilute 1 CUP OF THE BEST APRICOT PRESERVES with 1 TABLESPOON OF CALVADOS OR WATER, and glaze the surface of the tart, spreading it carefully on the apples with the underside of a spoon. Serve at room temperature, cut into little wedges, just plain or with sour cream, crème fraîche, or ice cream.

Chocolate Tartlets with Candied Grapefruit Peel

YIELD: 8 TARTLETS   PICTURED ON PAGE 226

Gloria is not fond of chocolate desserts, and her preference in chocolate is for milk chocolate. I like deep, strong, dark chocolate with about 70 percent cocoa—the richer the better. A big treat for me as a kid was a piece of *ficelle*, or "string" bread, which is classically about 1½ inches thick, but long, like a baguette. These thin *ficelles* were very crunchy, and my brothers and I loved to eat a piece of the bread with a bar of dark chocolate. It was Meunier chocolate, a bar of chocolate made up of ten equal-size connected segments. We would shove those pieces into our bread, or eat the chocolate along with it. It was our special 4 P.M. snack when we got home from school.

I've always made chocolate desserts, everything from chocolate soufflés to chocolate mousses, and a few years ago I started making hot chocolate terrines or small cakes with runny or soft chocolate centers. In this recipe, the chocolate mixture is poured into small tartlet molds lined with a delicate sweet dough, or *pâte sucrée,* and baked. This dough can also be used to make cookies, and it is the classic dough for fruit tarts made with precooked shells filled with pastry cream and fresh fruit, from orange segments to raspberries. I make my *pâte sucrée* in a food processor, roll it out, and then let it rest awhile before cooking it; otherwise it tends to shrink or bubble too much while cooking.

Uncooked tart shells can be frozen and cooked as needed right from the freezer. Conventionally, a piece of aluminum foil is pressed into dough shells before they are baked to prevent the sides from collapsing, although this isn't necessary for my recipe. Be sure to press the dough firmly into the molds with your thumbs, so it extends up the sides of the molds to the edge. Any excess can be crushed and cut even with the top edge of the mold, making it adhere enough so that the dough doesn't collapse in the oven. This dough is like modeling clay, so any tears can be patched by pressing the dough into place where needed, something you can't do with *pâte brisée* or puff pastry.

I usually melt my chocolate in a microwave oven, heating it a couple of times, for 1 minute first and then letting it sit briefly before microwaving it for another minute. This is a good way to melt all the ingredients for my filling. When the chocolate mixture is in the tartlet shells, it takes only 5 minutes to cook in a 350°F oven. These tartlets shouldn't be overcooked; the centers should be slightly soft and creamy.

The tartlets can be served on their own, although I like them with candied peels of citrus fruit. Orange is the classic choice with chocolate, but I also like candied grapefruit peel, which has a little bitterness that I like with the chocolate. The candied peels are relatively easy to make and can be kept in a jar in the refrigerator for months. They make a nice garnish for a soufflé and can be added to fruit desserts.

The recipe is composed of three preparations: the tartlet dough, which can be used for other things; the chocolate mixture, which also can be cooked on its own in small soufflé molds; and the candied grapefruit peel, which can also be served on its own or with other desserts.

dark chocolate and crunchy baguette, the snack of my youth

CHOCOLATE TARTLETS | For the dough, put 1 CUP OF ALL-PURPOSE FLOUR in the bowl of a food processor with ¾ STICK (6 TABLESPOONS) OF BUTTER cut into pieces, 3 TABLESPOONS OF CONFECTIONERS' SUGAR, and A DASH OF SALT. Process for 10 to 15 seconds, until well mixed. In a bowl, mix together 1 LARGE EGG YOLK and 1 TABLESPOON OF MILK. Add to the processor bowl, and process for another 10 to 15 seconds for the dough to form into a ball. Roll out immediately or chill for an hour or so before rolling.

I like to roll this dough between sheets of plastic wrap (which works quite well) to a thickness of about ¼ inch. It should be rolled no thicker than that. (There probably will be extra dough, which can be frozen for later use or shaped into small cookies and baked.)

Arrange the 8 tartlet molds (3-inch diameter with fluted edges), one next to the other on the table. Roll the dough between the plastic wrap, and then remove the top sheet of plastic wrap. Lift the remaining piece of plastic wrap supporting the dough, and invert the dough over the tartlet molds. Using your fingers, carefully press the dough through the plastic wrap into the molds. Peel off the plastic wrap, and trim off excess dough between the molds. Using your thumbs, press the dough into the molds until it adheres well, patching where necessary. Refrigerate for a couple of hours. Bake in a preheated 350°F oven for about 10 minutes. The dough should be just light golden. Leave the oven on.

Meanwhile, put 5 OUNCES OF RICH BITTERSWEET OR SEMI-SWEET CHOCOLATE, in pieces, into a 4-cup glass measuring cup with ⅔ OF A STICK OF BUTTER cut into pieces, and 2 TABLESPOONS OF SUGAR. Microwave for 1 minute, leave it for a few minutes, and then microwave it again for 1 minute. It should be all melted. In a small bowl, mix together 1 WHOLE EGG and 1 EGG YOLK. Whisk the egg into the chocolate mixture to combine.

Divide the chocolate mixture among the 8 tartlet molds, and return the molds to the oven for 5 minutes. The tarts should be eaten at room temperature, not ice cold, so the centers are slightly soft inside.

CANDIED GRAPEFRUIT PEEL | Remove 8 TO 10 STRIPS OF PEEL FROM A GRAPEFRUIT (preferably a Ruby Red) with a vegetable peeler. Take care to remove only the surface of the skin or zest and not the white pith underneath. Pile the strips up together, and cut into ¼-inch-thick julienne strips. Drop the strips into a saucepan, cover with about 2 CUPS OF WATER, bring to a boil, and boil for 5 or 10 seconds. Drain in a strainer, and run the strips under cold water in the strainer.

Return the drained julienne to the saucepan with about ⅓ CUP OF SUGAR and about ⅔ CUP OF WATER. Bring to a boil, and cook, uncovered, until the mixture starts to thicken, about 8 minutes. At this point, the syrup should be a bit gooey and thick, and the peels should be almost transparent.

Spread a good ⅓ CUP OF SUGAR onto a tray. Remove the grapefruit peel from the pan with a fork and put it in the sugar on the tray, Toss carefully in the sugar, separating the pieces with your fingers and a fork, so the individual strands are coated with the sugar. Transfer them to a plate, and let dry for at least half an hour. Store refrigerated, in a jar with a tight-fitting lid. To serve with the chocolate tartlets, sprinkle a few strands of the julienned peel in the center of each tartlet.

there is freedom and innovation in flower painting

BUGNES

Similar to beignets, *bugnes* are a specialty of Lyon made on Mardi Gras or Fat Tuesday, the last day before the forty days of Lent leading up to Easter. When I was a child, my mother and my aunts would make *bugnes* that day, and all the bistros in Lyon featured big platters of *bugnes* on all the tables for their customers to celebrate Mardi Gras.

The *bugne* is a fritter made with strips of thin dough flavored sometimes with orange water, rum, or vanilla, and deep-fried. Some are made with yeast, which makes them spongier, so they absorb much more oil. I like my version without yeast. Drier and crisper, it is covered generously with confectioners' sugar. I also like to sprinkle vanilla sugar on top of my *bugnes*. I always have some leftover vanilla beans that I put in a jar at home, cover with sugar, and leave there to flavor the sugar. I dust some of it on top of my *bugnes*, and then sprinkle on some confectioners' sugar, which sticks to them. Beautifully dusted with the sugar is just as I remember them when my brother and I fought over big plates of them at the restaurant.

I make my *bugne* dough in a food processor and then roll it very thin. My mother mixed the ingredients in a bowl with a wooden spatula to make a dough that was quite soft. My dough is also soft, and it can be used right away, although it is a bit more tender when made ahead and allowed to rest. Use flour and a rolling pin to roll the dough, even though it can practically be extended with your hands because it is soft and easy to roll.

Bugnes are fried in regular vegetable oil; I like to use corn, peanut, or canola oil. They cook quite fast, in a couple of minutes. If you are making a lot of them, the best way to drain them is on a wire rack, and they should sit there for a minute or two to cool off a little before you put them on plates and dust them with the sugar. In Lyon, they are usually cut with a wooden wheel with a crinkled edge, called a jagger or a *roulette* in French. Sometimes, however, they are cut by hand with a knife into various shapes, usually little rectangles about one inch wide and four or five inches long. Often a lengthwise incision of about two inches is cut down the middle of these dough rectangles, so that when they cook the dough separates, giving it a nice look and crunchy edge. Also, sometimes one of the ends of the rectangle is pulled through the incision to create a ribbonlike shape that is classic for *bugnes*.

Well-made *bugnes* will stay crisp for hours at room temperature. Bistro customers enjoy them with a glass of white wine or a *blanc cassis*, which is a little cream of black currant mixed with white wine. I made *bugnes* for my daughter, Claudine, when she was small, and I look forward to making them for my granddaughter.

————————————————

Measure out 1½ CUPS (ABOUT 8 OUNCES) OF ALL-PURPOSE FLOUR, picking it up directly into measuring cups from the bin, leveling it off, and putting it into the bowl of a food processor with A DASH OF SALT, 3 TABLESPOONS OF SUGAR, and ½ STICK (4 TABLESPOONS) OF ROOM-TEMPERATURE BUTTER. Process for about 10 seconds, and then add 1 TEASPOON OF LEMON ZEST, 1 TABLESPOON OF DARK RUM, 1 TEASPOON OF VANILLA EXTRACT, and 2 EGGS. Blend for another 15 seconds, or until a soft dough forms. Transfer the dough to a lightly floured work surface to roll immediately, or let it rest, refrigerated, for an hour or so.

Place a piece of dough about the size of an egg on top of the floured surface. Spread it with your hands, then turn the dough over, and extend it further with your hands. Spread or roll lightly with a wooden rolling pin until the dough is no more than ⅛ inch thick. Using a crinkle-edged wheel or a knife, cut into rectangles (or other shapes, if you prefer) about 1 inch wide by 4 inches long. Leave as is, or cut a 2-inch slit down the center of each rectangle to make a hole that will spread open as it cooks. If you like, slip one of the ends of the rectangle through the slit, and pull it back to give a kind of spiral or corkscrew effect to the strips of dough. Work quickly because the dough is very soft and delicate to handle. If you have a problem with it, cool the dough in the refrigerator to firm it up.

In a shallow skillet, heat about 3 CUPS OF VEGETABLE OIL to 325 to 350°F. The oil should be about 1½ inches deep. Put 8 to 10 of the dough strips into the hot oil at a time, and cook for about 1 minute on one side, then turn with tongs and continue cooking for another minute. Lift the *bugnes* from the oil, and place on a wire rack while you repeat the process with the remaining dough.

Sprinkle the cooked pastries with A LITTLE REGULAR SUGAR, VANILLA SUGAR (if you have it), or, if you like, CINNAMON SUGAR (not used in France, but appreciated in the United States). Then sprinkle with CONFECTIONERS' SUGAR on both sides. Pile up on plates, the *bugnes* are now ready to be enjoyed.

CANNELÉ

Cannelé are little cookies from the Bordeaux area of France. They are called *cannelé* after the little molds they are cooked in, which are fluted or ridged, and they are made from crêpe batter with a lot of sugar, which eventually crystallizes on the outside during the long cooking, making them crusty on the outside and creamy inside. You can find *cannelé* in the markets of southern France, and they are highly addictive. They are always the fastest disappearing dessert on my buffet table.

Cannelé pans are tiny, ridged muffin pans, with each cavity holding about 1½ tablespoons of batter. I remember as a child that the original molds were made of copper lined with tin, and it was difficult to get those cookies out of the molds. The chef seasoned them, like iron skillets for omelets, and no one was allowed to use these molds for anything else but *cannelé*. Now, with molds made of silicon (the same nonstick material used for cookie sheet liners) and sold under the brand name of Gastroflex, *cannelé* are a cinch to make. They should have a crisp exterior and a soft interior, and they are best at room temperature. They do not freeze well.

I have varied my recipe a few times, like not letting the batter rest as long as the recipe indicates, but I've concluded that it is necessary for the batter to rest for at least twelve hours or a bit longer.

Put 2 TABLESPOONS OF BUTTER and 1 CUP OF MILK in a large glass bowl, and microwave for about 1 minute, until the mixture is warm and the butter has melted. Combine A LARGE WHOLE EGG, 1 EGG YOLK, 1 TEASPOON OF VANILLA (if using Mexican vanilla, which is quite strong) or 1½ TO 2 TEASPOONS OF REGULAR VANILLA EXTRACT, and ¼ CUP OF DARK RUM. Mix well with a whisk. Add to the milk-butter mixture, and mix well.

In another bowl large enough to hold the finished batter, combine ½ CUP OF ALL-PURPOSE FLOUR with ⅔ CUP OF SUGAR. Pour about ⅓ of the milk mixture into the flour-sugar mixture, and mix well with a whisk. (The goal is to make a thick mixture that becomes very smooth as the whisk threads go through it. If all the liquid is added at once, the batter will be lumpy and require straining.) Add the rest of the liquid to this thick mixture, and mix it in; there is no danger of it becoming lumpy at this point. Cover, and refrigerate overnight.

The next day, preheat the oven to 300°F. Fill the small Gastroflex molds with the batter. Notice that the batter has thickened slightly. There should be enough to make 20 to 22 cookies. Bake for about 30 minutes, and then increase the heat to 400°F, and continue baking for another 40 minutes or so, until the *cannelé* are puffy, dark brown, and crystallized on top and around the sides. Let cool on a wire rack for a few minutes, and then unmold and cool on the rack until serving time.

CARAMELS

When I was a kid, one of the big treats that my brothers and I had on Sundays after church was a little bag of caramels. Some were hard, some were very soft, and my preference was for the softer ones. We usually bought these at a *patisserie de boutique* in Bourg-en-Bresse, a store that specialized in making caramels along with puffed and blown sugar confections, chocolate candies, and small fancy pastries.

I have tried through the years to make caramels, with different rates of success. The recipe that I have here is almost foolproof, and the caramels freeze quite well. All you need is a good candy thermometer, which is available at any hardware store. I mold my caramels in a nonstick loaf pan. I oil the pan very lightly, and put a strip of lightly oiled parchment paper in the middle with the ends extending over the

edges of the pan. The paper should be oiled on both sides, underneath because it makes it adhere well to the pan, and on top to make the caramel mixture release.

If you like your caramels very soft, take them out of the refrigerator a couple of hours before eating. I like to package them individually in plastic wrap or little squares of waxed paper or parchment paper. Bring these as a treat when you are invited out to dinner; they always get raves.

I also love chocolate caramels, usually made by adding cocoa powder to the mix. Yet dipping one end of each caramel from the recipe below into the best quality melted bittersweet chocolate is easier and yields a great result.

Combine 1 STICK OF BUTTER (8 TABLESPOONS), cut into pieces, and ¹⁄₂ CUP OF HEAVY CREAM in a small glass bowl, and microwave for about 1¹⁄₂ minutes, until hot. Set aside.

In a small stainless steel saucepan, combine 3 TABLESPOONS OF WATER, ¹⁄₄ CUP OF LIGHT CORN SYRUP, and 1 CUP OF SUGAR. Stir just enough to moisten the sugar. The goal is to avoid having the mixture collect on the sides of the pan, which happens when you mix with a spoon or shake the pan; it tends to crystallize where it touches the sides. Pouring the water and syrup in first and then adding the sugar allows it to get wet by the liquid without splattering the sides. Heat over medium-high heat until the mixture comes to a boil, and then cover with a lid for a minute or so to create moisture in the pan and melt any sugar that may be clinging to the pan sides.

Place the candy thermometer in the pan, and cook for about 6 minutes, or until the sugar reaches a temperature of 320°F, at which point it will begin to take on a light golden color around the edge. At that point, pour the butter and cream mixture gradually into the pan, adding about a third of it at a time, and stir, using the base of your thermometer to incorporate it. Continue cooking for another 5 or 6 minutes, until the mixture reaches a temperature of 240°F on the thermometer, the soft-ball stage. (This will create a relatively soft caramel; if you bring the temperature to about 245°F, the caramels will be hard. So make adjustments based on your own tastes.)

As soon as the caramel reaches the desired temperature, pour into an oiled loaf pan with a base that measures about 7¹⁄₂ inches long by about 3¹⁄₂ inches wide lined with a strip of oiled parchment paper that is long enough to extend up and slightly over either end of the pan. Cool, uncovered, at room temperature, for about 4 hours. Invert and unmold onto a sheet of parchment paper or waxed paper (pulling gently on the paper strips, if necessary). If the caramel is still too soft to work with, refrigerate for an hour or so to firm it up. Cut into strips about ³⁄₄ inch wide, and then cut the strips into 1¹⁄₂-inch lengths to have about 20 caramels. Wrap in squares of plastic wrap or waxed paper and enjoy immediately, or refrigerate or freeze for eating later.

To make chocolate-dipped caramels, let the cut caramels firm up overnight, uncovered, in the refrigerator. Drop A FEW SQUARES OF YOUR BEST BITTERSWEET CHOCOLATE into a glass measuring cup and microwave for 1 minute. Wait a few minutes, and then microwave the chocolate for another minute. It should be thoroughly melted at this point.

Dip one end of each caramel into the melted chocolate, so that it covers about half the caramel, and place the caramels on a piece of parchment paper to harden. When cool and hard, wrap the caramels and store them in the refrigerator.

the best buttery caramel ever!

CARAMEL CUSTARD

YIELD: 4 TO 6 SERVINGS

One of my oldest and most favorite desserts is crème caramel, or caramel custard, what the home cook calls flan in France and Spain. When I was a kid, it was flavored with vanilla or coffee, and sometimes with chocolate.

The flans that my mother made were cooked at fairly high temperatures. They had a little caramel in the bottom, and she used to serve them in her restaurant. I remember that the outside looked like a sponge, full of tiny holes. I realize now that it was because it was cooked at a high temperature in a bain-marie, with water boiling all around it, so the protein in the dessert expanded, and it ended up with air bubbles around its surface.

In all my years in the kitchen, I have tasted hundreds of caramel custards, some richer than others, some made with cream only, some containing egg yolks and/or whole eggs as well as milk, and some with starch or evaporated milk, as is done in South America. Crème brûlée, a richer version of caramel custard that is more English than French, is often made with cream, sugar, and egg yolks. It is a softer custard than crème caramel and is eaten unmolded. A crust of sugar is made just before serving by sprinkling light brown sugar on top of the custard and sliding the dessert under a broiler or "burning" the topping with a torch until a crust is formed.

When I was a young man working in Paris, we cooked *petit pots de crème* flavored with vanilla, chocolate, or coffee. Molded in beautiful little custard cups with a handle on each side, these were basically the texture of a crème brûlée, but without the sugar crust on top.

Petit pots, caramel custard, and crème brûlée are variations of the same dessert; the *petit pots* have no caramel on the top or in the bottom, the caramel custard has caramel in the bottom, and the crème brûlée has a sugar crust on top. Along with the apple tart and the chocolate mousse, these variations are probably the quintessential desserts of a good family home in France.

Caramel custard is a great dessert choice, first because it is best when made the day before. Second, everyone loves caramel custard—smooth and shivering, with a silky, shiny sauce underneath. Set out in the middle of the table, there is nothing better or more beautiful. Simple, straightforward, and satisfying, this elegant dessert is perfect served with a couple of cookies or a slice of brioche. I flavor my caramel custards with thick, soft vanilla beans from Tahiti. I always have the best results when I use organic eggs from a farm next door. Higher in lecithin, the yolks are thicker, creamier, and better tasting than most supermarket eggs. If you don't have a farm near your house, look for organic eggs at your market; they yield excellent results.

Slit ONE VANILLA BEAN in half lengthwise with a sharp knife and place both halves cut side up on the table. Then, using the dull side of the knife, scrape out the creamy seeds inside. You should get about 1 teaspoon of vanilla pulp from the inside of one large bean, which is about the amount needed for the recipe. Process the pulp in a mini-chop with A COUPLE OF TABLESPOONS OF SUGAR to keep it loose, and put the leftover shells of the beans in a jar of sugar to flavor it. At some point, the bean shells become dry enough to be processed in a mini-chop with some sugar to create a powder, which is a great way to flavor desserts.

Use a whisk to mix 5 LARGE EGGS with ⅓ CUP OF SUGAR, 2½ CUPS OF MILK, and ½ CUP OF HEAVY CREAM. Strain through a fine sieve into a bowl, and then add the vanilla pulp and sugar mixture, plus 1 TEASPOON OF VANILLA EXTRACT. Years ago we used to bring the milk to a boil (and you can still do this), because one out of three or four times, the milk would curdle. Milk is much more reliable nowadays and can be used without boiling it first.

The caramel is an important part of the recipe. Put ⅓ CUP OF SUGAR and A COUPLE OF TABLESPOONS OF WATER in a small saucepan or skillet, preferably stainless steel, and bring to a boil. Stir the mixture for a few seconds first to be sure it is well combined, then boil on top of the stove without stirring; if you stir it, the sugar tends to crystallize into cloudy, whitish lumps. However, it is not a catastrophe if the sugar crystallizes. Sugar crystallizes at about 310°F before it takes on a caramel color. If you keep cooking the mixture beyond 310°, the crystallized lumps will melt, and it will turn a caramel color. You can have a pale, light caramel, or a deeper, yellower caramel, my preference, and this occurs when the mixture reaches about 317°. Any crystals will have melted at this point.

Conventionally, custards are cooked at 350°F. Pour the caramel into a 5- or 6-cup clear ovenproof glass or porcelain custard or soufflé molds. It should cover the bottom of the mold in a clear, shiny, thick layer. Set aside for 5 or 10 minutes to harden, and then pour the custard on top. Set the mold in the center of a saucepan or roasting pan large enough so that there are 2 or 3 inches between the edge of the mold and the sides of the pan. Add tepid water to the pan, so it comes almost up to the level of the custard in the mold, and put the pan in the oven. The water around the mold should not reach a temperature of more than 160 to 170°F. This is a slow cooking process, but it produces custard with a wonderful texture, absolutely smooth and silky, and without the spongelike holes of the custards of my youth.

Bake the custard for about 1 hour, or until it is set. To see if it is ready, test with a toothpick or a paring knife. If using a knife, take care not to plunge it completely through the custard and into the caramel underneath. It could create a hole in the top of the unmolded custard that may cause the custard to split open after unmolding. When a toothpick or knife inserted into the center of the custard comes out clean, the custard is cooked. Let cool for 1 hour, and then cover tightly and refrigerate until you are ready to unmold it. It is better made a day ahead.

To unmold the custard, run a sharp knife around the edge of the mold, taking care not to twist the blade and cut into the custard. I find that pushing my knife in tightly against the edge of the mold at one spot and then holding the knife steady and rotating the mold (rather than moving the knife) gives a better result. Cover with the serving plate you plan to use, and invert the mold. If not serving the custard immediately, leave the mold in place, and refrigerate until serving time.

At serving time, remove the mold, and spoon the custard with some of the surrounding caramel onto dessert dishes. Served with your favorite cookie or a slice of soft, buttery brioche, there is nothing better.

the dessert of my Sunday meal as a child

Cheesecake with Peach and Blueberry Sauce

YIELD: ONE 8-INCH CAKE (8 TO 12 SERVINGS, DEPENDING ON PORTION SIZE)

I never heard of cheesecake when I lived in France as a child. I had tasted *tarte au fromage*, or cheese tart, in the Alsace region of France. Baked in a regular piecrust, it was savory, made with farmer's cheese, salt, pepper, eggs, and, sometimes, herbs and Swiss or Parmesan cheese. One version or another of this tart is still served in Alsace. My first exposure to cheesecake as a dessert was when I worked at the St. Regis Hotel in New York. It was served plain, with strawberries and whipped cream, or with chocolate sauce. I was also introduced to graham cracker crusts there, and these have been a component of my cheesecakes ever since.

I first learned how to make cheesecake when I went to visit Craig Claiborne at his house in East Hampton in the early 1960s, and I have prepared this recipe many times through the years and put it in books. I have probably made half a dozen versions of cheesecake, but this is the recipe that Gloria has been making for more than forty years—and she doesn't want any other version. She wants this one. It is a true favorite in our family.

I think it is important to cook the cheesecake in a bain-marie, that is with water around it, so it doesn't cook too fast and doesn't expand, staying dense and compact. Some people object to its cracking on top, but I think it looks appetizing this way. It's important to let the cheesecake rest for at least 30 minutes in the oven after it has cooked, so that it can cool slightly and set. Then it should cool completely or at least for a few hours before it is unmolded.

There are different sauces that I have served with this cheesecake, from a custard to a chocolate to a berry sauce. Yet I still return to a fruit sauce that is best done with peach or apricot jam and fresh blueberries. For the jam, I use my own, cooking peaches (see Peach Jam, page 252) or apricots slowly in the oven, so there are pieces of fruit in the jam. There is no comparison between this and what is available at the market.

PEACH AND BLUEBERRY SAUCE | Combine 1½ CUPS OF PEACH OR APRICOT JAM with about 1 TEASPOON OF GRATED LEMON ZEST, the JUICE OF THAT LEMON, and 2 OR 3 TABLESPOONS OF COGNAC. The cognac will dilute the sauce to the right consistency, but if you want it a little thinner, add 1 TABLESPOON OF WATER. When it the way you like it, stir in 1½ CUPS OF SORTED FRESH BLUEBERRIES. (Do not use frozen blueberries in the sauce; they look fine when frozen, but they bleed as they thaw and will discolor the sauce.) The fresh berries will appear as dark blue jewels in the golden sauce.

CHEESECAKE | Use an 8-inch pan, either a ring mold, a springform pan, or a soufflé dish that is at least 4 inches deep for the cheesecake. In the bowl of a food processor, combine about ½ CUP OF GRAHAM CRACKER CRUMBS, about 2 TABLESPOONS OF ROOM-TEMPERATURE UNSALTED BUTTER, and 1 TABLESPOON OF LIGHT BROWN SUGAR. Process until crumbly. Press the mixture into the bottom of the cheesecake mold.

Preheat the oven to 325°F. I think a food processor is best for making the cheesecake. Put FOUR 8-OUNCE PACKAGES OF CREAM CHEESE into the bowl of a food processor with 2 TABLESPOONS OF FRESH LEMON JUICE, 1 TEASPOON OF VANILLA EXTRACT, and about 1 CUP SUGAR. Process these ingredients until smooth, and then add 4 LARGE EGGS (preferably organic). Process for 1 minute or so, or until the mixture is smooth again. Pour it into your mold, and place the mold in a large skillet or roasting pan. Surround the mold with water from the tap, so that it extends at least halfway up the sides of the mold. Bake for a good hour. The cheesecake should be almost set at this point. Turn off the oven and allow the cheesecake to remain there for 30 minutes longer. Then cool completely on a rack before unmolding directly onto a serving platter.

If you are using a springform pan, the cake will come out very easily. If removing it from a soufflé mold seems difficult, run a paring knife around the edge of the mold, taking care to press the sharp blade of the knife against the mold, so it doesn't cut into the cake. The best way to do this is to hold the knife steady in the correct position, and then, using the other hand, turn the mold around against the knife to loosen the cake around the edges. Place a serving plate on top of the cake, and invert it to unmold. If it doesn't want to come out easily, run a kitchen towel under hot water and wrap it around the mold to help it release.

At serving time, top the cheesecake with most of the sauce, letting it fall over the sides with some of the blueberries. Serve in wedges with a little extra sauce. This is a very rich cake, and a small portion goes a long way. A family favorite, we enjoy it mostly in the fall or winter.

POUND CAKE

We didn't have many desserts when I was growing up, and the classics were only for special occasions. These included the apple tart, chocolate mousse, floating island, caramel custard, and the pound cake, which was a real standard.

In France, this traditional cake is called *quatre-quarts*, meaning "four-fourths," because it is made with the same amount of flour, sugar, eggs, and butter. Yet it was made in different ways by my mother, aunt, and cousin, with some versions lighter, some denser. Some were more like a classic genoise, the basic sponge cake used by most bakers, while others were closer to the *gateau de Savoie*, where the yolks are beaten with the sugar and the flour, and beaten egg whites are incorporated into the batter. I like my pound cake relatively dense, but still make it with a little *levure Alsacienne*, or Alsatian yeast, which is actually baking powder.

Pound cake is used in different types of fruit desserts, even cut into little strips and served as cookies with ice cream. It is also used to line charlotte molds before filling them with a mousse or a buttercream, and I have added candied peel of lemon, lime, and grapefruit to the batter to make a standard fruitcake. I also love pound cake soaked with a lemon syrup. However, my favorite preparation is slices dipped in a strong espresso coffee.

This recipe makes a large pound cake that should be baked in an 8-or-10-cup mold, either a conventional loaf pan or a round pan. The batter can also be divided between two 4 or 5 cup pans, to produce two pound cakes. If cooking them in two smaller pans, they will bake faster.

Put about 2½ STICKS (10 OUNCES) OF SOFT UNSALTED BUTTER in a mixing bowl with 1¼ CUPS OF SUGAR and 1 TEASPOON OF VANILLA EXTRACT. Beat by hand or in a mixer fitted with a whisk attachment for about 1 minute. Add 6 LARGE EGGS, preferably organic, beating them in two at a time for 10 or 15 seconds before adding more. When the eggs are incorporated, add 2½ CUPS OF CAKE FLOUR. (Cake flour tends to form lumps, so it is a good idea to sift it. For this recipe, I measured the flour before sifting, so there are probably 2 or 3 tablespoons more flour by the time it is sifted.) Incorporate the flour, and then add ¼ CUP OF MILK and A DASH OF SALT. Beat with the whisk for 20 seconds or so.

Preheat the oven to 325°F. Butter an 8-or 10-cup loaf pan, and put a strip of parchment paper in the bottom that extends up the sides and beyond the edge of the pan to help with the unmolding later. Pour the batter into the pan, and place the pan on a cookie sheet. Bake for about 1 hour. It should just be set inside. Test for doneness with a toothpick. If the toothpick emerges wet, turn off the oven and allow the cake to sit in the oven for 20 or 30 minutes, or until it is set. Cool completely on a rack before unmolding. Cut into slices and serve.

The cake freezes well. Cut it into large chunks, freeze, and thaw as needed. Not too sweet, it is always a great accompaniment to your café au lait or expresso for breakfast.

Peach Jam

In the summer, we always make jam from strawberries, cherries, apricots, and sometimes from plums and peaches. I have tried several methods of making jam, often with my friend Jean-Claude at his Catskill house in the summer.

We go and pick apricot "seconds" at a farm near his home. These are from fruit that falls off the trees—some are small, some big, some ripe, and some not so ripe. We use the ripe fruit first, making a small batch of jam with it. The other fruit is used as it ripens, and within a few days the jam is made. Often we break the pits of the apricots, remove the "almonds" from the inside, and slice them to put in our jam for a nutty, crunchy, slightly bitter taste.

Cheap commercial jams have up to twice as much sugar as fruit. Conventionally, homemade jam has a one-to-one ratio. Our jam, made with really ripe fruit, has half the amount of sugar as fruit, and it is still quite sweet.

We experimented a number of years ago with a recipe someone gave me for "strawberries cooked in the sun." The idea was to cook sugar and water to about a soft boil, 130 to 140°F and then add hulled strawberries (big ones cut in half; small ones left whole) to the sugar syrup mixture, and then bring this to a boil for a few seconds. This mixture would then be poured into a large roasting pan, covered with a screen to keep out insects, and placed out in the sun for three or four days. The liquid around the berries evaporates slowly until it reaches the point where the berries, which were very soft to begin with, start to plump again as they absorb some of the syrup. When ready, the syrup will be relatively heavy and thick when the pan is inclined back and forth. At this point, the jam is poured into clean jars, covered with a little melted wax, and stored in the cellar for the winter. The resulting jam is good, but after experimenting with different fruits, we have found an even easier way to make jam. Our recipe follows.

Use 4 POUNDS OF VERY RIPE UNPEELED PEACHES, cutting each into 8 wedges and discarding the pits. Put the fruit in a bowl, and stir in 2 POUNDS OF SUGAR. Leave the mixture at room temperature for an hour or so, tossing it occasionally. By then practically all the sugar will have melted and mixed with the fruit.

Pour the mixture into a roasting pan to form a layer $1\frac{1}{2}$ to 2 inches thick. Place in a very low (about 160°F) oven to evaporate most of the syrupy liquid around the fruit. The oven is even more reliable than the sun, and you should "cook" the jam this way for about 24 hours. Check occasionally to see if the mixture is thick enough; it should have the texture of corn syrup.

Arrange the jars and lids on a cookie sheet, and place in a 170°F oven for 15 minutes to sterilize them. Alternatively, sterilize the jars in the dishwasher, running them through the rinse cycle. Spoon the jam into the sterilized jars. To keep the jam for winter, melt some beeswax, which comes in tablets, and pour a $\frac{1}{2}$-inch layer on top of the hot jam. It will harden within an hour or so, becoming opaque and white. Cover each jar with a lid, and place in the cellar until ready to use.

This is a great recipe to serve with baguettes, croissants, or brioche for breakfast, or as a dessert on top of ice cream, or with a ripe piece of Gorgonzola cheese.

Homemade Jams are always the best

Cheese, Fruit, and Nut Platter

YIELD: 8 TO 10 SERVINGS

Very often when we have a big backyard party at my house, or a picnic at the beach or the river, I serve a big wooden board filled with a mixture of cheese, fresh fruit, dried fruit, and nuts, with crunchy baguettes on the side. The combination of nuts with grapes or apples, for example, along with a piece of Gorgonzola or a wedge of Brie or aged Gouda, is possibly the best way to finish a meal. Often, I sprinkle some whole basil leaves on top for taste as well as a color accent.

Follow the seasons. Use hard cheese, like Parmesan, in warmer seasons, and soft cheese, like Brie or Stilton, when it is cooler. If your gathering is during the summer, add fresh apricots, cherries, grapes, white peaches, and the like, and in the fall, apple or pear quarters sprinkled with a few drops of lemon juice to prevent discoloration, and dotted with freshly ground black pepper.

Dried fruit, like figs, apricots, cherries, or cranberries, is wonderful, as are walnuts, almonds, hazelnuts, and Brazil nuts in the shell. Nuts roasted in their shells stay fresh for several weeks, not becoming rancid as they would out of the shell, and the roasting wonderfully intensifies their flavor. Spread the nuts in a roasting pan, and brown them in their shells in a 350 to 375°F oven for 12 to 15 minutes. Let cool for a while before serving, and don't forget the nutcracker.

Use ferns or maple leaves to line a big piece of barn wood, and arrange your CHEESES (2 OR 3 IN LARGE WEDGES OR WHOLE) on top first. Place some FRESH FRUIT, WHOLE OR IN WEDGES, around the cheese, and add DRIED FRUIT AND NUTS. Finally, sprinkle on some whole LEAVES OF BASIL, TARRAGON, or MINT. Let the guests enjoy themselves.

APRICOT AND RASPBERRY
PÂTE DE FRUITS (FRUIT PASTE)

YIELD: ABOUT 36 JELLIES

Pâte de fruits are very expensive in France. Usually made with pure fruit, they are sold in high-end *patisseries,* or pastry shops, or *chocolateries* when there is an abundance of fresh fruit, often by an establishment located in the south of France. These treats can be enjoyed anytime as a snack but are often served as a petit four at the end of an elegant meal. The highly concentrated fruit taste contains the fragrance and perfume of spring and the flavors of a summer orchard. This is the ultimate fruit taste but, sadly, these fruit paste confections are rarely available in the United States.

There are three ways for a fruit paste to set up and hold its shape. The first is through reduction, the bringing of the mixture of fruit to a paste by cooking it to 230° to 235°F, close to the soft crack temperature, to set up into a jellied state. This is not easily done at home. The boiling mixture goes to 210°F in a few minutes, but raising the temperature from 210° to 230°F may take as long as 2 hours, during which time it will darken, possibly scorch, and lose its bright color. In commercial operations, this is done with a vacuum system at relatively low temperatures to keep the color as well as retain the intensity of the fruit.

The second alternative is to use pectin to jell the fruit. It comes in powdered or liquid form in pouches. This approach works best with mixtures that are not too thick, like fruit juices or even jams. The fruit puree in this recipe is quite thick and concentrated, and the pectin doesn't work as well as a jelling agent as the third alternative—unflavored granulated gelatin.

Depending on its ripeness, moisture content, and acidity, some fruit jells better at certain times than others.

The finished fruit paste can be cut into different shapes and rolled in crystallized or sanding sugar. Readily available in France, crystallized sugar has crystals that are four to five times larger than regular table sugar here, which makes it cling to the *pâte de fruits* without melting. When we use regular or superfine granulated sugar for this purpose, it is so fine that if there is some moisture still left on the *pâte de fruits,* often the case, the sugar will melt and make the tops of the jellies wet. So keep the jellied mixture covered with plastic wrap and refrigerated. When ready to serve, cut it into shapes, and roll in granulated sugar before arranging on a platter.

Many pastry chefs make *pâte de fruits* from a puree of apples, high in pectin, to which other fruit puree is added along with a little more pectin. I make these confections with apricots and raspberries, my two favorite *pâte de fruits* short of quince, a fruit that is more readily available in France. I use less sugar than conventional *pâte de fruits* recipes, and I concentrate the taste of the apricots by using dried apricots with canned apricots and apricot jam. Peach jellies are made in the same way, using canned and dried peaches and peach jam. Strawberry *pâte de fruits* are made the same way as the raspberry paste. It takes one envelope of gelatin (two teaspoons), to jell a cup of the cooked fruit puree to the proper consistency.

APRICOT PÂTE DE FRUITS | Use A 15-OUNCE CAN OF HALVED APRICOTS IN SYRUP. Reserve the apricots and pour the syrup, about ¾ cup, into a medium saucepan. Add 12 DRIED APRICOTS, and bring to a boil. Cook for about 5 minutes, until most of the liquid has evaporated and the apricots are just moist.

Transfer the apricots to the bowl of a food processor and add the canned apricots, A 12-OUNCE JAR OF APRICOT PRESERVES, and

½ CUP OF SUGAR. Process for 10 to 20 seconds, or until the mixture is smooth. Transfer to a sturdy saucepan, and bring to a boil, stirring constantly with a rubber spatula; the mixture tends to stick and will scorch if not stirred as it comes to a boil. After the mixture is boiling well, it tends not to stick as much, but stir it with a spatula every minute or so. Cook for 8 to 10 minutes to reduce the liquid and concentrate the flavor.

Pour ⅓ CUP OF COLD WATER into a small glass bowl, and sprinkle 2 ENVELOPES (4 TEASPOONS) OF PLAIN GELATIN on top. The gelatin will sink into the water and get thoroughly moistened by it, with no white spots visible. If necessary, stir with the point of a knife. Microwave for 20 seconds, until the gelatin is melted. Stir into the hot apricot mixture. You should have about 2½ cups of the fruit puree. Pour into a lightly oiled rectangular loaf pan lined with a strip of waxed or parchment paper, lightly oiled underneath and with the ends extending beyond two ends of the pan to help in the unmolding of the *pâte de fruits*. The fruit mixture should be about ¾ inch thick. Cool for a couple of hours at room temperature, and then cover with plastic wrap and refrigerate overnight.

The following day, unmold the fruit paste in one block onto a sheet of plastic wrap, using the paper liner in the pan to help in the unmolding. Wrap it thoroughly in plastic wrap, and refrigerate until ready to use. When ready to serve, cut into strips about 1¼ inches wide and then into triangles or squares so you have between two and three dozen pieces, depending on size. Put about ½ CUP OF SUGAR in a bowl, and roll the jellies in the sugar until they are coated on all sides. Arrange on a platter, and serve.

RASPBERRY PÂTE DE FRUITS | Put TWO 12-OUNCE PACKAGES OF IQF (INDIVIDUALLY QUICK FROZEN) RASPBERRIES in a food processor with 1 CUP OF SUGAR and ONE 18-OUNCE JAR OF SEEDLESS RASPBERRY JAM. Process until smooth, and push through a food mill first to remove most of the seeds, and then through a strainer (not double mesh) set over a sturdy saucepan. Begin by banging the sides of the strainer with the palm of your hand or a wooden spatula to make the mixture "jump," so that most of it runs through before the seeds clog the holes. When most of the mixture has passed through the sieve, press with a rubber spatula to get as much puree from it as possible. You should have about 4 cups of puree.

Transfer the puree to a deep saucepan and bring to a boil, stirring constantly with a flexible rubber spatula so the puree doesn't stick to the bottom of the pan. When it comes to a strong boil, stir occasionally, and boil for 30 minutes (longer than the apricot mixture because the raspberry puree has a more liquid consistency) to reduce to about 3 cups and concentrate the taste.

Meanwhile, pour ½ CUP OF WATER into a small glass bowl, and sprinkle 3 ENVELOPES (2 TABLESPOONS) OF PLAIN GELATIN on top. Make sure that all the gelatin is moistened, and microwave for about 20 seconds. Combine with the raspberry puree. You should have about 3 cups. Pour into a lightly oiled loaf or square pan lined with a strip of parchment paper lightly oiled on the underside. Refrigerate overnight to dry, and proceed as you would for the apricot jellies. This makes about three dozen.

THE MOST FREQUENTLY ASKED QUESTIONS
in Cooking Classes

I love to teach cooking. During the 1970s and '80s, before appearing regularly on television, I used to spend up to forty weeks a year teaching in private cooking schools all over the country. I have been teaching at Boston University for more than twenty years and at The French Culinary Institute in New York for nearly that long, and I still enjoy giving classes at both places. Nothing is as good as being close to the students and getting a reaction firsthand, feeling the excitement and enthusiasm learning can bring. There can be no job as rewarding as this one. I always learn when I teach, and it forces me to keep current in regard to what is going on in the world of food.

Twenty years ago, the most genuine interest in cooking in the United States was generally found on the East and West Coasts. The incredible variety of restaurants in New York City, the sophistication of diners, the amazing ethnicity of the city, and the "everything is possible" attitude made it a magnet for chefs and restaurateurs, and it was one of the greatest food centers in the world. The opportunistic and spontaneous attitude of the West Coast joined with the availability of an amazing array of beautiful and fresh vegetables and fruits year-round that stimulated sight and smell, enticing people to the stove.

Today this food passion has spread throughout the entire country, and one may eat in stupendous restaurants from Chicago to Philadelphia and from Dallas to Miami. Weekly newspaper food sections, cookbooks, and cooking shows proliferate, and Americans are taking cooking classes in record numbers. However, if thirty years ago, 90 percent of attendees in these classes were females, cooking classes are now often 70 percent male. It seems that men have ventured into the once strictly female territory of the home kitchen and the once male-dominated world of professional cooking is now occupied by women who have turned to it as a career. Often my classes at Boston University and FCI consist of between 60 and 70 percent women looking for careers in the food industry.

Throughout the country, small cookware shops and cooking schools are doing well, and most colleges have now added extension programs in the culinary arts for people who want to sharpen their cooking skills or meet other "foodies." As a cooking teacher, I like people to ask questions. It makes the classes lively, friendly, fun, and relaxed, and usually one question leads to another. Following are the most frequently asked questions and my answers:

1. "CAN I FREEZE IT?" | I jokingly answer that "Can I freeze it?" will be the title of my next book! However, this is a question that is perfectly legitimate in some instances and doesn't make any sense in others. Certainly, soups, bases, stocks, and some meats, particularly raw meat, freeze perfectly well, while many vegetables, fruits, and pâtés are altered badly in the process. When we get fish fresh from the sea, we often vacuum-pack them or wrap them very tightly in plastic wrap and freeze them as quickly as possible. When ready to use, I defrost them very slowly in the refrigerator overnight with excellent results. Freeze as fast as possible, and defrost very slowly so you don't lose too much moisture. Make sure you place the food to be frozen in a freezer that is not too crowded. If you shove it into a place that is already very crowded with food, it will take much longer to freeze and bacteria can develop during the freezing process. Of course, when "Can I freeze it?" addresses itself to a just-finished, piping hot spinach soufflé, the question of freezing can be ludicrous!

2. "HOW FAR AHEAD CAN I PREPARE IT?" | As with the previous question, it sometimes makes sense and at other times it doesn't. Working people want to know when a dish can be partially prepared ahead and finished at the last moment. Probably 90 percent of dishes can sustain partial preparation ahead, but this varies with each dish.

Asparagus, for example, can be cooked ahead, particularly if you serve it cold, but better, it can be peeled ahead and cooked at the last moment, whereas most stews can be completely cooked ahead with their vegetables and just reheated at the last moment—with a gain in flavor as a bonus. Most professional kitchens work this way.

The so-called *mise en place* is where commis and prep cooks will peel vegetables, slice and arrange them, bone out fish, meat, prepare the stock, etc. This means that when the chef gets to the stove at mealtime, nothing is cooked but everything is ready to be cooked. So how long does it take you to grab a tablespoon of chopped shallots, put them in a skillet with a fillet of fish that is waiting there for you, add some sliced mushrooms, a dash of white wine, and finish it with herbs that are also ready for you? It will take only seconds to prepare, and a couple of minutes at the most to create something very fresh, because most of the ingredients are prepared ahead. It is a question of common sense. However, when one admits that a particular dish can be prepared ahead, the next question is, inevitably, "How far ahead?" Again, the answer can rarely be very specific. A freshly roasted chicken is best consumed soon after it comes out of the oven. If it is covered with aluminum foil, it steams and gets a reheated taste. It will not be as good within an hour and will slowly and gradually lose its "tastiness" as time goes on.

However, many dishes can be partially prepared a day ahead. Even a fish can be put in the cooking vessel with sliced mushrooms, herbs, onion, scallion, and tomatoes around it, along with butter and seasonings, and refrigerated for most of the day. Then in the evening, it can be sprinkled with white wine and baked for 20 or 30 minutes, depending on size.

3. THE QUESTION OF SUBSTITUTION IS OFTEN RAISED. | "Can I use margarine instead of butter?" There is no replacement for butter, especially if the butter is fresh and unsalted, but if it cannot be used, there is nothing better than oil: olive oil or, for a different flavor, maybe hazelnut or walnut oil, or a good peanut or canola oil to finish a dish or a salad.

"Can I use milk instead of cream?" Milk will give one result and cream another. Sometimes it is possible to substitute milk, sometimes it is not. I like a caramel custard made with milk rather than cream, which makes it too rich for my tastes. My mother made *gratin dauphinois* with milk only, but adding a little cream makes the dish better (see *Gratin Dauphinois*, page 212).

Often the answer cannot be generalized. "Can you use dried herbs in place of fresh herbs?" Dried parsley, dried chives, and dried chervil are totally flavorless, while thyme, laurel, and oregano are excellent dried. I like frozen baby peas, which are usually picked off the vine and put into a bath of salted water. The small ones, less starchy, come to the top of the water, while the larger, starchier peas sink to the bottom. So these tiny frozen peas can be very good, although not as good as their tiny, fresh counterparts. Also, there is nothing like fresh haricots verts, asparagus, and broccoli; these vegetables are never as good frozen.

cook with friends and share a glass of wine

4. "WHAT KIND OF KNIVES DO YOU USE?" | My answer to this is always "sharp knives." Whatever the brand or the metal—stainless, high carbon steel, or ceramic—a dull knife is useless. Less expensive knives with thinner blades are easier to sharpen than heavier, thicker-bladed knives. "How do you sharpen your knives?" Anything that cuts is made of tiny teeth, whether a scalpel or saw, and when you bang your knife on the table to chop, these teeth get a little out of whack. Running the blade of your knife on a sharpener realigns these teeth. However, after a while those tiny teeth get worn out and disappear. A new edge must then be formed on the blade, and this is done with a grinding stone, or the knives can be sent to a professional sharpener.

5. "DO YOU PREFER TO COOK ON A GAS OR ELECTRIC STOVE?" | Gas, most certainly! First, it is easier to control. There is something visceral about cooking on an open fire outside or in an old country kitchen, where you can see the flame. Yet I prefer an electric oven to a gas oven. The electric oven tends to stay more accurate and equal in temperature than a gas oven does.

6. "WHAT KIND OF POTS AND PANS DO YOU USE?" | There are so many choices of quality cookware on the market now that it is hard to go wrong. However, there are advantages and disadvantages to different materials: Copper is a great heat conductor but it is expensive and heavy. Make sure any copper pots you buy are all copper with a liner of stainless steel. Aluminum is a good heat transmitter, but unlined aluminum tends to discolor some food after a while, so buy thick, heavy aluminum lined with stainless steel. Stainless-steel pots tend to be lighter and easy to care for, but thin stainless-steel skillets develop black spots and burn the food. Yet stainless steel is what I prefer for bowls and other kitchen equipment. Cast iron is good but, unless used continually, it will rust and it also discolors some foods. Enameled cast iron is very good for slow cooking, but it is heavy, the enamel can chip if the pan is dropped, and, eventually, it discolors inside.

There are better and better nonstick pans. One from France, called Cybernox, looks like a stainless-steel pot, but it is nonstick. There are also pans called "permanent nonstick," which have a much stronger coating inside, and one can use some abrasive cleaners on them without damaging the nonstick surface. There are also silicon pads now for lining baking sheets. Cookies and other baked foods won't stick to these, so they are quite useful.

7. "CAN I DO IT IN THE FOOD PROCESSOR?" | This question applies generally to the techniques of mincing, chopping, and so forth, and the answer is "yes." To puree soups and certain vegetables, a food processor is fine. There are many examples where the food processor is better than doing it by hand, such as when preparing shellfish, meat, or liver mousse, which used to require pounding in a pestle with a mortar when I was an apprentice.

For making purees with herbs, from basil to parsley, a small mini-chop or blender is better than a food processor, as the blades turn faster. Also, a grinder is better than a food processor for grinding meat, which tends to become pasty in a food processor. To make a tartare of fish, for example, it is best to cut the salmon or other fish by hand rather than in the food processor, where it tends to get gooey quickly. An electric mixer is always great for making anything from bread to different types of dough or for mixing pâtés, and I do use a microwave oven to cook bacon, melt chocolate or caramel, and reheat food.

8. "CAN MY BUTCHER OR FISHMONGER DO IT?" | This question usually applies to trimming a saddle of lamb, dressing a rib roast,

cutting up lobster, or boning fish, etc. The answer is usually yes, but make sure the butcher or fishmonger is willing to do it your way.

9. "WHAT IS YOUR FAVORITE DISH?" | This is a question I am always asked, and for me, it is unanswerable. It presupposes that in any season, at any time of the day, I would feel the urge for one particular dish. I have many favorites, depending on the season, the weather, what I am in the mood for, who I am with, what I am drinking, the occasion, and the availability of ingredients at the market. For example, I often go to the market with the idea that I am going to make a gratin of cauliflower—only to return with artichokes, because they are beautiful, in season, and readily available that day.

10. "WHAT IS YOUR FAVORITE RESTAURANT?" | Where they know you, to paraphrase James Beard. There is a great deal of truth in this; when you are known somewhere, they do take care of you. Another response is that "my favorite restaurant is home," as certain foods never taste the same at a restaurant as they do at home.

11. "HOW DO YOU PAIR FOOD AND WINE?" | One doesn't have to match a particular dish with an exact wine. As a cook, I usually start with the food, and then see what I have in my cellar to go with it, visualizing the ingredients in the dish and the type of wine that would complement them. I tend to like Rhône-type wines, like Syrah, that are fairly big and heavy.

12. "WHAT IS THE PROPER WAY TO SERVE CHEESE, AND WHERE SHOULD IT APPEAR IN A MENU?" | In a classical menu it comes after the salad at the end, or sometimes with the salad, if the dressing

is extremely mild rather than acidic. Cheese usually demands a good wine to accompany it.

13. "WHO DOES THE COOKING AT HOME?" | This changes, depending on who gets to the stove first. After more than forty years of marriage, Gloria and I often cook together, but we have our parameters in the kitchen and we do our own things in tandem together without getting into each other's way. I particularly enjoy her Chicken with Rice (page 142) from her Puerto Rican heritage, or her black beans and ribs from her Cuban heritage.

I often raise the question of leftovers when I teach, to make people understand that if you know the process of cooking, you can create food with what you have left from other meals. The word "leftovers" is often a pejorative term, but making a recipe from leftover fish that you flake and combine with butter, a little onion, and white wine and serve over pasta, or turning it into a quiche works much better than trying to reheat the dish in its original form. Someone who can create dishes out of leftovers shows a great knowledge and comprehension of food, as well as imagination and economy, and these qualities are important in a professional kitchen as well as in a home kitchen. Questions about food costs are usually asked out of curiosity rather than real concern, unless one cooks with exorbitantly priced ingredients, such as black or white truffles, foie gras, caviar, or saffron.

These questions illustrate how much people all over the country are enjoying cooking classes, discussing recipes, and cooking at home. To finish, I would like to ask my question: Is there any better way to enjoy friends and family than around a table loaded with good food and wine?

CONVERSION CHART

WEIGHT EQUIVALENTS

The metric weights given in this chart are not exact equivalents, but have been rounded up or down slightly to make measuring easier.

AVOIRDUPOIS	METRIC
¼ oz	7 g
½ oz	15 g
1 oz	30 g
2 oz	60 g
3 oz	90 g
4 oz	115 g
5 oz	150 g
6 oz	175 g
7 oz	200 g
8 oz (½ lb)	225 g
9 oz	250 g
10 oz	300 g
11 oz	325 g
12 oz	350 g
13 oz	375 g
14 oz	400 g
15 oz	425 g
16 oz (1 lb)	450 g
1½ lb	750 g
2 lb	900 g
2¼ lb	1 kg
3 lb	1.4 kg
4 lb	1.8 kg

VOLUME EQUIVALENTS

These are not exact equivalents for American cups and spoons, but have been rounded up or down slightly to make measuring easier.

AMERICAN	METRIC	IMPERIAL
¼ teaspoon	1.2 ml	
½ teaspoon	2.5 ml	
1 teaspoon	5.0 ml	
½ T (1.5 teaspoons)	7.5 ml	
1 T (3 teaspoons)	15 ml	
¼ cup (4 T)	60 ml	2 fl oz
⅓ cup (5 T)	75 ml	25 fl oz
½ cup (8 T)	125 ml	4 fl oz
⅔ cup (10 T)	150 ml	5 fl oz
¾ cup (12 T)	175 ml	6 fl oz
1 cup (16 T)	250 ml	8 fl oz
1¼ cups	300 ml	10 fl oz (½ pt)
1½ cups	350 ml	12 fl oz
2 cups (1 pint)	500 ml	16 fl oz
2½ cups	625 ml	20 fl oz (1 pint)
1 quart	1 liter	32 fl oz

OVEN TEMPERATURE EQUIVALENTS

OVEN MARK	F	C	GAS
Very cool	250–275	130–140	½–1
Cool	300	150	2
Warm	325	170	3
Moderate	350	180	4
Moderately hot	375	190	5
	400	200	6
Hot	425	220	7
	450	230	8
Very hot	475	250	9

(Page numbers in italic indicate photographs of recipes)

EDITOR: Julie Stillman

DESIGNER: Susi Oberhelman

PRODUCTION MANAGER: Jacquie Poirier

The text of this book was composed in Filosofia and Sackers Gothic.

PRINTED AND BOUND BY
Elegance Printing & Book Binding, Hong Kong